Holding My Own in No Man's Land

M O L L Y   H A S K E L L

Holding My Own in No Man's Land

Women and Men and Film and Feminists

· ·

New York   Oxford

Oxford University Press

1997

Oxford University Press

Oxford   New York
Athens   Auckland   Bangkok   Bogotá   Bombay
Buenos Aires   Calcutta   Cape Town   Dar es Salaam
Delhi   Florence   Hong Kong   Istanbul   Karachi
Kuala Lumpur   Madras   Madrid   Melbourne
Mexico City   Nairobi   Paris   Singapore
Taipei   Tokyo   Toronto

and associated companies in
Berlin Ibadan

Copyright © 1997 by Molly Haskell
Published by Oxford University Press, Inc.
198 Madison Avenue, New York, New York 10016

Library of Congress Cataloging-in-Publication Data
Haskell, Molly.
Holding my own in no man's land : women and men and film and
feminists / Molly Haskell.
p. cm.   ISBN 0-19-505309-5
1. Women in motion pictures.
2. Feminism and motion pictures.
I. Title.
PN1995.9.W6H32   1997
791.43'652042—dc20   96-18850

9   8   7   6   5   4   3   2   1

Printed in the United States of America
on acid-free paper

FOR MY MOTHER

Contents

Literary Heroines

The Nineties: Where Do We Go from Here?

Holding My Own in No Man's Land

Introduction

It's a Wednesday in late April, a chilly spring day at Columbia: a cluster of students on the steps of Low Memorial shout through a bullhorn, demanding an ethnic studies department. Since 1968, and the Balkanization of the American campus into single issue identity groups, student activism has become the annual rite for the release of seasonal high spirits and raging hormones. Inside Dodge Hall, where I teach a course on the Image of Women in Film, I'm trying to negotiate my own buffer zone between politics and aesthetics and find some common ground between my love of movies and their complicity in so many social injustices.

Today I'm showing *Gentlemen Prefer Blondes*, Howard Hawks's gaudily pagan 1953 musical in which Marilyn Monroe and Jane Russell play bosom buddies who strut their stuff on an ocean liner, fishing for men and diamonds. Monroe is of course Lorelei Lee, the golddigger created by Anita Loos in 1925, whose linguistic tropes ("Thank you ever so," "A girl like I") charmingly conceal a canny capitalistic brain; and Jane Russell is the good-time girl whose frustrated pursuit of "love" with the narcissistically buffed-up Olympic team leads to one of the funniest, slyest numbers ever to have come halfway out of the celluloid closet.

In this Darwinian world, where women exploit their assets while they've got them, flaunt their wares, measure their leverage according to the age, buying power, and availability of the men, Russell, having lost a whole shipload of prime-meat males to sexual indifference, makes a quick calculation and readjusts her sights. When Malone, the private detective, tries a pick-up line that offends, then asks for forgiveness, she grants it ("there's a shortage of men on this boat").

These two showgirls from Little Rock, only one of whom (Monroe) is in quest of a bigger rock, are out to get husbands, a career that might not pass muster with today's feminists, but one for which these shipboard strutters are uniquely well equipped. They harmonize so well and noncompetitively because they've carved up the field of men into two types, hunks and millionaires, corresponding to their own contrasting yet complementary images.

One of my favorite scenes has the two women—Monroe in red, Russell in black—descending the grand staircase of the first class dining room like two legendary gunfighters entering a saloon, their weapons (bazooms and bottoms) cocked and ready to fire, their eyes surveying the quarry. In the saloon, a hush falls, ice tinkles nervously in glasses, and there's an audible intake of breath. No one's going to try and outdraw either of these babes.

I can sense the uncertainty of my students—should they deplore or applaud these women's shenanigans? I of course opt for the latter and endeavor to persuade them.

My approach, for someone teaching a gender-related course, has been idiosyncratic, to say the least. Though there's plenty to object to in the representation of women in the male-dominated art form of the twentieth century, I've increasingly come to look for and cherish the heroic or contrary images of women that go against the grain of oppression—either slipping cunningly through the cracks of a patriarchal world order or defying it outright. As glorious monsters, Muses, femmes fatales, worker bees, queen bees, and sweet and sour dames, movies are full of women in convention-stretching roles that contravene a simple dialectic in which the active male gaze transfixes and objectifies the supposedly passive female.

In 1991, while preparing to teach my first course at Columbia, I found in a quarterly on feminist film theory a discussion of my 1973 book, *From Reverence to Rape: The Treatment of Women in the Movies*. It was treated as a sort of prehistoric text, once important but—now that theory had come to save the day—obsolete. The writer noted that for all my strengths and weaknesses, everyone had missed my one fatal defect: I was "an uncritical celebrator of heterosexual romance."

After the first moments of irritation and amusement passed, I thought, yes, I plead guilty to the charge. This was, after all, the early seventies when the term heterosexual had not become problematic, one item—and presumably the least hip one—on the lifestyle menu or the academic agenda.

In 1973 gender studies and gay activism had not yet arrived on the scene to make us aware that the word "heterosexual" did not describe a timeless and absolute institution but a temporal and mutable one, a habit whose "naturalness," having led to the exclusion and opprobrium of homosexuality, was now open to question. But the political thrust of the new gender studies was to cast heterosexuality as "straight" man, secure, complacent, and comfortable, in a somewhat false dialectic on the other side of which was its rebellious, neurotic, angst-ridden opposite, homosexuality. Homosexuality got all the good lines, while "straightness" was the starchy and repressive puritanical foil. And romanticism—a word which had become synonymous with Hollywood/Hallmark kitsch, with soft-focus repression and happy endings—was the ultimate heavy, the opposite of honesty, sexual freedom, autonomy. In my experience, so-called "straightness" is never all that straight, but a tortuous and insecure route to some compromise negotiation with what is known optimistically as sexual fulfillment, its various "orientations" occupying shaky and shady positions on the spectrum of sexuality, along with, and sometimes overlapping, homosexuality.

The unarguable contention was that the stars, always in the configuration of the heterosexual couple, didn't include most of us—the short, the swarthy, the rotund, the ethnic, the homosexual, the nerdy, the awkward, those of us—who didn't have a date on Saturday night, which was all of us some of the time and some of us most of the time. They were a patrician ideal, impossibly smooth and glamorous, the creation, ironically, of a group of short, swarthy, cigar-smoking Jewish moguls who were only one generation away from the shtetl and who projected their assimilationist yearnings onto the stars whose careers they owned and tended.

In an impulse which went against the grain of feminist thinking at the time, I wanted to show how women had in fact been better served by the notoriously tyrannical studio system than they were in the newer, freer, hipper Hollywood of the (then) present. This has since become a truism, but in 1974 it was heresy.

However unreflective of the actual social power of women, the female stars of the thirties and forties radiated an enormous sense of authority and had the salaries to back it up. The spirited and challenging woman, if not a universal reality, was a powerful and ever-present *idea*. (And there were enough female headliners in politics, sports, the arts to give resonance to the authority and swagger of stars like Dietrich and Garbo, Davis, Crawford, Hepburn, Dunne, Rosalind Russell, Colbert.) If fictional heroines wound up following the traditional line on what women should do—settle down and become compliant wives—they nevertheless offered enough subversive resistance along the way to indicate that all was not peaceful and placid in the supposedly natural order of things. As a metaphor for the way movies would serve up the obligatory happy ending, but with an acrid aftertaste, I pointed to *The Moon's Our Home*, a 1936 comedy in which Margaret Sullavan, playing an actress who has agreed to give up her career for her Park Avenue husband (Henry Fonda), suddenly bolts, goes to "Idlewild" (now Kennedy) and is boarding a plane to Hollywood when Fonda comes with some paramedics to capture her. The last shot of the film has Sullavan in a straitjacket, in the back seat of the ambulance, looking up at Fonda with the smile of the blissfully subdued.

Not coincidentally, two of the movie's screenwriters were husband and wife team Dorothy Parker and Alan Campbell, possibly the most undomestic couple ever to be joined in marriage and housekeeping. My original point was that, as with many such films, what we remember is not the scene of surrender but the previous ninety minutes in which the heroine more than holds her own in the battle of the sexes. As in Shakespeare's plays, the happy ending is a convention that satisfies a need for order and resolution while leaving ample room for doubt as to the completeness of the promised joy.

For most feminists, there is and has always been a split between the forward-looking conscious self, politically progressive and "emancipated," and the dark recesses of our fantasies, in thrall to the past and to the movies that provide a pathway back.

With a bow of acknowledgment to Sandra Gilbert and Susan Gubar, who used the phrase somewhat differently as the title of one of their collections, I had begun to think of myself as stranded in No-Man's-Land, like a soldier caught in that exposed area between Allied and German trenches in the First World War. Or a tennis player, caught in the one position on the court where you have no purchase on the ball—too far from the net to volley, too close to try for a ground stroke. To me, my engaging with film on a feminist basis left me in a friendless place. For the film buffs, film critics, and journalists with whom I had most in common, film was a first priority and the issue of women entered into it secondarily. Film was my first allegiance as well, but I couldn't help responding in an unusually intense way to the man-woman relationship and its meaning for both sexes. It seemed to me so much what film was all about, so much what had drawn me to film in the first place, and, in some as yet undeciphered way, so much the secret of my choice of metier, that I was incapable of pulling away to a more detached, less emotional position; no more could I use film—as so many intellectuals do—as slumming escapist fun while I used my mind for more "serious" things.

I felt a strong rooting interest in women, in what enabled them to rise above the limitations imposed on them, in how they found succor, in their camaraderie, in the radical urges that lay germinating, concealed beneath correct behavior or erupting into wild remarks, comic confrontation, swagger, seduction, and battles of independence.

"Women are compromised the day they're born," says a rueful Paulette Goddard in *The Women*. I wanted to know how they handled the compromise, wrested some triumph from the deal. And how each case, each movie, each director differed; even within the career of a director known as misogynist, different actresses changed the coloring and therefore political meaning of a character and film.

What I *was* culpable of, it seems to me—along with most people who were discussing culture from a feminist viewpoint—was subscribing to an oversimplified dichotomy between male and female, oppressor and victim, which implied a utopian agenda. Equality could be won because the enemy—the "patriarchal oppressor"—was without. No doubt if we hadn't believed in and given voice to certain rhetorical simplifications—using the pronoun "we," for example, to embrace blithely and without fear of contradiction the hopes and grievances of one-half of the human race—we never would have spoken out in the first place.

It seems obvious, now, that if gender parity has not been realized overnight, it is because the impulses that give rise to inequality lie deep within, ancient and universal. Patriarchy is a symptom, not a root cause, of the need to deny and repress the matriarchy into which every child is born, the maternal womb from which we issue, the maternal presence that overwhelms our early life.

Our image-saturated culture everywhere presents examples of our ambivalence toward powerful women and our lingering inability to see older, authoritative women as desirable in the way that older men of consequence surely are. The double standard of aging that allowed Cary Grant and Fred Astaire to play Romeo to increasingly younger Juliets, decade after decade, has not changed much when we accept De Niro and Pacino, Redford and Eastwood, playing lovers of much younger women, while reviewers absurdly reproach Emma Thompson for being too old to play the older sister in *Sense and Sensibility*! From our discomfort with the idea of mature women as models and magazine covers, our preference for young bodies in love scenes, can't we infer that the older woman holds some residual terror for both sexes, and that if there is a "backlash," some of its energy may be coming not just from patriarchal white males but from women themselves?

Having not yet found the conceptual path to understanding these various conundrums, I nevertheless tried to suggest in *From Reverence to Rape* some of the difficulties inherent in taking a strict feminist view of a form as complex, as full of contradictions, as hooked into the secret closets and shadowy recesses of the viewer's psyche, as movies. This wasn't a popular idea with those theoreticians who saw film simply as another arena in which women were used, abused, or oppressed.

For seventies feminists, the career woman of thirties and forties movies was a stock figure of ridicule. Invariably, she was a workaholic or spinsterish professional (Ingrid Bergman as the bespectacled psychiatrist in *Spellbound*) who, finding the right man, shed her glasses, and, like a female Clark Kent, blossomed into a figure of desire. The idea that career had to be surrendered on the altar of matrimony or that there might be a conflict between the two was, to latter-day feminists, anathema, an example of Hollywood propaganda in favor of patriarchy and the propagation of the species. The possibility that this drama might *also* express a conflict within women themselves, or that there might be some downside in releasing women, and men, from their different and time-honored roles safeguarding the family, was not to be countenanced.

So persistent is the fear of the powerful woman—the demonized feminist, the she-monster who proliferates in decades of significant progress by women—that it must reflect a deep-seated taboo against combining the awesome biological power of motherhood with status outside the home. It violates some fairness doctrine, an innately held belief in the division of powers. The absence of mothers, as others have noted, in genres that celebrate sexual equality (the screwball comedy) or female ambition, is significant. It's impossible to imagine Katharine Hepburn's Dorothy Thompson-like journalist in *Woman of the Year* as having a mother. Hers died when she was young, and she has acquired, in her feminist aunt Ellen (Fay Bainter), an idol and surrogate parent. When Bainter accepts Hepburn's widowed father in marriage, Hepburn—whose marriage to Spencer Tracy is a sham, a structure designed to allow her to remain essentially as she was—is crushed. "I always thought you were above marriage," she tells Bainter in one of the movie's most poignant moments. Being a mother or even a loving wife draws on different energies and emotions than being a newspaperwoman does (although, in a rose-colored bit of male chauvinism, Tracy is granted prowess in all three domains).

Still, there's a difference between *Woman of the Year*, where, in an ending demanded by the studio, Hepburn has to pay for her presumption by making a mess of breakfast, and the late-eighties version of the she-monster with retributive ending, *Fatal Attraction*. Glenn Close's sexually uninhibited career-woman-turned-psychopath so elicits the blood lust of the audience that she has to be cut down to size literally, with a knife and a gun.

I was less interested in categorical signs of oppression and victimization than in diversities of sickness and health; less interested in how "Hollywood" defined women than in how Woody Allen or Ingmar Bergman defined them, or how different women survived the Pygmalion-like hold of these complex, women-obsessed artists. How Eva Dahlbeck might give weight and meaning to one aspect of womanhood, and Harriet Andersson to another, how some actresses profited from these mentors while others were, if not destroyed, used up by them, and unable to forge careers apart from them.

To other critics, women characters might seem to be, if not an afterthought, just one of the many ingredients "produced" by the story, whereas to me they were its fulcrum. A writer came up with a story in order to wrestle with feelings about women, to present a certain view that would contain *and* assuage, enhance, adore, lust for, avenge, ridicule, destroy, surrender to, the image of woman he carried within him. The inextricable link between the woman on the screen and the feminine side of the artist, and, no less important, the identification of females in the audience with males on the screen, made the whole process of film viewing considerably more complicated than a simple male-vs.-female equation could account for.

Try as I might to keep aesthetic considerations paramount, I could never separate John Huston from his view of woman as a creature who in looks and entertainment value came second-best to a fine Irish thoroughbred. That women are less fun than guys or horses—or the current boys' toy, bombs—is of course a typical adolescent view. I should know: I once held it.

Not just men but women, too, find refuge in all-male stories and fantasies of male rescue. The fact is, we are all, in some measure, more comfortable with maleness than with femaleness.

The wider moral latitude granted men in all areas of life begins at a deep emotional level but is evident in film after film, where the sleaziest of male characters (especially if played by a charismatic actor) is forgiven, even swooned over, while a wicked woman is beyond the pale, rendered witch-like, then blown away to cheering approval.

When, in a Women in Film Noir class, I showed *The Maltese Falcon*, the students, feminists and sympathizers all, forgave Humphrey Bogart everything and Mary Astor nothing. The fact that the lying Bridget O'Shaugh-nessy was a woman of scant resources, trying to stay afloat by guile and sex appeal, carried no weight with them, while Bogart, professing pious alle-giance to his dead colleague, could have murdered twenty people and gotten away with it. Charm he had in spades, and he was a man. The myth of male superiority is an enormously stabilizing force, as we can see from the increased violence and instability in the relations between the sexes that has accompanied every step in the movement for equality.

Do they really have more charm, more value? Or must we overvalue and romanticize them in order to create superior creatures worthy of the compromises we make for the sake of love, marriage, and family? The stories are legion of powerful intelligent women—Simone de Beauvoir, Hannah Arendt, Mary Wollstonecraft come to mind—who overlooked the flaws or exaggerated the attractiveness of lovers or husbands, who placed their minds and consciences in *chador* in order to invest their men with aphrodisiac power and feel comfortable as females beside more pow-erful men. By all means let us talk about the ways in which men threaten, subdue, overmaster us, but let us also look at the ways women belittle themselves and invite belittlement.

Why is it that stories of fathers and sons melt us while mothers and daughters must struggle not to be banal? Because when men, stoical and given to hiding their emotions, suddenly break through, the moment is charged with an intensity of pent-up feeling nothing else can match. Women, nurturers by definition, are expected to exude feeling and com-passion. If the story of a woman struggling to hold down a job and raise a kid on her own were at the center of *Kramer vs. Kramer*, there would be no story. The chronicle of a man's discovery of the woman in himself is a tale of expanded horizons, leading in films like *Woman of the Year* and *Tootsie*, to funny and heartwarming epiphanies. A woman's access to her masculine side is, however, a nastier proposition, a cautionary tale of shrinking hu-manity *and* loss of femininity.

SUCH CONSIDERATIONS FORM LITTLE part in the academic discussion of film, which is dominated by what is popularly known as "theory," a mixture of semiotics and deconstruction by way of psychoanalysis. I am obliged, *faute de mieux*, to give my students reading lists of essays with titles like "The Inscription of Femininity as Absence" and "Enunciation and Sexual Difference." These essays, and above all Laura Mulvey's influential "Visual Pleasure and Narrative Cinema" (according to which the female on the screen is pinned like a helpless butterfly by the castrating male "gaze"), dominate reading lists.

Of course, there's some truth, as there always is, in what is basically Marxism in feminist drag; for instance, one essay on *Gentlemen Prefer Blondes* diagnoses the women as being "objects continually on display for . . . the film audiences' voyeurism and fetishism," in what the author sees as a "machine to entertain." But this fails to capture both the spirit of the film and the camaraderie of the women (and, in disavowing its female parentage, becomes party to the patriarchal usurpation it criticizes!).

You might talk about the exploitation of women; on the other hand, you might observe that jostling up against the spectacle that *seems* to serve them up as objects is the subversive manner they have of turning things to their account . . . and the satiric humor that allows them to tease and expose male lechery without becoming harridans or she-monsters. Like conscious and unconscious motivations, text and sub-text don't lie in easily stratified layers, but constantly shift; once the hidden becomes visible, something else is repressed. The theory, seductive and concealing, that embraces fetish runs the risk of itself becoming a fetish.

In the face of such earnest deconstruction, one wants to cry, Hey, this is a Hollywood musical. We're engaged in a process of identification, admiration, and amusement, send-up and celebration, not in the alienation effect. There's a far more knowing and critical appreciation of the "system"—of the mating game as a commodities exchange—in this musical than in any plain-Jane critique or Maoist ballet with dancers romping and stomping in figure-concealing tunics.

Still in search of secondary material, I find another, later essay which takes the gals' point of view, but in terms that simply transfer the jargon, leaving the formulaic dichotomizing intact. The heroines, the writers argue, "appropriate the space around them, refusing to yield it to the male gaze." Of course, there were in Mulvey's essay as in John Berger's earlier, eloquently accessible analysis of women as visual commodities in *Ways of Seeing*, some timely and acute observations about the cultural meaning of what it means for the female to grow up feeling herself observed and having to internalize this sense of what Mulvey calls the woman's "to-be-looked-at-ness."

But the esoteric rhetoric of semiotics and psychoanalysis becomes yet another form of that puritanism that has lurked around movies, that most sensual of mediums, since their beginning. Silent movies, then talkies, were found evil, or dangerous, precisely because of their rakishness, their celebration of adventure, outlawry, glamor. The film theoreticians are the descendants of the bluestockings, refusing to acknowledge that women create excitement on the screen through their sexuality, not their virtue. Mae West might be speaking for the wayward charms of cinema itself in her first screen wisecrack (in *Night after Night*, 1932). A woman seizes her wrist and exclaims, "Goodness, what diamonds!," and West proudly retorts, "Goodness had nothing to do with it!"

In refusing to enjoy the sexual and emotional appeal of movies, feminist film academics occupy the (peculiarly male) high ground of Cartesian rationalism and cut themselves off precisely from the fleshy reality of women in these films—their bodies, their womanliness, their vanities and frailties and sensuality.

The male "gaze" was invariably presumed to turn woman into an object serving not just his pleasure but some pathological defense mechanism, with no allowance made for the part women play in creating and enjoying their own desirability, or for the pleasure women viewers take in watching women . . . or men.

In fact, until the fifties, women and men liked and responded (in varying degrees, of course) to the same stars. Davis and Crawford may have been favorites with women, Edward G. Robinson or James Cagney a little too short and funny-looking to be romantic heroes; many of the exotic or independent women we love today became "box office poison" in their time; nevertheless, with some strains, audiences were integrated in their tastes. In the fifties, as the studios were being dismantled as star-making systems, so did tastes begin to fragment. Monroe may have been the beginning, the first big star who polarized audiences. My own band of tomboyish teenagers just starting to date were appalled at what she represented and what her strutting, breathy, needy, neurotic self said about not just female, but male, sexuality. Earlier bombshells and beauties—Rita Hayworth, Jean Harlow, Gene Tierney—had appealed to both women and men. Their gorgeous but concealed bodies hadn't been fetishized, one aspect spotlighted to the exclusion of the rest. Unlike today's supermodels who have replaced actresses in the glamor roles, movie stars weren't physically perfect specimens but women with very definite personalities, idiosyncrasies, speech patterns. Like painting, film is a visual medium that satisfies a need as old as humanity: we will always want to *look at* bodies and faces, bodies clothed and unclothed, faces of all shapes and kinds of beauty.

If women don't want to pose, then men—in Calvin Klein ads and Mapplethorpe's photographs—will.

In the eyes of the theoreticians, the cinema's naive drama could be passed through the grid of Lacan/Freud and feminism and made scientifically respectable. I used to see this in students who came to film for its gender revelations and sins rather than out of any deep enthusiasm for film itself. They were in love with oppression, they saw it everywhere.

I'm reminded of a remark by Alfred Kazin. Visiting an Ivy League college, he'd chosen to read from *The Four Quartets*, only to be challenged by the professor afterward. "How could you endorse the work of an anti-Semite like Eliot?" the professor asked. "I decided long ago," Kazin replied, "that I would side with what I cared for rather than what made me unhappy."

I'm psychoanalytic enough to believe that we arrive at our political and aesthetic positions, our—let's face it—*biases*, via routes that lead back to our early lives and buried childhood emotions, fears, and yearnings that we can know only obliquely from the way they determine the present. Even the professions we choose, choose us, and the movies we are drawn to, and the way we are drawn to them, seem intimately bound to early childhood. The voyeurism of the movie buff or critic is no doubt hard-wired into the core fantasy life from some primal experience, whose intensity we continue to seek in movie after movie.

The "heterosexual" couple of classical cinema encompassed within them and between them all sorts of shifting alliances: dyads, triangles, quartets, the great stuff of Freudian narrative, concealed and revealed. You don't *have* to see the perverse shadings and alternative readings in the old films, but they are there: to deny all the homosexual, bisexual, and heterosexual possibilities inherent in the coming together of, say, Dietrich or Garbo and their lovers; Grant and his; or practically all of the screwball couples; or practically all star couples, is to read film literally and to insist on making unequivocal something whose very charm, whose layered inferences, were based on the equivocal.

We believed in the couple because we believed in the family, yet ironically it was the glamor and allure of the couple that heralded and even contributed to the weakening of the family by placing their mutual happiness above the subordination of self required for creating and sustaining a family. They were a Nietzschian pair, waltzing above the muck and mess of domesticity.

This enshrinement of elective affinities in the name of romantic love was the historical outgrowth of women's emancipation. For the last couple of centuries, and until the very recent wholesale entry of women into the workforce, romantic love—as opposed to arranged marriages—was the first step toward any kind of sexual equality. Beginning just before and abetted by the Industrial Revolution, and reflected in the heroines of Jane Austen, women were beginning to exercise choice in matrimonial matters that had customarily been arranged by their families. The idealized union, depending on an inner mandate rather than external claims, was a huge advance, creating a state of mind in which women ceased to regard themselves as property and more as free agents.

The apotheosis of the couple in Hollywood movies—or the premium placed on the "woman's domain" of love in the woman's film—was a powerful argument for the importance of love itself and of women as its votaries. If women were the presiding geniuses in the realm of emotions, if they were what Simone de Beauvoir, in writing of the heroines of Stendhal, called "the militarists of love," theirs was a transforming power in an arena that more and more determined our daily lives.

As the brain scientists and philosophers now tell us, memory is a far more subjective and fluid affair than we have previously thought. Traditional models of the brain—a storehouse, a copy machine—are being rejected, while we come more and more to understand the active role we play in constructing the images that pass for memories. We go back to a film seen in childhood and find we have it all wrong—the tunnel was shorter and not as dark as we remembered; the shower scene was less explicit than our shrieking and bloody recollection. Not only that, but there were opposing images in a single film, a single frame: women were constantly being objectified and oppressed. Women were constantly holding their own and calling the shots. In fact, of course, both are true—woman as victim, woman as victor—but one view or the other will predominate according to changing political contexts and complicated and elusive personal agenda.

In considering some of the stars whose profiles I might include in this collection, I began to see how much I had "created" them, having responded to them, through identification, as extensions of myself. Hence my opting to include pieces on Doris Day and John Wayne, whatever the risk in terms of bucking cultural prejudices. In the confessional salons of my New York, it is easier to admit to self-mutilation or masochistic sexual perversions than to a serious liking for Day or Wayne. They are so déclassé in the minds of the liberal left that their names are practically code words—she for the perpetual virgin of glossy fifties comedies, he as some Neanderthal male symbol of right-wing jingoism.

While most knowledgeable film writers appreciate Wayne and Day as two of what French cinephiles called "axioms of cinema" (both having far richer and more varied careers than they are generally given credit for), this might not have been enough to stiffen my resolve if the two hadn't great personal meaning for me, both in my evolution as a film critic/feminist, and through this, to a phenomenon I see as essential to the way we see, remember and talk about movies: the process by which we choose and construct and revise movie memories along the way, blaming them, celebrating them, using them to buttress and illuminate the changing narratives of our lives.

The idiosyncratic British Freudian Adam Phillips has written that "if sex is the way out of the family, falling in love is the route back, the one-way ticket that is always a return."

Some individuals are more successful than others in leaving the family behind, loosening its grip on the unconscious, but the struggle continues. I'm quite prepared to confess that something in my own particular childhood, some toxic mix of yearning and guilt, plus the Victorian scruples of my Southern Wasp background, may have predisposed me toward films in which love revolves around taboo and the unobtainable, and renunciation sends noble shivers down the spine. The tug o' war between the erotics of concealment and of revelation, between denial and fulfillment, operates at every cinematic level; even the history of cinema reproduces it in the ongoing tension over censorship. Films made under the Production Code (the thirties to the sixties) reflect traditional values of virginity, chastity, and, tied to sex's indissoluble link with marriage and reproduction, woman's power to say No, while the films made in recent permissive decades, featuring nudity and copulation a-go-go, presumably celebrate women's sexual autonomy, thanks to feminism, the pill, and the severing of sex from procreation, yet show a corresponding loss of leverage in the mating game.

The same power shift can be seen in the making of movies, with women no longer at the center of male power fantasies, or even holding decent chips at the bargaining table. With women scorned, both as actresses and as target audiences, moviemaking, Hollywood style, has become a high-stakes macho poker game played by producers, agents, directors and superstars. Virility is measured in terms of the length of zeroes stretching after a digit, as in a $70,000,000-budget or 5 mil. for a first screenplay, a figure then dutifully publicized and quoted, like a mantra, on *Entertainment Tonight* and in awed tones in the culture pages of our newspapers.

My students feel more alienated from these high-explosive blockbusters than from the most lachrymose weepers of the thirties and forties. They don't approve of heroines' sacrifices in the name of love, yet their sheepish responses to such films as *Letter from an Unknown Woman* and *Stella Dallas*, or the more schematic *Vertigo*, suggest that suffering for the "wrong man" is not unknown to them, nor are the themes—women's complicated and often self-destructive ambition to serve as muse, model, Galatea to charismatic men—completely outdated.

Still I was surprised, in looking over long-ago articles in order to make a selection for this book, to realize how often (despite my "uncritical celebration of heterosexual romance") I had written about woman-to-woman relationships: in the occasional "summer reading" book reviews I did for the *Village Voice* (of *The Bostonians*, Colette, *Emma*); in my highlighting of the loving and tortuous female bonds in the comedy of Carol Burnett and Lucille Ball. I think my attraction to those sustaining female relationships was partly the influence of my mother, a frustrated painter and a woman who chafed under the social requirements of being dependent on a man.

And it was also the fact that, having been educated for sixteen years at all-female institutions, I was used to having female friends. *Clueless* is one of those rare movies that shows how female bonds are the first line of defense against enslavement to men. Years at a single-sex parochial school also left me with a sneaking envy for those odd women, spinsters, schoolteachers, who, however restricted their lives might seem to the world of heterosexual couples, had escaped thralldom to a man.

I consider these articles, which come out of my own "couplings" with my subjects and with cinema, a kind of continuing set of ruminations, encounters, insights, and images of people and characters who, as themselves and as representative of currents beyond themselves, have had an influence in our lives.

Movies operate on so many different levels—it's why no single theory or approach can ever encompass all of cinema. Conditions under which we view them, the Zeitgeist, whether they've been overpraised or underrated, all play an enormous part in our perceptions of a film. But when we come to discuss or review a movie, we talk and write about it as if it is a mutually agreed-upon stable thing.

We have to do this, otherwise we would be lost in a chaos of qualifications and miscommunications. And so we go on talking and writing, projecting and receiving fantasies, hoping to occasionally discover a mutual truth. Exiting a century in which marriage, monogamy, and the church no longer anchor our existence and entering one in which we can choose the sex of our children, prolong or end our lives, possibly redefine marriage or abandon it, we hardly know where we are going as a species, much less as individual men and women. But that's what makes our surrogates in the movies so endlessly fascinating. If roles for women have declined, or splintered into subdivisions of class, ethnicity, and age, talking about them is a means of keeping sexual issues both on the table and mediated through the prism of a popular art form that belongs to us all. A collection is a devious way of entering the gender and culture wars without committing to print a book purporting to advance a definitive line. Feminists continue to bemoan the lack of a theory of female sexuality, but why should there be one? Why must we *answer* the question What Do Women Want?—a question posed by a man demanding a single, obvious explanation along the lines of male sexuality, a man who had said, more profoundly, that desire is by its very nature inacapable of being satisfied . . . and, just as pessimistically, that men and women are always a phase apart.

It seems to me there must be a certain melancholy tinge to all our polemical assaults and clarion calls for change, a sense that some deep pull within us resists that change. The subtext of most critiques, including my own earlier one, is that Society (or the System) is at fault and Something Must Be Done. I no longer see clear lines of guilt and responsibility but more often paradox: something lost, something gained; unconscious yearnings thwarting conscious aims. And so, in the articles and essays collected here, you will find that a sense of paradox in the playing of roles unifies writing on a variety of subjects, literary heroines as well as cinematic ones, and for an even greater variety of publications, which may be either a reflection of my own scattered sensibility or the exigencies of freelance writing.

Although interviews constitute a small portion of my overall writing, I included a sizeable number here, because they seemed to transcend their journalistic mission. Unless the subject was someone who interested me exceptionally, I shied away from interviews. A career journalist or reporter, used to going for the jugular, could pose personal questions that by deeply ingrained reserve I was incapable of asking. If I felt emotionally engaged, however, the artificiality of the format melted away, and the whole enterprise seemed less a ritual for mutual exploitation than a conversation between two people who might in other circumstances have been friends . . . or (in the case of Lina Wertmuller) antagonists.

The pieces constitute something like a personal narrative and testify to my continuing belief that there are many ways to talk about the cinema, which is, after all, life and truth, and sometimes even love, at twenty-four frames a second.

Dames

. . . .

Icon of the Fifties

DORIS DAY

A Terence Davies movie of several years ago, *The Long Day Closes*, came close to expressing the quasi-religious ecstasy induced in me by certain fifties movies. The story of Davies's Liverpool childhood as the youngest member of a large, close, Catholic working-class family (and, though unmentioned, gay filmmaker to be), the movie shows his young alter ego sitting in church, the liturgical music swelling and metamorphosing into the by no means out-of-place romantic songs sung by Doris Day ("Once I Had a Secret Love") and Debbie Reynolds ("Tammy"). Terence Davies no doubt had a secret love, and so did I (my father? my mother? one as forbidden as the other). The camera is high in the apse, the filmmaker unafraid to link religious loftiness with a popular song. The little boy is transported out of the loving, messy, disturbingly intimate home life and his sexual confusion into a world of clarity and romantic fulfillment.

Movies were at once a substitute and an escape hatch, supplying an emotional release from the sexual confusion of adolescence. I was in the process of losing my religious faith and my father (the first because of the second) and giving up my first career ambition—to be a minister—conceived before I realized preaching was not a calling intended for females. That was a great deal of loss for a teenager to confront head on, and I didn't.

Movies in the still worshipful atmosphere of the large, cathedral-like theaters of the fifties (often with organ music), could allow communion between star and spectator that was like transubstantiation at the altar rail. We drank and ate of their radiance, and, like miniature female impersonators, copied their looks, their expressions, modeling ourselves on women just ahead of us in years and development.

My first movie star crushes were Roy Rogers and Trigger (forget Dale), and the Lone Ranger and Silver, the cowboys (and horses) with whom as rider and horse-lover I could feel both identification and covert attraction. These complex, changing attachments seem to reflect Simone de Beauvoir's idea that "the adolescent girl wishes at first to identify herself with males; when she gives that up, she then seeks to share in their masculinity by having one of them in love with her." All the popular love songs of the day romanticized obsessive love and devotion. Only movies offered something in between—glamorously *active* women like Esther Williams and Sonja Henie. And, when the young girl was finally nudged by hormonal and social (and Darwinian) imperatives into the dating arena, stars who seemed to combine romantic desirability with some kind of spunky resistance—to wit, Doris Day and Audrey Hepburn.

I became interested in Day a second time around, in the early seventies, when, thinking about her performances in movies like Hitchcock's *The Man Who Knew Too Much*, I saw the repressed ambition and neuroticism that had been there all along. Appreciating the proto-feminist boldness of some of her working-girl characters, I became suspicious of the quickness with which most people dismissed her. Why the refusal to take her seriously? What was so threatening about her? Was it that her all-American whole-someness in the anti-Amerika sixties had become an embarrassment? Her cheery optimism and determination were not only qualities we had lost but ones we felt ashamed of having entertained in the first place. Or was it that she was too close (for many of us) to something we had been or wanted to be in the fifties and now were running from for our lives?

To many women, she was like a hundred-watt reminder of the exces-sively bright and eager-to-please feminine masquerade of the fifties. She was that for me, but I had found refuge in the masquerade in ways I had yet to completely fathom. Outsiders could pay their respects unambivalently: she was remote enough from their inner struggles. Men, for example. John Updike, in a long and elegant mash-note-cum appreciation of her career, could admit to being attracted to her as "sheer symbol—of a kind of beauty, of a kind of fresh and energetic innocence, of a kind of banality," someone who "fascinates us with the amount of space we imagine between her face and her mask." He touches on her sexiness, the deceptive sexiness of the girl next door, quoting James Garner's memorable acknowledgment that the two greatest, i.e., sexiest and most giving, stars to play love scenes with were Day and Julie Andrews, both "notorious girls next door." For men (and, subtly and subconsciously for women), there is a kind of covert and disguised eroticism, the buoyant readiness, the hourglass figure hinted at beneath the calico frocks or tailored suits. Updike sums it up: "The fact of the matter probably is that star quality is an emanation of superabundant nervous energy and that sexiness, in another setting, would be another emanation."

The Canadian actor Brian Bedford, in an interview in the *New York Times*, credited his eventual migration to the United States to his boyhood love of Doris Day and the vision of family and domesticity enshrined in her movies. Family and domesticity? This wasn't part of my Doris Day mental scrapbook, but Bedford wasn't the only one who followed the siren call of Day cheerful, if not barefoot, in the kitchen. At a feminist luncheon at the Waldorf Astoria sometime in the eighties, the woman sitting next to me launched into a near-tirade about how her life had been blighted by "those films of the fifties in which Doris Day ended up in the kitchen, glued to the frying pan and her apron." She, following this example, had made a traditional fifties-style marriage, lived the indentured life of the "feminine mystique," and spent a decade undoing the damage.

While sympathetic to the woman's tale of woe and the social pressures behind it, I felt Day was more convenient than appropriate as a symbol of oppression of women. The suburban nesting phenomenon was far more a staple of television shows than movies.

Of course, this woman chose to emphasize the stickier aspects of Day's persona that I had conveniently forgotten, like her frantically domestic doll-wife in *Send Me No Flowers*. It's as if she has to pay for her seething career ambitions with bouts of hysterical housewifery. My affinity with Day and the selective way I remembered her embodied a kind of denial, and it's difficult for me to read the interview I did with her because, like a schoolgirl diary, it reveals a self I'd rather disown. We weren't so far apart—if she had a mask, so did I. She had found in Christian Science a way out of depression that I had found (without yet realizing it) in movies. We both had black belts in stiff-upper-lip cheerfulness. It was the Wasp way.

This was the first piece I did for *Ms.*, and my revisionist view of Day went very much against the feminist grain. Not only was she politically incorrect, but women were now supposed to be above the raptures of fandom; nevertheless, to their credit, a savvy editor and the staff responded to the idea and supported me all the way.

BETWEEN 1948 AND 1968, Doris Day made some forty films: the first third—until roughly 1953—as a musical leading lady, and the rest as a star. The fact that as late as 1968 she played heroines who were still "in the running" as far as men were concerned, makes hers one of the longest female careers in the business.

Certainly her method of survival was not, like Joan Crawford's, to adapt herself to changing tastes and mature with her audience. On the contrary, she represented conservative values that went defiantly against the grain of the swinging sixties. Nor did she evolve, like Bette Davis, into offbeat roles. On the contrary—again—she seems to have survived largely by *not* changing, by remaining fixed in a firmament of shooting stars. But *how* she survived and what she was fixed *as* are best explained by what she was not: by not being identified primarily as a sex object or a romantic fantasy—she played mothers, teenagers, and romantic leads in no particular logical, or chronological, order—she remained invulnerable to the mutability that such fleshly fantasies are heir to.

Like most stars (and movies) who arrive on the cusp of a decade, Day combines qualities of both eras. Her emotional intensity, just this side of hysteria, is a throwback to those tearful, heartbreakingly feminine heroines played by June Allyson and Margaret Sullavan in the forties. But where they were yearning, even masochistic, Day is direct and forward-moving, constitutionally incapable of succumbing to melancholy.

From singing with big bands, she went straight to singing in the big band movies that Warner Brothers was churning out. She was the blonde in the white blouse and pleated skirt—even in *My Dream Is Yours* (1949), with a fatherless son. When paired with other females, it was always they who were tough, or sexy: Lauren Bacall in *Young Man with a Horn* (1950) and Ginger Rogers as her older sister in *Storm Warning* (1951).

Next came the tomboy phase, from 1951 *(On Moonlight Bay)* to *Calamity Jane* in 1953, the year I tuned in. I had a "secret love" and, at the age of

*This interview/career essay first appeared in *Ms.*, January 1976. Permission to copy granted by *Ms. Magazine*. Copyright © 1975 by Molly Haskell.

thirteen, was strenuously resisting the pressures to stop climbing trees and convert myself into that passive figurine of womanhood, the "lady." Doris Day's freckles, the lumberjack shirt, the blue jeans, the athleticism, and the occasional shrill notes of incipient womanhood may not have struck movie critics as the last word in art or glamor, but they constituted a shrine at which my barely adolescent anxieties could find relief. If she was to be pitted against the sexually blatant Marilyn Monroe type—as she was implicitly, and later (in *The Thrill of It All*) explicitly—then I was wholeheartedly on her side. She would not twist herself out of shape to win men's love, and find instead only lust.

Looking at her career with more detachment, it was in the mid-fifties that she played her most dramatically interesting roles: Ruth Etting in *Love Me or Leave Me*; and, in Hitchcock's *The Man Who Knew Too Much*, the hysterical American mother abroad, overattached to her son and overdependent on pills.

One of the marks of a great director is the ability to capture the side of an actor that has remained hidden. Hitchcock was a genius at exposing the neurotic underside of his star's image. With uncanny prescience in *The Man Who Knew Too Much*, Hitchcock painted a portrait of a woman who wouldn't be defined as a type, or analyzed as a trend, until ten years later. In Day's anxious young mother, we see the neurotic overcompensation of a woman who has given up her career (the stage) for marriage. Obsessed with her son, she has become an emotional invalid of a wife, as if to punish the man (the husband played by Jimmy Stewart) who had forced her to make such a choice. And with further insight, Hitchcock gave to Doris Day, in the song "Que Sera, Sera," what I was to discover was her philosophy of life.

It was in the late fifties and early sixties, when she herself was in her late thirties, that she won her reputation as the eternal virgin, a crystallization of those traits that had endeared her to masses of Americans and damned her forever with the cultural arbiters. The films in which she *did* accept her years and matronliness with wry equanimity, like *Please Don't Eat the Daisies*, were not as successful as those in which she resisted her fate. Likewise, her more subtle musicals and comedies *(The Pajama Game* and Billy Rose's *Jumbo)* were ignored by audiences and critics for the increasingly abrasive confrontations of the Fox and Universal farces *(Pillow Talk, Move Over, Darling*, and so on), in which Day and a lover/antagonist would enact sexual duels as horrifying, in their folksy way, as the arma-geddons of Strindberg.

In these films, virginity and masculinity were the citadels under siege. But for all the coy plot devices contrived by screenwriter Stanley Shapiro to keep Day from turning into Night, the lady herself was willing to surrender—as long as she could cloak her deed with the missionary pur-pose of reclaiming one faltering soul to manhood. If these films made us uncomfortable, surely it was partly because they touched upon anxieties we all felt, in a society and a decade in which women were little encouraged to expose themselves sexually. To lose one's virginity was to lose everything. Small wonder that Doris Day clung to hers with something akin to desperation.

But when I remember her roles in these films, it is as one of the few movie heroines (and one of the last) who had to *work* for a living. Grace Kelly and Audrey Hepburn, bless their chic souls, floated through life. Voluptuous Ava Gardner ran barefoot and bohemian through exotic places. Marilyn Monroe was the sexual totem for the various fetishes of fifties America. Kim Novak and Debbie Reynolds and Shirley MacLaine, who, like Day, were not goddesses and hence had to exert themselves, still sought a man to lean on. One never felt in them the driving, single-minded ambition one felt in Day—the very strength that was used as a weapon, in the sex comedies, to impugn her femininity.

She had excellent positions—as an interior decorator in *Pillow Talk* and an advertising executive in *Lover Come Back*—and she worked because she loved it, was good at it, and needed the money; not just to find a husband. She had come to the big city to make her way. And thus she seemed to be resisting, in a way that would find its voice in the Women's Movement, the creeping paralysis of adult womanhood as it was coming to be defined in the fifties. It is surely from this period of suburban migration and domes-ticity as a consuming vocation that the reductive notion of being "just a housewife" dates.

But gradually the hardening process set in. Her brisk, no-nonsense approach was institutionalized through farcical exaggeration. Her later films—*The Ballad of Josie*, *Where Were You When the Lights Went Out?*, *With Six You Get Eggroll*—were all of the "Oh, here comes the nutty lady" variety. If her natural talents never left her, neither were they permitted to develop within the coy vehicles and overproduced comedies designed to keep her afloat in the sixties. But in even the silliest roles—from damsel in distress

(*Julie* and *Midnight Lace*) to feminist of the Old West (*The Ballad of Josie*)—
she kept her head, and saved her face, when all around her were losing
theirs. She remained true to herself: for that alone she deserves more than
passing interest.

I HAD ADVANCED, IN public and in print, the novel idea that Doris Day
ought to be treated with several degrees more seriousness than has charac-
terized most articles and critiques of this—I think—underrated actress.
Not only was I defending her talent, but, more preposterously, her
movies—something not even her best friends would buy. "If only her
career had been different," they would say, shaking their heads. "If only
Hollywood . . . "

What they and Day's detractors are referring to, of course, is the
superannuated virgin of the sexless sex comedies, protected by cameras
coated with seven veils of Vaseline from growing old before our eyes. With
the aid of the rejuvenating techniques at the disposal of the film industry
and her sunny inviolability, Doris Day would seem to remain forever a girl
on the brink of experience. With disconcerting obviousness, Hollywood
dedicated its know-how to arresting the aging process that, for women
particularly, is the nightmare underside of the American dream of eternal
youth. The filters, fine as they were, were still too coarse. They reminded a
ruthlessly youth-oriented audience that Doris Day—who hadn't the grace
to retire like Garbo or the sense of timing to take her life like Monroe—
was growing old and pretending not to.

But the image of the eternal virgin is one-sided. At the same time, Day
was challenging, in her workingwoman roles, the limited destiny of women
to marry, live happily ever after, and never be heard from again. The fate of
women to contract spiritually and finally to disappear into the miasma of
male fantasies, as they did on the screen in the sixties, was one to which she
would not resign herself.

And so it was this career, and not some hypothetical one, that I felt was
worth examining in some detail—a feeling, I am here to report, not shared
by Day herself. If she has little desire to talk about her life, she has an
almost pathological aversion to discussing her films. As a consequence of
which we found ourselves sitting across the table in the charming den of
her Beverly Hills home with not much to say.

"I don't want to look back at my movies," she explained. "It's too soon.

You just want to do things differently. It's a waste of energy. What you put down was right at the time."

"But you've just been going over them, haven't you?" I asked her. "In the process of doing your autobiography with A. E. Hotchner? I heard it was a painful experience for you."

"No," she replied casually, "not really. I just don't like any of my movies. [The chasm opens, closes again.] I'm sorry to say that, because it sounds like ego. I might be wrong. If other people like them, who am I to say?"

The hope, in my interviewing her, was that if she didn't "tell all," she would at least express feelings, thoughts, and perhaps a self-awareness that had been given little breathing space on the screen.

"Don't they [*Ms.*] know I don't give interviews?" she said.

"Well, I don't do them either," I said reassuringly, "but I'm a fan of yours and they thought . . . you know—" Why didn't I say, "Look, you've given interviews to other magazines. And you've just told your life story to A. E. Hotchner in a biography that will surely contain at least a few revelations that don't accord with the official Doris Day." Because, well, I was sitting in her house drinking her home-brewed decaffeinated coffee and eating a coffee cake that her secretary Ruth had gone to the bakery to get.

I was casting about for a common bond, for there was one passion— unfortunately, the one dearest to Doris Day's heart—that we did not share: dogs. I had already made a slight gaffe and betrayed, I thought, the hostility I was trying to conceal. But first, let me set the scene.

I passed through the electronically controlled gate and entered the one-story house with some trepidation, having read up on her obsession, and her menagerie. She is tirelessly active in a group called Actors and Others for Animals, which rescues stray and mistreated animals and tries to place them in homes. She has a varied collection of her own, which I can report are an extremely well-behaved lot. Instead of my being greeted, on entering the cheerful, L-shaped living room, by howls and a cascade of tongues and teeth, most of the dogs were out on the patio, their noses pressed against the pane in a portrait of canine harmony.

I was first introduced to Ruth, then Doris Day, then Doris Day's chipper, eighty-year-old mother, and then, at my request, I was presented to "Bubbles," in Ruth's arms.

"How old is Bubbles?" I asked. (I know enough to get the name first, so I don't betray my ignorance of gender, and thus of life itself, by asking

"How old is she?" or, worse, the blatantly bluffing "it" when it's a he. If only they wore pink and blue dresses, like humans.)

"Eighteen months," Doris replied. "They're all eighteen months."

I hesitated. "You mean like women are always twenty-nine?"

"Exactly."

I was nonplussed. I'll have to tread carefully, I thought. She then told me she'd nicknamed one of the dogs Toughy Brasuhn, after a particularly scrappy roller-derby queen. This sign of humor was encouraging.

There were occasional glimmers of irony, but there were few "slips." A woman totally in command of herself and her every utterance, she consciously projects not so much a self as a state of mind: one of unalloyed harmony, joy, mental health as its own reward.

This determined euphoria, or mind control—for it is a product of will, not intuitive faith—is the end result of Christian Science principles adopted early but since modified to a less orthodox and more personal code.

She was receptive to Christian Science, she said, "because I'd been thinking that I should be happier than I am. This was when I was singing with Les Brown. There has to be a better way, I thought. One ought to be able to control one's thinking instead of having depressions—one day you're up, the next you're down. I didn't want that kind of life, but I didn't know how to change it."

She made her first picture in Hollywood, *Romance on the High Seas*, in 1948; then her ex-husband (George Weidler, her second, also a musician) came to visit. He seemed completely changed.

"I asked him what had happened, and he introduced me to the teachings of Mrs. Eddy. The essence is that God is spirit. He—or She—is not material and neither is man. It was a turning point in my life. My husband came and went. I believe he returned to give me this pearl.

"I'm no longer orthodox. Christian Science can be very rigid. I'm not a church person. You can pray anywhere, riding on a bicycle. But it was perfect for me, because it started my life in Hollywood with a whole new way of thinking. It was a complete protection. I've lived happily here and enjoyed all my years, and yet I've no sense of competition. There *is no* competition."

Her conviction forms an invisible but impenetrable wall around the most frivolous conversation. She is a daisy drawn with a heavy pencil—the border's too thick for a flower, especially one so simple and spontaneous.

Throughout our interview—four hours one day, two the next—and beneath our bantering, I know she mistrusts me. Perhaps she is right—after all, I pretended to love dogs. The sense of a barrier is all the more intriguing because of her apparent openness, and our apparent rapport.

Here is a woman who has lived a fascinating life: a singer, married to a musician when she was seventeen (in 1941); divorced in 1943, and, with a small baby, making her way with big bands; married in 1946 to another musician; divorced in 1949; goes into movies and soon becomes a star; married in 1951 to Marty Melcher, who until his death in 1968 manages her career; discovers after his death that they have both been swindled of some $22 million by their lawyer-manager Jerome B. Rosenthal; discovers the IRS has overruled a multimillion-dollar tax shelter, goes to court, wins her case, takes her career in hand; remains active, doing television work, recording her autobiography, adding to and decorating her house, seeing friends and befriending animals.

And yet all her experiences have been converted into spiritual bromides, chopped up and purified in the blender of Higher Understanding. They have merged into a life plan which is ultimately beyond her responsibility." "Que Sera, Sera."

"I never wanted to become a performer," she told me. "But when I was fifteen, I was in a car accident and had to give up dancing. Somebody suggested I take up singing. I ended up with a wonderful coach—I used to go over on crutches. She thought I had promise but felt I should have three lessons a week, and we couldn't afford it. She gave me three for the price of one. I feel now that it was simply meant to be."

This woman is intelligent, even shrewd. No vapid, spaced-out star is she, no freak or faddist. There are contours and lines to her mind, and yet she is busy atomizing life's bulk into weightlessness. People and episodes no longer have the thick, nubby texture of whole experiences, but have been shaved to fit a completed puzzle of spiritual beatitude. Her second husband was not (as he was reported to be at the time) the great love of her life, but the man who brought her the "pearl" of Christian Science and vanished.

At least, that is the self she presents to me. And considering that I, after all, am associated in her eyes with the four things she turns out to regard most suspiciously—contemporary films, her own films, critics, and the Women's Movement—I suppose we get along surprisingly well.

The house buzzes with activity. The houseboy comes. Ruth has to go to the dentist. The swimming pool man arrives. Doris is in some pain because a dog accidentally bit her finger two nights before, the same finger she had smashed in a car door a few years back. The house—sunny, open, furnished in early American and bright colors—is modest by Beverly Hills standards (though not by mine). If the paintings are not gallery material, we can, according to a recent *Wall Street Journal* story, thank the crooked ex-lawyer Rosenthal, who advised the Melchers not to put their money in art and the home, as he had better plans for it.

We began talking about the changing status of women, a subject on which she has conflicting feelings.

"I could reel off a list of the ways women are relegated to being homemakers—it starts out early in life," she said. "But I wanted that. At least I wanted a nice house. And I wanted my husband to be the—" she looked for a word.

"Authority?"

"No, no," she said quickly. "To have the good position. I wanted to be a source of strength and support. And manage a nice home and run it well. Not that I wanted to do all the work. I had the same idea most young Americans have—that you'll have somebody to come in.

"It's not bad when it works. But it's better now that women are getting out of the home and finding fulfillment.

"Between marriages, I stayed at home with the baby. I never lived it up enough. I was always guilty about not being a good mother. Motherhood is a super experience, but it shouldn't take up all the time." (Day has a close, friendly relationship with her son, Terry, a record producer who has recently married.)

She stopped for a second. "My husband was a musician. We were traveling all the time and didn't have much money, so I couldn't just call home to Mother to find out how to do things. I didn't know how to cook a steak or when to put in the potatoes to make them come out at the same time. My husband would come home with four hungry musicians, probably having told them I was a great cook."

Here she stood up and with a natural dramatic flair began acting out the story. "I couldn't eat. I would hover over them [she moves around an imaginary table], they would be ready to cut the steak. The blood was draining out of my face.

"'It's terrible,' I would say, before they'd even tasted it. 'I'm really just not a cook. I don't mean to be learning at your expense.' Then I would run into the kitchen. My husband would come rushing back and say, 'You've just got to relax.' I never did.

"Maybe if I'd stayed in Cincinnati those early years and had a nice little apartment near my mother, I'd be the Perle Mesta of Beverly Hills."

What she turned out to be is a beautiful, active woman of fifty who looks forty and is perhaps a little more vain about her youthful looks and sensational figure than she lets on. She is wearing blue pants, a cream knit top, and a scarf that matches her blue eyes. She has thin, well-proportioned legs, a small waist, and an enormous bust—the biggest shock, because who ever knew she had it? She usually wore the kind of gear—lumberjack shirts, suits, or shirtwaist dresses—designed to conceal it. When I suggest this to her, she plays dumb.

(If I had known, in my anxious adolescent years, that Calamity Jane not only had a secret love but also a secret bosom the size of Marilyn Monroe's, I think I would have turned away in misery. She was a tomboy and therefore on one side—my side—of the chasm that separated the "women" from the "girls" in that most sexually schizophrenic of decades.)

I asked her about her so-called image.

"I don't think I have one. Being blond, blue-eyed, and having a lot of energy is an image that people connect with the girl next door. Actually I'm one of the few women who had children in films. Most women refused to play mothers.

"Also, it might have to do with coloring. Generally, with the exception of Marilyn Monroe, dark women are considered sultry and sexy. There's the old joke about the bank teller with glasses being the great lover."

(Was she suggesting that she was the female equivalent?)

"What about reviews?" I asked her. "What about your ego?"

"I don't have an ego," she said. "I don't read reviews. I was under contract to Warners, and I figured they were paying me, so they would find the right thing for me to do.

"They didn't allow us to see the rushes. They didn't want us to come knocking on the door because a strand of hair was out of place. Still, maybe if we had seen them, it would have enabled us to improve. When you finally saw the whole thing, you wanted to go through the floor.

"I never read critics. I think they ought to simply describe a play or movie, not pass judgment on it. The world will decide."

It was on the subject of critics and current movies that she betrayed the only intimations of anger I was to see.

"I don't go to movies very much. I don't want to see junk. If I want realism, I'll become a social worker. But to come out thinking it's a shitty world . . . it's like people who stop to look at an accident; they're not aware of what it does to them. I know what I want, and I know what I don't want. In this country you can do what you damn well please."

One of the dogs came up and her whole manner changed. She leaned over to talk to him, then murmured to me, "They're so spiritual. So perfect. They've got it all together." She tells me the story of a dog that was brought to America from Nazi Germany and taught to love after only feeling hatred.

I asked her what her life was like after losing the husband she'd been so close to, and dependent on.

"The first year was really, really hard. But time heals everything. I didn't think I'd ever get over that and I did. I like being free. Oh, that doesn't sound right. But I like making my own decisions."

"What about the lawsuit against Rosenthal? Was that a terrible ordeal?"

"Yes. But compared to losing somebody that you love, I would say not. Having all your money taken from you is no joke, but you have to put it all in its proper place. I told my son, I have so much to be joyful about. That man is not going to take away my joy for any minute of any day. I'll do what I have to do, but I'll go about it in my way.

"No matter what comes, it's for a reason. With Marty, things got a little one-sided. He took over too much and didn't tell me enough. If I ever get married again, it'll be the best. I would have more insight into what a marriage should be.

"I have grown, and in growing you change your reactions to things. Life is nothing but a series of reactions. I want to do good things, and I want to be used. Do you know how many people have been helped by my case? Women read about it, and they all said, now I'd better check with my lawyer and my accountant, I'd better get involved. If my experience did that for people, then it's worthwhile."

Sitting back in her chair, she seemed to luxuriate in the ordeal and well-being of her world.

"Now I'm a peaceful lady. I love my house, I love being in it. I swim twice a day in my birthday suit. I love my dogs, and I'm glad I can do something for animals. That's all a name is good for."

The next day over breakfast at the Beverly Hills Hotel she pursued the same theme.

"I always felt that making a living wasn't the easiest thing in the world, and I decided I was going straight ahead and try to be as uncomplicated as possible. The important thing in life is just living and loving. So many people feel that if they're not in show biz or writing a book, they've been cheated, or wasted. People say, 'Oh, *you* can talk because you're a star.' But I never wanted that. I get the biggest charge when I know that an animal has been placed in a good home. It just thrills me."

Then, as if by design, on the way home from the hotel we encountered a German shepherd, wandering lost and hungry three doors from Doris Day's house. She seized his collar, and they were off with an alacrity that left me trailing in the dust. Was it really meant to be? Could she be *right*?

No Angel to Her Daughter

MARLENE DIETRICH

M arlene Dietrich was not the classic Narcissus of myth. When she looked in the reflecting pool she saw more than an image to fall in love with; she saw one that needed improving. She and Josef von Sternberg, the mentor, discoverer, and director with whom she made seven sumptuous films, were meant for each other. Slipping in and out of the roles of master and slave, slave and mistress, they fashioned an image of Dietrich that would withstand time, aging and self-parody. Whether it will survive this memoir by her daughter Maria is another question, but my guess is yes.

Those of us enamored of Dietrich—by no means everyone—have always known that no star was more aware of her effect she created than she and more shrewd and knowledgeable in developing and sustaining that effect through artifice: the light held three inches above and in front of the forehead to dramatize cheekbones. But the extent of that artifice and of the gap between image and reality had to await exposure by the one person who had both the privileged viewpoint and the compulsion to tell the tale. *Marlene Dietrich*, by Dietrich's only child, is the ultimate act of demystification, a startling and riveting work, completing—rather than competing with—the portrait begun by Dietrich's previous biographies, including Stephen Bach's recently published *Marlene Dietrich: Life and Legend* and Donald Spoto's *Blue Angel*, not to mention Dietrich's own charmingly unforthcoming account of her life, *Marlene* (1988). Maria Riva's revelations will incense a great many people—indeed, they apparently already have. Friends, fans, and perhaps relatives have been shocked by the comprehen-

---

*This article was first published in the *New York Times Book Review*, February 7, 1993. Copyright © 1993 by Molly Haskell.

sive catalog of lovers (most startlingly, if not incongruously, are Edward R.
Murrow and generals James M. Gavin and George S. Patton). Lovers are
caught in their boxer shorts, traipsing in and out of trailers, hotel rooms,
hideaways, and, when Maria is little, disappearing and reappearing at breakfast for Marlene's "famous scrambled eggs." A law unto herself, Dietrich
was romantic rather than sexual in her passions and so omnivorous that the
word promiscuous seems pale and petty. Maria writes of her childhood
with a chilling detachment:

> I was accustomed to my mother always having someone around. I
> never questioned their gender, or what they were actually there for. If
> they brought me expensive dolls and made a fuss over "the beautiful
> child," I didn't like them and stayed out of their way. If they saw no
> reason for courting the child simply because they were "busy" with the
> mother, I respected them as I did von Sternberg and Gabin, years later.
> If they treated me as an entity all on my own and judged me
> accordingly, as Brian Aherne did, I loved them. . . .
> I have never judged my mother for her emotional gluttony, only for
> the way she treated those who loved her. Occasionally, the rapidity of
> her turnover of bed partners became embarrassing, but that one learned
> to ignore over the years. I would have hated her habits more had she
> been motivated by sexual appetite. But all Dietrich ever wanted,
> needed, desired, was Romance with every capital R available, declara-
> tions of utter devotion, lyrical passion. She accepted the accompanying
> sex as the inescapable burden women had to endure. She would ear-
> nestly explain this to me. I was a grown woman, with a family of my
> own, but she felt I needed some sex education nevertheless:
> "They always want to put their 'thing' in—that's all they want. If
> you don't let them do it right away, they say you don't love them and
> get angry with you and leave!" She preferred fellatio, it put into her
> hand the power to direct the scene. Besides, European women were
> expected to have great skill in that department.
> Dietrich also adored impotent men. "They are nice. You can sleep
> and it's cozy!" Adopted American expressions were always pronounced
> in italics. Those "cozy" men naturally worshiped her. Her lack of
> concern, her obvious enjoyment despite their affliction, usually brought
> about miraculous cures. It was only when they regained their sexual
> equilibrium that she had enough and left them . . . flat!

She continued to have affairs into her sixties and beyond, but her romantic "gluttony" became unseemly only when, in her eighties, she began confiding indiscreetly in copious letters to a stranger in California, a fan whom she made her epistolary lover. Ms. Riva does not, I think, take into account sufficiently the alteration (or pathological exaggeration) of personality that can come with old age and disease—even to a human being as superhuman as Dietrich. The description of Dietrich's death, an undignified descent into drunkenness, meanness, and squalor, is particularly upsetting, and very different from Stephen Bach's more decorous picture of her sipping scotch, making records, and chatting on the phone, or even the disdainful diva of Maximillian Schell's documentary film, *Marlene*. Yet I not only believe every word in Riva's account, I also came away convinced of her right to tell it as she has.

We live in an age in which the hordes of people who want to "know all" create the demand for the number who want to tell all. Our ambivalence toward this transaction seems to express itself in a special hostility toward the memoirs of the surviving children of dead movie stars, not so much out of sympathy for the parents, whom we hypocritically claim "aren't here to defend themselves" (and if they were, what indeed would they say?), as from a *lack* of sympathy for the offspring raised in such gilded environments.

Who are they to tamper with our fantasies, or to claim to be writers when material simply falls into their laps! And yet, as Maria Riva's account of life with "mutti" demonstrates, they are the ones whose need to disentangle the Hydra-like hold of their mythic parents is most compelling. Stars are role-players by definition, and never more so than in that most alien environment, the home. The child is born into a stage set and into a role over which she has no control, without an agent to negotiate a decent deal for her. Dietrich's domiciles—luxury hotels in Europe, a series of lavishly appointed rented houses in Hollywood—were particularly unhomelike, just as Maria's role was particularly unchildlike. What made it more difficult was Dietrich's success in persuading the world that she was the most maternal of beings, a first rate cook, a perfectionist housekeeper, a "hausfrau," as well as, in fact, the financial mainstay of her daughter's family.

Maria was a girl who was chubby, who photographed badly, and who always looked older than her age, for the very good reason that her mother had subtracted two years from her daughter's age and her own. Losing two years to her mother's vanity was a sort of figurative foot-binding to which was added a literal body binding: Dietrich decided the girl's legs weren't growing normally and had them encased in braces every night for two years.

Once in Hollywood, Maria was not allowed to attend an American school and was discouraged from learning English (it was von Sternberg who insisted, and he gave her lessons), but she did go to the set with her mother and, with an eye as sharp as Dietrich's, became adviser, lady-in-waiting, and sounding board for her mother's consuming aestheticism regarding her own presentation.

Dietrich and her husband Rudolph Sieber played husband and wife till they died—he owing the bed he slept in and the farmhouse he lived in to her controlling munificence; she with a brand new store-bought wedding ring on her hand in order to make her exit as a faithful wife instead of the voracious and inexhaustible lover of men and women she had been. We learn from Steven Bach's biography that Dietrich's marriage, aside from being a necessary concession to Hollywood decorum in a puritanical age, was intended to preserve the fantasy of her and Sieber as romantic newlyweds, while we learn from Ms. Riva that she showed or dispatched to Sieber all the letters she received from her various lovers and carbon copies of those she sent in return. Excerpts of these are published here. Dietrich and Sieber confided all to each other, called each other *Mutti* and *Papilein* in their letters. But the daughter's memoir, full as it is of delicious and scathing disclosures cannot be dismissed as a Mutti-dearest, or even smutty-dearest, account.

Ms. Riva's book acquires a certain majesty through the quality and sharpness of remembrance and despite, rather than because of, the author's method of interspersing global news bulletins with the details of Dietrich's life, as if to broaden the picture and give it heft. Yet gradually even these passages become less awkward, more poignant, their childish tone suggesting the young person's desire to escape Dietrich's smothering world and the hothouse bitterness of the showbiz survivor genre. Also what I take to be an ironic attempt to discredit her mother by setting her self-absorption against the pageant of history does not work. Dietrich *is* part of history, and her right to belong there becomes self-evident. She is simply too interesting —cultivated, European, disciplined, furiously energetic, and sharp-witted (her wicked comments on various stars and movies, though highly self-serving, are no less astute for that).

And Riva is her mother's daughter, not just in intelligence and breadth of experience but also in her seeming objectivity. If Dietrich saw herself in the third person, so Maria has arrived at a point where she can contemplate her mother through bifocals: the luminous goddess who casts a spell over fans, lovers, and friends (even in those earliest films that disappeared from her filmography, Dietrich always knew how to turn to the light), and the Dietrich who was hidden from view, the Dietrich of the imperfect body (how endearing to know she had impossible breasts that she kept aloft with a high-tech foundation garment), the bigoted, racist, and imperial Dietrich. Dietrich as a destroyer of lives—the fate of Tami, the Russian woman who was Rudi's live-in lover and occasional servant, is a tale in itself. So is the horror story of the mother leaving her teenage daughter in the charge of a lesbian lover, identified only as "the rhinoceros," whose solicitous concern for Maria and her budding acting career suddenly took a malevolent turn. Night after night the woman forced herself on this girl, who had been trained to be obedient and compliant, in an act that she only later understood to be rape.

Ms. Riva is perceptive about her own complicity in the charade, about the reasons, when given the choice at various points in her life, she chose not to leave her mother's side. She understands how the sins of the mothers are visited on the children, sees herself pathologically reliving with her own children the childhood she did not have, to the point of playing with their toys at school, getting their mumps and chicken pox.

Maria Sieber did go into the theater and, between bouts of alcoholism and a brief marriage, established a minor career as an actress and director. It was during a stint at the Fordham University theater department that she met and fell in love with the university's teacher of scenic design, William Riva. They married and began having children, and although Ms. Riva continued to work in theater and television, this adored husband and the miracle of their marriage became the emotional center of her world. The book, however, is the lifework by which she establishes her own identity apart from yet somehow including the legacy of her mother.

If Maria-the-child got little joy from Dietrich's humorous interludes, Maria-the-writer triumphs over her past by recognizing the jewels when she sees them and presenting them with an eye for setting and style. I love the portrait of Dietrich and Mae West, in neighboring dressing rooms on the Paramount set, visiting back and forth, laughing and strutting their costumes and lovers like two gunfighters comparing technique. Or Marlene always referring to Cary Grant, because in his early days he peddled haberdashery on the set, as "the shirt salesman."

Dietrich inherited backbone and character from her stern bourgeois mother and a soldier's mettle and gallantry from her father, a patrician army officer who died in World War I. Her discipline and energy were famous. In one of the book's funniest interludes, this woman who had never sat behind a steering wheel learned to drive on her lunch hour for a scene that required it. Energy may well have been, as it often is, the largest component in her genius; it seems to have isolated her as well, as Erich Maria Remarque, one of Dietrich's lovers, beautifully understood when he gently reproached Maria after the girl had admitted she didn't love her mother.

"You must. She loves you as she perceives love. But her r.p.m.'s are a thousand a minute, whereas ours are a normal hundred a minute. We need an hour to love her, she loves us as well in six minutes and is on to everything else she must do, while we are wondering why she isn't loving us as we are loving her. We are mistaken, she already has."

When the press reported she had fainted on the set of *The Garden of Allah*, she called David O. Selznick in a rage. "I am *not* some delicate female who droops. That 'old lady' [Charles] Boyer does that enough for every-body." Even her bladder did her bidding, and she never played victim until, in old age, she began to deny reality. Her tyrannies and self-deceptions were grandiose: she eliminated unwanted people, including her sister, from her biography, just as she had erased her early films The credit for her leaving Hitler's Germany as early as she did should really go to Sieber, Ms. Riva says. But her derision of her mother's war activities comes across as petty and beside the point.

She understands that Dietrich, in war uniform complete with service ribbons and combat boots, had "the best part she was ever given," appear-ing before rapt and cheering soldiers in the United States, Algeria, Italy, and France. But in her disenchantment, Ms. Riva fails to appreciate the importance of the grand gesture to war as well as in theater and seems to find the honors and medals Dietrich won for her war record hopelessly disproportionate to her actual bravery. Yet Ms. Riva admits her mother was "fearless," and who can resist Dietrich flying out of La Guardia with her U.S.O. troupe in a hailstorm and getting herself to Algiers in order to track down Jean Gabin? This is how the daughter remembers the North African episode through her mother's eyes:

There was a rumor that the front had been reinforced by an armored division of the Free French. She commandeered a jeep and a driver from the motor pool, went searching for a tank division and, before dark, found it. . . .

"I ran from tank to tank—crying his name. Suddenly, I saw that wonderful salt-and-pepper hair! He had his back to me. 'Jean, Jean *mon amour!*' He spun around . . . jumped to the ground and took me in his arms."

They stood in their passionate embrace, oblivious to all those longing eyes envying the gray-haired man holding a dream. The kiss went on—they doffed their corps berets and cheered their approval, tinged with jealousy.

The sound of tanks starting up their engines finally broke them apart. He kissed her once more, "We go, *ma grande, ma grande, ma vie,*" held her to him for one timeless moment, then let go and leaped back onto his tank and down into its belly. . . . She stood in the clouds of dust they churned up, shielding her eyes, trying to catch one last glimpse of him, afraid she might never see him again.

She had managed to turn World War II into a movie, and who is to say the soldiers were less emboldened by this gallant woman than by the pep talks of their generals?

The heroism is offset by more than enough anecdotes revealing her corrosive disdain for people beneath her. Yet with all her fraying seams and rusty zippers exposed, she's still so much more interesting than that other blond sex goddess, Marilyn Monroe, whose very lack of definition and self-will has allowed her to become an all-purpose symbol, icon, and tool of popular culture. Monroe has provoked reams of fatuous prose by rescue fantasizers on the one hand and feminist victim-seekers on the other, whereas Dietrich, even at her most wretched, refuses pity, never begs for love, and defies us not to be stunned by her.

She does, however, put men on a pedestal. Riva points to the contradiction of this enormously powerful woman insisting that men were superior beings "whose authority must be endured with resignation." She finds irony in Dietrich's somehow believing that she was "an exception to the rule of female inferiority" (their brains were "too small" and they were prone to excessive emotionalism, exaggerated passions) even as she sat waiting by the phone for Yul Brynner's calls.

But this retreat by powerful women into protestations of inferiority and subservience to male "gods" obviously fills some need on their part to restore the "balance of nature" and atone for their own hubris. It reassures them, and us, and the men whose approval and love they seek, that they are after all "just women." It may also be that what these "superior" women secretly boast and inwardly cherish as their virtue (Latin: *virtus*) is the man in themselves, those qualities of body and mind—the soldier, the stoic, the philosopher—deemed manlike, so that even a man's way of loving becomes superior to the abject ways of a woman.

Riva seems to subscribe to this dualism when she describes her working with her mother on her Las Vegas show: "Once she was in tails, I gave her material that she could relax with, could enjoy. . . . She had fun with 'Whoopee,' indulged her favorite fantasy of the lonely lover in 'One for My Baby,' and explained love as she perceived it with 'I've Grown Accustomed to Her Face'—Dietrich could always sing real love to a woman better than to a man. Sentimental love, *that* she did better as a woman."

Dietrich's beauty is itself seen as trivial (because "feminine"?), not worthy of the adulation it inspires. As her mother did literally, Ms. Riva falls figuratively at the feet of talented and artistic men, while expressing dismay that anyone should worship at the equally famous but in her view less worthy feet of her mother.

If she denies her mother's awesome magic, she denies her own role in its creation. Yet the delight she must have felt, as a small child with a precocious sense of style, comes through in some of the book's most lyrical passages: vividly detailed descriptions of the step-by-step collaboration of mother and daughter, often in conjunction with costume designer Travis Banton, thinking up the wild and exotic ideas, finding the fabrics, fusing them into elaborate and camera-defying creations which von Sternberg nevertheless found ways of photographing.

Riva endorses Kenneth Tynan's axiom that Dietrich "has sex without gender," but I would say she is both genders, and she existed at a moment in time in a censored medium—romantic rather than sexual, glorying in a language of innuendo rather than clinical categories—when it was possible (in the Sternberg-Dietrich masterpiece *Morocco*) to kiss a woman on the lips and run off after a man in the desert sand, to be love object and love subject simultaneously. She makes us wonder, safely, without having to lose sleep over it, what is a man and what is a woman, after all, if so much of one can exist harmoniously in the other?

Hiding in the Spotlight

MERYL STREEP

No one could accuse Meryl Streep of playing to the galleries or pandering to the lascivious appetites of a male audience, but her delight in disguise—in bizarre wigs, unorthodox get-ups, and foreign accents—and in playing women who are outside the normal range of audience sympathy may have reached some high water mark in *A Cry in the Dark*. Can even Meryl Streep, astonishing talent that she is, get away with this one? She plays Lindy Chamberlain, the woman accused and convicted of killing her baby on a camping trip in central Australia in a murder trial that had the whole country in a stir in the early eighties. Most people think it was one of the most bizarre miscarriages of justice in modern times, some scholars even calling it a witch hunt (though a small minority is still convinced of her guilt). A case was concocted against her for a crime that seems to have been the work of a dingo (a wild dog), largely, it seems, because she and her pastor husband didn't behave properly. The sentence was suspended when exonerating evidence turned up, but not before Lindy had served three and a half years in prison and not before a large part of the public had gotten their kicks savaging Lindy with T-shirts and bumper stickers and other obscene mementos of mass hatred and hysteria.

The performance is an acting triumph, one of Streep's finest. The theme, as it emerges in the movie, is that the verdict was reached not through evidence but through the image of Chamberlain that came through in bite-size media snatches and in the trial. People didn't *like* Chamberlain, the way her eyebrows pointed upward, the fact that she didn't show

*This article first appeared in *Ms.*, December 1988. Permission to copy granted by *Ms. Magazine*. Copyright © 1988 by Molly Haskell.

sufficient grief; that her face was a mask of self-control; that she and her husband, Seventh-Day Adventists, took their religion's attitude of philosophical resignation toward their child's death; that they were too eager to cooperate with the press. And then, Lindy was a little too tough, too sensual (shades of our own Alice Crimmins), not "maternal" enough. In sum, Lindy Chamberlain didn't satisfy the public's myth of what a woman and mother should be.

It was a natural challenge for Streep, an actress who has delighted in playing unconventional, even unpleasant women, and who has made a fetish out of not giving the public what it wants and expects from a star. Still, there's something awesomely perverse in choosing a character who, though a byword in Australia, is remote from moviegoers' experience to begin with, and then giving her disconcertingly uningratiating characteristics. This is no small act of defiance when you consider that *Plenty* and *Ironweed*, two of Streep's recent films, were box-office failures, and she could have used a more conventionally romantic vehicle, something on the order of *Out of Africa,* to shore up her waning audience appeal and keep her career afloat.

But if there's one strand running through Streep's chameleon-like range of roles and impersonations, it's precisely this "alienation effect," her determination to be an actress rather than a star in the old-fashioned sense and to do idiosyncratic, theatrical roles in a medium in which success depends on being loved by huge numbers of people. In her willingness to forgo easy identification, Streep brings to dramatic point something that has been nosing its way to the forefront of consciousness for some time: the whole issue of a woman's lovability.

Stars are women who are always on display, always "on trial" for their femininity. As women, in real life and on the screen, choose roles that exude authority, strength, obsessiveness, ambition, secretiveness, power, self-interest, as opposed to the traditional (and often hidden) female qualities of openness, vulnerability, niceness, surrender, do they automatically risk losing their sex appeal, hence acceptance?

Streep is not alone in this. Recently, major actresses have played parts so unsympathetic, so "unwomanly" by conventional standards they would have given Louis B. Mayer apoplexy, and in projects that no studio head would have "greenlighted." Barbara Hershey, as the activist anti-apartheid heroine of *A World Apart*, places politics ahead of her family and deprives her teenage daughter of love and attention. Sigourney Weaver as the primatologist Dian Fossey so identifies with "her" gorillas on an African mountaintop that she takes leave of her fiancé, a lover, and her own sanity, and ends up looking more like a gorilla than a woman. Natasha Richardson, playing Patty Hearst as an enigmatic cipher, refuses to express anything more than contempt for the public that mythologizes her, a public that includes the audience for the film. But no one has more steadfastly refused to look like a dish or invite audience identification than Meryl Streep.

In *Manhattan* she was Woody Allen's furtive lesbian ex-wife who'd written a tell-all book about their marriage. In *Kramer vs. Kramer* she was a housewife who, with only the vaguest notions of self-fulfillment, abandoned her family and eventually gave up her son after a custody trial. In a quintessential Streep moment, the scene that won her that year's Oscar for Best Supporting Actress, she sat on the witness stand, her pale face masking all emotion, unrepentant. Okay, you'll say, that was the beginning of her career, before she had become a star, while she could still play around with her image. But instead of capitalizing on (or being imprisoned by) the stardom she attained for such relatively romantic roles as the mysterious Sarah in *The French Lieutenant's Woman*, Sophie, and Isak Dinesen, she went on to play the feisty lower-middle-class troublemaker and whistle-blower of *Silkwood*, the sanctimonious idealist in *Plenty*, and the derelict of *Ironweed*. The determination to be different—each role not only different from each other, but different from what we assume Meryl Streep, Yale Drama School graduate and the mother of three, to be—is the one constant of her career. An anti-star mystique seems to govern her life and her roles, a convergence, perhaps, of her seriousness as a performer and the inhibitions of a well-bred Protestant.

"God forbid I might be thought to be hogging the spotlight!" she might be saying with her reclusive life style, her reluctance to give interviews, her apparent indifference to billing (Redford, rather absurdly, received top billing for *Out of Africa*), and the fact that instead of imposing her ego on a project, she elects to be a part of some larger design: Africa in the twenties; the hidden history of the Holocaust; the battle against nuclear power; postwar England. In fact, these films in which she serves some larger purpose or is remote in time and place are her most effective. Her least successful roles have been contemporary and urban and (ostensibly) closer to home: the upscale reporter with marital problems in the failed comedy *Heartburn* and the suburbanite and adulteress manquée in *Falling in Love* (the misguided "remake" of *Brief Encounter*).

The aura of the old stars radiated out of a sense of self, a core identity projected into every role. However varied the performances of Bette Davis, say, or Katharine Hepburn, or Margaret Sullavan, we always felt we were in the presence of something knowable, familiar, constant. They had recognizable voices, ways of reading a line, even certain expressions that remained consistent from film to film. Comics could do imitations of them, and you either responded to them, unambivalently, or you didn't. Streep, chameleon-like, undercuts this sort of response by never staying in one place long enough for you to get a fix on her. Stretching the bounds of type, Bette Davis went in for costume (Elizabeth in *The Virgin Queen*) and period *(The Old Maid)*, but she was always Bette Davis, and no one would have thought to want it otherwise. Like Streep, she even dared to play unlikable, morally ambiguous heroines, her greatest being that of the wife of the planation owner in *The Letter* who murders her treacherous lover in cold blood, then refuses to confess or repent. The difference is that Davis fused with the role, poured her own passion and intensity into it. Her heroine is as icily proud and implacable as Medea—which may be why members of the Academy denied her the Oscar she deserved in favor of sweeter and tamer Ginger Rogers for *Kitty Foyle*—but Davis makes us respond to the fire within. It's hard to imagine an actress like Streep, who remains at a safe distance from her roles, rising to such heights . . . or falling to such depths. Moreover Streep inhabits a different world, one in which women don't throw themselves away on men . . . or don't publicize it if they do.

Instead of merging with her roles, Streep metamorphoses, changing herself completely, tying up all the loose ends so that she is perfectly hidden, an exemplary preceptor of the middlebrow injunction against "playing oneself." Playing ugly, equating disguising one's good looks with seriousness has always had a certain dubious vogue: Olivia de Havilland won points for occasionally looking plain, even dumpy. But for the most part it was men who went in for disguises, since it was men who felt more defensive about acting in the first place. Stretching themselves out of shape was a way of showing their seriousness and their superiority to a profession that was "second nature" to women, who were narcissists after all, but anathema to real men. Marlon Brando doing Okinawan in *Teahouse of the August Moon*. Laurence Olivier concealing his matinee idol sex appeal under Othello's blackface and Amos 'n' Andy voice or the crippled and ugly body of Richard III. Even his blond Hamlet was a refugee from the "real" Olivier. Paul Muni is reported to have shown up for Beverly Hills dinner parties in makeup.

But when women go out of their way to distract attention from themselves, in what's known as the Helen Hayes syndrome, it generally signals an inferiority complex about their appearance. Streep's off-center looks may not conform to traditional notions of beauty, which may be one reason she was less than effective as the archetypal woman of mystery in *The French Lieutenant's Women*. But it's precisely the ambiguity of her looks that are tantalizing—is she beautiful or is she strikingly plain? what does *she* think?—and how do people react to that milky, man-in-the-moon face, round and flat in certain lights and, in others, full of shadows and contours. Does she obscure her "beauty" in order to be taken seriously, or are her disguises distractions from what she perceives as a lack of beauty? Or is it just "play-acting"—a refusal to play the movie star game? The enigma remains.

"There's such a thing as the willful destruction of one's looks," said a friend of mine, as we looked at a still photograph of Streep, round-faced, with a black mop-like wig, and looking frumpy in gingham dresses and running shoes. Streep acquired an accent that was a cross between New Zealand, where the Chamberlains were from, and Australian, reportedly the most difficult there is, and gained weight for the part. It's one thing for De Niro to put on poundage to play a heavyweight boxer, but a woman? My friend had just spent three months taking off twenty pounds she'd gained during a black period of her life when, for whatever semiconscious reasons, she had "wanted" to look bad. And here, looking less like herself and more grotesque than ever, was Streep, doing another disappearing act, an actress who seems, as a British critic wrote of Olivier, to be "hiding in the spotlight."

Her talent is the stuff of legend. "She can do anything," says Robert Benton, who directed her in *Kramer vs. Kramer* and *Still of the Night*. "She has more ability and more range than any other actress." Most directors would agree, yet many would probably also agree that her gifts are more theatrical than cinematic. "Transcendent" and "electric" are words used by people who have seen her performances in even marginal stage plays. They also speak in hushed tones of her "stillness" and "quietness," words you wouldn't use to describe her screen work, which is busy in the extreme. The playing with the hair, the abrupt turning of the head, even the sound of wheels clicking as her mind calculates its next move in compiling a "brilliant" performance.

One feels a certain condescension in Streep, as if she were slumming, coming to cinema to save it from its own vulgarity. Movie critics have blown hot and cold on her, overpraising the early performances and then, in a predictable round of backlash following her premature canonization, ignoring her later performances or blasting them as "too technical." In fact, they were always "technical" and never more so than in her Oscar-winning performance in *Sophie's Choice*. Although the role is a setup, Streep brings it off dazzlingly, the way she twirls the English around in her mouth or falls to the floor, yellow-faced and anemic, or waddles through a Concentration Camp, her hair hidden in a kerchief, or, finally, the way she forces painful memories upward, like vomit. As she portrays Isak Dinesen, we feel the thinking processes, the "choices," of the actress ("Will this work?" "How's this going to look?"), but they coincide with the choices of a character who is discovering her destiny, fine-tuning her own sensibility. And similarly, Karen Silkwood is a woman awakening from small-town provincialism to a political vocation. Indeed, if there is a theme in Streep's films, it's precisely this: women in flight from one self, one identity, and in search of another.

Her heroines, like Streep herself, are masters of secrecy and evasion. Think of the furtiveness of the wives who become ex-wives in *Manhattan* and *Kramer vs. Kramer*; or the multiple enigmas behind the startling facade of Sophie, the Polish "shiksa" who is concealing not only the truth about her anti-Semitic father but her betrayal of her own daughter. The fiercely moralistic ex-Resistance fighter in *Plenty* seeks and never finds an arena for her ambition. The bubble-gum-chewing factory worker of *Silkwood* has left her home and lost custody of her children, eventually losing the good will of her co-workers and even her boyfriend when she finds her vocation as the uncompromising opponent of Kerr-McGee's nuclear negligence.

None of her heroines are feminist, strictly speaking, yet they uncannily embody various crosscurrents of experience in the last twenty years, as women have redefined themselves against the background of the women's movement. The discontented wives of *Manhattan* and *Kramer vs. Kramer* belong to those early days when women felt shackled by oppressive domesticity or unsatisfying marriages, yet hadn't found the jobs or careers that would justify rebellion. Isak Dinesen, eccentric and gifted as she was, was also the prototype of a woman adventurer who "invented" herself anew. Susan Traherne in *Plenty* and Karen Silkwood might be seen as representatives, without portfolio, of the politically idealistic strain of feminism; Silkwood and Lindy Chamberlain of the women who were neglected in the first wave of feminism because they didn't have middle class education and aspirations, but are now increasingly its focus.

There are unusual sexual arrangements: Isak Dinesen's expedient, yet unusually charged, marriage to Klaus Maria Brandauer's Baron von Blixen; the "scandalous" menage of *Silkwood*: Karen with her lover (Kurt Russell) and pal (Cher as the lesbian roommate). In the annals of female camaraderie, there is no moment more touching than her scene on the front porch with Cher, when the two fight and then teasingly make up.

I wouldn't want to press the parallels too far, but even the spectacle of failure that Streep raises in *Ironweed* has its resonance for those who've been burned, or burnt out, by the excessive hopes of fulfillment raised by the women's movement. Her Depression-era derelict, fallen from her upper-middle class perch, can still fake her former elegance when she runs into a friend from the old days, or enthrall a roomful of rowdies with a singing voice not completely ruined by drink. (She's got a wonderful voice, but like everything else, she won't give it to you straight. She'll sing bad-good, just as she'll look bad-good, and you're never quite sure which it is.) But the portrait of degradation makes us uncomfortable, because it reminds us of the hidden worm in the rhetoric of upward-striving: failure, spectacular failure. Again, Streep has touched a topical nerve: there are women in the streets, drunk and deranged, who once had "expectations."

And what of a mother's ambivalence toward her children, and the fear that any defection raises in the society around her—an explosive issue that crops up with remarkable frequency in Streep's movies? With the myth of mother love dictating that nothing less than 100 percent will do, it's no wonder that child abuse elicits such murderous outcries and such willful absence of understanding from the public. Honoring and enshrining the one "perfect" love in an imperfect society, movies have made sure we never glimpsed ambivalence: the fury a mother feels when confronted by a colicky baby or a recalcitrant ten-year-old; the unimaginably deep frustration of a woman who has had to abandon her talent, surrender her own ambitions to raise her family. Or a mother's instinctual preference for one child over another (generally, the male over the female)—a preference that (*Sophie's Choice* suggests) the mother would be bound to make under duress, which is why the ending of that movie is still such a shocker.

How are we to regard this woman, finally, who has assembled a gallery of women who are difficult, ambiguous, testy, ambitious, lonely, whose intelligence and sexuality are complicated and often contradictory parts of their lives, yet who fail to move us in accustomed ways. Hardcore movie lovers and aestheticians have always resisted Streep. Andrew Sarris sounded the note of opposition when he wrote that he preferred more intuitive and less controlled actresses, women with a sense of abandon. But intuitive actresses require someone to use them correctly. Debra Winger, Jessica Lange, Kathleen Turner are dependent on others and have their ups and downs, while Streep endures, her performances independent of her directors. Control is, of course, a key word with Streep. It's what prevents us from warming to her, yet it's part of her mystique. She's like someone acting in a glass house wired for sound: you see perfectly, hear with crystal clarity, but you never quite "feel" her. A friend of mine said his favorite Streep moment is the scene in *Out of Africa* when she's confronted by the lion.

"You suddenly see . . . there's somebody there," he said.

More than Olivier, Streep sometimes appears to be running for cover while displaying her wares, hiding behind her talent rather than enjoying it. Acting is the art of revelation as much as concealment, and Streep reveals little of herself. If she were to reveal more, she might involve us in the destinies of her characters, make us feel what it is we share with them rather than what divides us. Yet it is that quality of imagination Keats called "negative capability"—the ability to get inside someone else and project their *differences*—that captures us. What is fascinating about Streep's Lindy Chamberlain is ultimately mysterious: the worse life treats her, the more brutishly people behave, the stronger she grows, and her strength seems to arise from some religious or spiritual wellspring within. She doesn't ask for our tears, but she gets them anyway.

Control—that unwillingness to reveal, or surrender, the self—is Streep's essence, and no small factor in her appeal. Young women are said to idolize her, perhaps the way even younger women idolize Madonna—not for any single role or moment, but for an image of strength; for the "chutzpah" of a by-no-means conventionally beautiful woman in seizing stardom (*whatever* she wants to call it) and shaping it to her own specifications. For years we have watched female stars fall by the wayside when their youth and beauty faded, while their male counterparts went on as romantic leads forever. If Streep can sustain her career by virtue of talent and will power, rather than sex appeal, can play unorthodox roles and get away with it, more power to her. For *that* kind of power, for the "aura" of longevity and endurance, who wouldn't give up a little of the other kind?

The Goddess as Ordinary Woman

LIV ULLMANN

It is not just the publicity releases that are comparing Liv Ullmann to Greta Garbo, Ingrid Bergman, and Jeanne Moreau. Along the length of Bloomingdale's Belt, where *Scenes from a Marriage* is playing at Cinema I, men can be found wandering in a daze. And some of them haven't even gotten inside to see the film. Women are more guarded in their admiration, but most admit that Ullmann is "together" in a way that seems to elude many of us at this transitional moment of history.

What is it about the Norwegian-born Ullmann, aside from the Titian hair and the blue eyes that one must resist translating into purple prose? If I hadn't been shamed by the interviewer from the woman's magazine in *Scenes from a Marriage*, who does just that, I would say they have the color and the astonishing pale brightness of cornflowers or a gray sky just clearing to blue. The color—as it happens—of the telephone she uses several times in the film. The color of the floor-length knit dress she wore the first time I saw her, when she came to Sardi's in 1972 to pick up a Best Actress award (for *Cries and Whispers*) from the New York Film Critics Circle. Not only the color but the slight angora-fuzziness of the dress emphasized her soft contours and ultra femininity and suggested the awareness of a woman in perfect harmony with her exterior and not above displaying it a bit.

I think the popularity of *Scenes from a Marriage* is largely explainable by her presence and an audience's gratitude for what is not just the first real woman in months of drought, but a particular kind of woman—a radiant,

*This interview/article was first published in *The Village Voice*, October 3, 1974. Copyright © 1974 by Molly Haskell.

soothing Earth Mother who appears to heal the wounds wrought by sexual enmity. I am not sure that the reconciliation isn't illusory, but the fact that we grasp so desperately at something that is more than a straw but less than a lifeboat suggests that perhaps our needs have been given too short a shrift in American movies.

In the simplest terms, there is underlying *Scenes from a Marriage* an assumption that we are in this together, that both sexes are plunked on this planet without a guidebook, and if we join our heads and hearts and the rest of our bodies we will probably do better than if we spend all our time and energy trying to prove we don't need each other. If in Bergman's films men need and revere women too much—thus imprisoning them in their "superior," traditional roles as mothers and nurturers—in American movies the reverse is true. Men, fleeing their own mortality and the love and knowledge that might redeem the pain of growing old, take refuge in gross-out humor, male rite-of-passage films (which manage to bypass women as part of the process), or greater and greater displays of violence. As has happened so often in the past, a European actress has come to fill in a gap in our own culture.

Ullmann is that anomaly, an international star—the only one in Bergman's repertory to make the cover of *Time* magazine—who has yet to make a good film outside Scandinavia. The uncharitable might attribute this to the famous *Time* cover jinx on movie stars, but I think it is rather that Bergman has probed the actress's psyche and sensuality and allowed her to reveal and extend herself in ways that no other director, including Jan Troell, has dared to do.

It is probably true, as she pointed out in our interview at the Pierre—that critics have been unwilling to accept her in non-Bergman pictures. "If it's not Bergman," their thinking goes, "it's no good." But once we have seen Liv Ullmann speak worlds just by narrowing her eyes or barely parting her lips in a Bergman close-up, how can we tolerate the distance she places between us and a fustian, posing Queen Christina (in *The Abdication*) who makes a mockery of woman's "search for fulfillment."

Having lived with Ullmann for some five or six years, Bergman knows her moods and contradictions and what it is like to watch television with her and sleep with her and help her wash the dishes, and it is this knowledge that seeps through the cracks of Johan and Marianne's crumbling marriage, filling the narrative frame with feelings and perceptions that are sometimes at variance with the middle-class stereotypes with which it is concerned. Although Bergman gives Ullmann a looser rein than here-tofore to "become her own person," the film is ultimately not about Ullmann/Marianne's growth in understanding herself so much as with Bergman's understanding of Ullmann—her strengths, her fantasies, her evasions, her shuffling drabness, her sudden, dazzling beauty. Her gestures towards the women's movement are not particularly convincing, nor does her career seem to play any great role in her life. But her vibrations and metamorphoses as that classical creature, a woman "made for love," have an uncanny aura of truth: the way she becomes more alluring when she has "gotten over" him and is no longer emotionally dependent; her increased sexual desire and abandon when she no longer feels possessive towards him or anxious about what he feels for her. It may also be the ultimate "woman's" film, and Bergman's revenge on same: Johan's exasperation is also Bergman's, Johan's fear of being swallowed up by a woman is also the dramatist's fear of being overwhelmed by dailiness and domesticity, the dramatist's edge polished into smooth uselessness by familiarity. In that, its made-for-television length allows for the playing out of every nuance of a relationship, rather than the focusing on confrontation of a more conven-tional drama.

Ullmann, who once exchanged identities with Bibi Andersson in *Persona*, radiates a poise and self-possession that both attracts and repels Bergman and that is strikingly unlike Andersson's more tenuously cerebral grasp of herself. The differences between the two, as they have evolved since 1966, are fascinating. Andersson suggests the insecurity of the more complex, intellectual woman, harboring an unresolved conflict between her sensual and spiritual selves. It is Ullmann's self-containment bordering on compla-cency that drives her crazy in *Persona* and that in *Scenes from a Marriage* galvanizes her into a momentary alliance with her despised husband. In Andersson, we think we glimpse the kind of woman who is constantly in search of something, who is tormented by doubts and driven by spiritual needs. Whereas Ullmann, even when she withdraws from the world in *Persona*, is responding simply, with a peasant sense of survival, by rejecting the world and its unanswerable questions.

As a woman who fulfills herself in love, she demands paradoxically less of men than Andersson, who requires that they engage her mind. An-dersson has sharp edges; Ullmann the mother, the solace, has none. But in her soft sufficiency she is invulnerable. The other side of her pliancy is what Johan/Bergman calls her "white, hard resistance." Perhaps she gives everything—and nothing. Only a great artist or a long relationship could uncover such cruel ironies, and with Bergman, Ullmann had both.

CERTAINLY, WHEN YOU MEET her in person, you are likely to decide that even such failings as the screenplay attributes to her are unthinkable. There is nothing hard or resistant in this woman in red pants and top who, when I meet her, is cheerful, voluble, curious, frank, and self-critical, and who betrays no weariness at having to confront yet another interviewer except to confess that she is sick to death of talking about herself.

When I arrive at their suite in the Pierre, she and her companion, Cecillia Drott, who did the makeup for *Scenes* and *Cries and Whispers*, are watching *The Mating Game* with that mixture of amusement and disbelief that makes American daytime television such a mind-blowing experience for Europeans.

Ullmann is still trying to recover from a show in which the wife, in the presence of the husband, was asked to tell the worst secret of her marriage, and she revealed, to her husband's horrified humiliation, that they had a lousy sex life.

"Yesterday I saw the Merv Griffin show," she said, "where Burt Reynolds and another he-man and a [laughing] he-girl were talking about what they would do to all the bad critics of their movie. I couldn't take them seriously—they are not like real people. If anyone ever came on a show and acted sincere and normal, he would look fake," she said with amazement. I was struck once again at how European actors and actresses are able to ply their profession with more dignity and less psychic dislocation—probably because they are treated like human beings rather than trained seals hawking their products.

Ullmann speaks beautiful English, having lived in New York briefly as a child and studied it in school. There is only a slight accent—she also has a Norwegian accent in Swedish—and an occasional marvelous neologism (or transposition of a Norwegian work into English), as when she told me that some poor plagiarist, whose book on Harlem had been much praised, had the "unluck" for somebody to discover the original.

I told her I had seen the two-hour, forty-eight-minute version of *Scenes from a Marriage*, as well as the four-hour version (itself cut from the original six-part, five-hour television special), and asked her what she thought had been gained or lost.

ULLMANN: The four-hour version was a compromise of the television version. There were many of the same kinds of scenes, only slightly different. There were moments of relaxation which you need in a TV show but not in a movie. The film shows all the important things that happen, but some of the emotional scenes are cut because you can't watch everything in that short a time.

MH: I found myself liking it much better the second time around. It was like watching it on television, getting to know and accept the people. In particular, I found the husband (played by Erland Josephson) more sympathetic.

ULLMANN: This happened in Sweden, too. The first time around, people had enormous discussions the whole week. Then the next time around [the whole cycle was shown three times], what you said happened. They had seen more of the husband and they understood his attitude in the first scene, his arrogance. They came to pity him, and they realized he was acting that way to hide his insecurity.

MH: My male companion (as we say) didn't understand why Johan would leave Marianne. "She's so beautiful and extraordinary," he said. But I think women understand it.

ULLMANN: Why he leaves her is that he suddenly feels afraid. He's trying to grab life while it's still there.

MH: It's something we've begun referring to [apologetically] as "male menopause."

Ullmann appreciates the term, and she and Drott nod vigorously.

ULLMANN: Yes, men have it harder than we do. We can call it something physical, can get pills, go to the doctor, get pity. But men do all these crazy things—they get divorces, they suddenly turn homosexual, they walk through red lights. They feel lost but they have nothing to prove what's wrong. It is much more difficult.

We are very lucky if we have a relationship where we feel fulfilled, but if we are unfulfilled, the warning lights keep flashing that age is coming on.

MH: In one of the film's most extraordinary scenes, you are interviewed by an elderly woman [actually Barbro Hiort Af Ornas, who was the nurse in *The Brink of Life*] who wants a divorce. Suddenly in the calmest possible manner, she confesses not only that she doesn't love her husband, but that she doesn't love her children, has never loved them; and that she feels her senses failing her—when she hears, sees, touches something it is remote, the "sensation is thin and dry." You start to say something, but then are silent. What was it?

ULLMANN: Bergman never told me, but I think it is that the woman touches a nerve in me, something that I am used to hiding.

MH: In the first scene, you and Josephson are being interviewed by a reporter, Mrs. Palm, from a woman's magazine. Some of the scene has been cut for the theatrical version.

ULLMANN: Yes, she runs and snoops around when they've left the room, she even peeks in the bedroom. It's a very funny moment, but you know she is that kind of woman without showing that scene.

MH: She reminds me of so many interviewers, when she pushes her glasses back on her head, and opens that enormous, all-purpose sack, the way she intimidates you with her clickety-click professionalism.

ULLMANN: All the interviewers for the gossip magazines in Sweden are like that, with their little skirts and big belts, always snooping.

MH: And you feel stupid because you can't respond in their terms, can't think of something cute and quick and "profound" about love and marriage. Having just endured a similar experience, I really appreciated that part, and the whole notion of the Happy Couple feature, which is predicated on the assumption that each partner was a cipher or a half-person until the marriage, which miraculously completed and transformed them.

But there are other things that have been cut, like our discovery that Mrs. Palm was an old schoolmate of yours. To me, it seemed an allusion to *A Doll's House* and the scene when Christine comes to see Nora.

ULLMANN [thoughtful, then delighted]: Yes, you're right. I never thought of that. I don't have anything to say to the interviewer, I don't feel friendly. I try to move away, and yet I never quite got the bit of business when we were shooting the film. But then, when I was doing *A Doll's House*, I suddenly remembered this feeling and I used it, I moved away from Christine more decisively. I believe I felt at the time (of *Scenes*) that if I ever have the opportunity, I will use this gesture. I remembered it and used it.

It's like when I was watching a production of *A Doll's House* a long time ago. It was a bad production, but a friend of mine, a good friend, was playing Nora. In the scene when she is decorating the Christmas tree, before Torvald is coming home, she suddenly starts decorating herself! At the time, most of us didn't understand, but when I came to do the scene, I started doing it, I started decorating myself. This is a woman who is always putting on masks for her husband.

MH: Another interesting, and related, factor is that Mrs. Palm is addressing most of her questions to Johan. When she asks you one that you *can* respond to, and you finally open up, she immediately interrupts and calls for a photograph! This becomes especially ironic when you know that she is an old friend of yours, and seems to confirm something that Johan says later, in a semi-facetious diatribe against "Women's Lib," when he claims that all women are out to get each other.

ULLMANN: Yes, but interviewers do that to men, too. With Bergman, they always interrupt him just when he is going to say something interesting, because they can't handle it. It doesn't fit, like a person suddenly acting natural on your TV game show. The interviewers come to get what they want to give their readers, so it is fake to begin with. It's like a bad director. When you at last find the right action or motivation, he will talk it out so much that you'll never find it again.

MH: Why do Johan and Marianne consent to the interview?

ULLMANN: Why does anybody? Because they think it will be fun. They've never done it before.

MH: What is Bergman's attitude toward the Bibi Andersson character? The scene seemed rather harsh on her.

ULLMANN: He likes her. I think he likes her. He feels sorry for the man but sympathy for her. He finds a kind of hope in the woman. Women are stronger than men.

MH: I think the fact that Marianne blossoms after the separation is proof of that.

ULLMANN: It's funny. One woman critic wrote that it was unbelievable— the man got more and more wrinkled and sad while she was lovelier than ever—but that's the point of the story. This is always happening in real life, women becoming more attractive after their husbands divorce them, or die.

MH: I think it's partly just discovering that they *can* make it alone that gives them strength. I also love the scene when, after they are separated, he comes for dinner. She brings out the journal that, at the encouragement of her psychiatrist, she has started to keep. [With that wonderful insight into her female vanity, Bergman has her wishing she hadn't stayed up till three on *that* night writing in it, as it has made her look tired.] She begins reading it to Johan, and he falls asleep.

ULLMANN: I've heard men say, heard Bergman say, they just want to leave when women go on and on about emotional things. This is a difference between women and men—men are tired, but women are always ready to go on and on about emotional things. That can be exhausting for a man. They are on another level, where everything is not that important, and when you start up they say "Oh, there you go again." He saw her like that.

MH: Yes, but she never does go on and on. Johan is always criticizing her for faults you never show.

ULLMANN: I agree, they say that about her, like when at the end he is surprised that she is not jealous. He thinks she is not jealous. I don't know where he got that idea. It's written in the character, but so he let them say it about her.

Everybody has her own interpretation. It's like your friend saying how could he leave her? I identify so closely with the woman, I felt it was natural that he should leave her. She's wearing those glasses and a night dress, she looks terrible and takes the marriage for granted while he wants somebody who doesn't. She's plain and very uninteresting. It's all in what you see at the time.

MH: There's a scene in the published screenplay that is one of my favorites that has been cut out of the shorter version. It's when he's divorcing her and they are discussing the details over breakfast. She mentions she'll have to tell the old housekeeper, and he stutters and finally he says you don't need to—she already knows. Marianne looks surprised, and shamefacedly he explains that there had been a change of his schedule that he didn't know about and he had brought his mistress home—the only time—and the housekeeper walked into their bedroom the next morning. On her face there's this incredible pain mingled with an attempt to see the absurdity of it.

ULLMANN: Yes, to me that's one of the most horrible things that happens to her, maybe the most horrible—more than the humiliation of finding that all of her friends know. The fact that the cleaning woman is such an old friend, and that the husband brought his girl to her home. But men don't feel it that way. Bergman had to choose between the two scenes, and he kept the one with her on the phone, where rage comes for the first time. The other one is actually worse. But the way the man is talking about it, he doesn't know how terrible it is. If a woman had written that scene, she would have made the lines more cruel, to bring out the horror of it. But the way Johan is talking, neither the man who acted it nor Bergman understood the impact of it. That's what makes the whole thing so interesting.

MH: How much freedom does Bergman give you?

ULLMANN: A lot. He gives you a direction: you pass through a room. But the freedom of expression is yours.

MH: I liked it when you just pulled the covers over your head, to make the whole thing go away. Did you think of that. It seemed such a reflex?

ULLMANN: I don't remember. It was probably something I had done or would do.

MH: And packing the husband's suitcase?

ULLMANN: I wouldn't have done that. But I have a friend [she says a name and turns to Cecillia Drott, who nods] who always helps her husband pack when he goes on his affairs.

MH: In the very last scene, there's a sequence in which you confess to Johan that early in your marriage you had affairs. That's been cut.

ULLMANN: I'm glad. I never saw her as having affairs. I guess Bergman wanted to think she was more exciting and open to adventure than she was, that she had been exciting all the time. I didn't want to say the line, so I asked Bergman if I could say it as if I were lying. That's what I'm trying to do. Now afterwards, Bergman has been very nice about it in interviews—he admitted I didn't want to say it.

MH: The abortion scene has been cut, but frankly I don't miss it.

ULLMANN: There's a lot of life left out.

MH: I would have liked to see the scene, cut from both versions, between you and your mother.

ULLMANN: So would the woman who played my mother. I feel very sad about that. At first I didn't have the heart to tell her it had been cut, but I guess I will have to now.

MH: I miss, too, the scene in which Johan admits to hating the children.

ULLMANN: Well, there are always things cut from every picture that disappoint you. As a matter of fact, I miss more in *The Abdication* than in *Scenes from a Marriage*. If you really care for a picture, there will always be those scenes on the cutting room floor about which you say, "There's where I really show this other side of my character." [Having now seen "The Abdication," I think she may be right. I'd like to think there were some footage somewhere that would show Ullmann as something other than a neurotic, posturing soap opera queen who makes decisions of state on whim and religious conversions out of displaced sexual longing.]

MH: What was it like doing *Persona*, your first film with Bergman?

ULLMANN: At first I was terrified. I blushed whenever Bergman said a word. If I had not had Bibi [Andersson] there—I lived with her and her then-husband—I wouldn't have gotten through. Slowly I understood that he was kind and nice. Then he got excited about the rushes and I got confidence. Bibi was nervous, too, at the beginning, and broke out in nervous spots. Bergman knew very little about me, he had only seen me on the stage. And there I was this young girl who was always blushing, playing a mature woman. Bibi and I heard later that there was a lot of talk during the first week about canceling the whole project.

We went to the island of Faro and redid all the scenes done in Stockholm. We had a wonderful time, always joking. We just thought we were making this small film on an island and nobody would ever see it, and then it became a classic. Bergman experimented a lot and let us be a part of it. The scene with the faces coming together, we didn't even know what was up until we went to the rushes. Bibi said, "Liv, you're marvelous." I said, "Bibi, you're fantastic." Then we saw the faces merging—it was the most frightening thing I ever saw in my life. Everybody has one good side and one bad side, or at least two different sides, one not as good as the other. Bergman had taken the worse side of each of us. To see this woman, moving her lips, and half of her is you! It's what schizophrenic people must feel. There were things like that all the time.

With *Cries and Whispers* we never had a somber atmosphere. Harriet Andersson was running around and making jokes in this little night-gown, and I was really getting worried, but when the camera said go, she looked dead.

MH: What about the character you play?

ULLMANN: She isn't really a sympathetic character. Someone says she's the kind of woman who goes through a room and never shuts the door after her, very selfish. When her sister needs her she can't give. And yet everybody still thinks she's sweet and nice—the audience, too. That's why she's dangerous.

Some people criticized and said Bergman is so bad what he does to me. I'm so stupid, I just thought it was the part's bad character, not mine. There is this streak of selfishness in me, though, that I wish weren't there.

MH: Although you were highly praised for your role as the pioneer woman in the Troell epics, I always think of you as contemporary, as belonging to modern times.

ULLMANN: Actually, I've done mostly period things, except for Bergman. Classical movies like *The Abdication* also reflect modern people. I like that mixture, although I guess I'd like to do more modern stuff.

MH: What about your American movies? One I haven't seen is *Zandy's Bride*.

ULLMANN: I love Gene Hackman. He is fantastic, very inventive. He played an unsympathetic character but he did wonderful things with him.

MH: One male critic told me he found you at your most attractive and most womanly in *Zandy's Bride*.

ULLMANN: Then he must be a misogynist, because I was asked to look thin and haggard. I was a mail order bride, after all, and no great catch. The first thing he says to me is you lied about your age.

MH: *Forty Carats?*

ULLMANN: I'd do it again, willingly. Only with a little more control.

MH: I didn't quite see you as the "older woman."

ULLMANN: If I'd only had Cecillia to help me. What happened is they were so afraid I wouldn't look old enough, that they made me look ugly instead of older. The boy would have easily gone off with someone forty but more attractive. Only in Greece did I look okay—I had a scarf on my head. I'd really like to do more comedy. I have a disadvantage of working in the Bergman pictures. All the critics think if it's not Bergman then it's wrong. It's unfair that I have to do seven American pictures that are as good as the Bergman pictures before they will accept me.

MH: The difference between you and, say, Garbo and Ingrid Bergman, was that they came here first, and their myths grew out of their American movies, whereas you . . .

ULLMANN: If I'd come here first, then nobody would have *ever* heard of me. Bergman and Garbo came at a time when they still made pictures for women in America. Joanne Woodward is the only actress who has scripts written for her. All anybody wants to see is Paul Redford. [We yelp with delight at this slip.]

MH: I'm afraid it's women as much as the men who go to see *The Sting.* They get two for the price of one.

ULLMANN: I guess women don't want to look at other women over thirty with the same problems.

MH: Why is the situation different in Europe, in European films.

ULLMANN: In Sweden, in Europe, they make more movies about women because they feel more interest in women's inner soul. On commercials here, nobody talks about the inner side of woman. They only do things to their outside, to their smell, their hands, their hair, for the husband when he comes home. That's their idea of attractiveness in a woman, while a man reads newspapers, does other things. They've made a myth of the American woman everybody wants to get away from.

MH: What about European commercials?

ULLMANN: In Sweden they don't have them at all. In England there is not the same emphasis. You don't have the same theme that all women must be this way. Here, it is really effective propaganda. When I watch for a while I feel I have to go out and get that shampoo. They talk even in a certain kind of voice because they know it works. There is this image of the sophisticated woman which very few of us are. All of us have to face the problem of what to do with ourselves, and what we are.

MH: What about the Women's Movement?

ULLMANN: I don't like the real militants. Their idea of what a woman is, is just as rigid. They have a fixed image that is even more frightening than the commercials. Everyone is afraid to show woman to herself. They think nobody will love her if she grows for herself.

MH: I was electrified at that point in *Scenes from a Marriage* when we see snapshots of you as a child and a teenager, just seeing what you looked like. Marianne's voice-over says she has always lived for others. Is that true of you?

ULLMANN: Very much. I have spent most of my life and still spend most of it living for other people, doing what is expected of me, being scared of doing my own thing. I've wasted oceans of time doing what other people didn't care about by doing for them, while they were doing the same thing for me.

In fact, Bergman got hold of these pictures without my knowing it, and his insights were a revelation to me. Like the one where I am all dressed up with the hat and the pocketbook and the big bosoms. That was taken when I was seventeen and I went to London to study acting. I lived at the Y.W.C.A. with older girls—only by about two years, but they seemed much older. All the time, I was trying to be grown up, wearing a hat, and padding my bust, all these things that had nothing to do with me, just to be accepted by the older girls.

Then there's a picture with me lying on the beach, and the speech says I was obsessed with sex. I certainly didn't think of myself that way, but I look at the picture and it proves it. After years of padding, I have finally started to get a bust, and I've crossed my arms to make the crease show. There again, I was preoccupied with sex so people will accept me, so early on we get into these things.

MH: How much of *Scenes* is your story, the story of you and Bergman?

ULLMANN: It's not my story. I was terrified everyone would think that, but everyone thinks it's *their* story. A producer here in America who had divorced his wife told Bergman that once she invited him home during the separation and that she started telling him she had gone to sleep with her psychiatrist, and about her soul-searching, and he fell asleep, exactly like in the movie.

Men have a facade. One part of women's nature is to be open to these emotional things, so they can see a film like this and fit it in, face it, but men aren't able to deal with it as easily. A man, a journalist, came here, he was very stiff and formal, but in talking about the movie he suddenly broke down. He had had a similar situation and was shattered by the film. He was so attractive when he broke down.

One reason a lot of women relate to it, is that I've drawn from so many women, from this friend and that one, I steal bits and pieces like a drawing. Things I've kept and collected I've used in this picture.

MH: The divorce scene becomes extraordinarily violent although Johan's hitting you occurs below the frame.

ULLMANN: Erland didn't want to do it, he didn't want to hit a woman. He just felt he couldn't do it and he felt sick beforehand, but when he got into the scene he lost himself. It wasn't that he lost control but suddenly he felt it was right for his character. It took a long time to get to that part, twelve minutes. But we start with hating, so we are already at a high level. He will be able to do a lot more now. That's why it's important to have a director like Bergman who will allow you to do anything. [I don't know. I remember the story of Gregory Peck not being able to bring himself to hit Lauren Bacall when they were doing *Designing Woman*. She told Bogey and the boys when she got home and they were supposed to have gotten a big laugh out of it, but I always thought Peck was the hero of that story.]

MH: The jobs seem unreal, subordinated to the relationship.

ULLMANN: Because love is more important than the job. You throw yourself into a job when you can't do other things, but deep down we want to talk about the human condition. Their story is really their marriage story, and that's also the reason the children—who wouldn't have changed what was between them one way or the other—are left out. It's *their* particular story. Some other couple, the children might have come between them.

MH: Isn't it really about a relationship rather than a marriage?

ULLMANN: Yes, it's very important that it's a relationship. Homosexuals also think it's their story. It's about a relationship and a longing for it, so even people who have never had one understand it.

MH: How long did it take to shoot?

ULLMANN: A very short time—eight weeks shooting. It was very hard, because there was a lot of dialogue to learn. We shot it in sequence, rehearsed for one week, then shot for a week. We couldn't have gone on like that much longer. There was no improvisation, for almost the first time with Bergman, who lately is very free. We were not allowed to depart one word from the script. This was important because there was a lot of silly, banal talk. If we had been let loose we would just swim out into sheer banality.

It was an extraordinary experience, fighting and crying. We got to know each other so well, we skipped all kinds of shyness with each other and with everybody on the crew. We worked intimately and discussed the scenes. Working on the island was so much fun, very relaxed. You had to walk for miles to a toilet and there was only cold water. We would meet in the evenings by the fire and drink and talk.

MH: Bergman, too?

ULLMANN: No, without him; he's a recluse in the evenings.

MH: And how is it since you have broken up?

ULLMANN: Much easier. Before, if we had an argument at breakfast, I would be upset all day in my womanly way. Now we have the best part of a relationship. [She hesitates.] Or almost. The best thing you can have with somebody you lived with—friendship and working together.

Belle Dame sans Merci

JEANNE MOREAU

With her knowingly enigmatic smile and her singleminded pursuit of passion, Moreau wasn't quite femme fatale as involuntary force of nature. She was more a thinking man's *belle dame sans merci*. When she stalks the nocturnal streets of Louis Malle's *L'Ascenseur à l'echafaud*, looking for her murderer-lover, she's a somnambulist in the clutch of her own fierce and unconditional vision of love. Although she and Maurice Ronet never appear together until the end of the film—and then, only in the photographs that incriminate them and seal their love in an irrecoverable past—her interior monologue runs like a sinuous thread through the story, binding him to her and making everything else irrelevant. Whereas Garbo got one giant close-up each as Anna Karenina and Queen Christina, Moreau's face dominates almost every frame, the engine powering *L'Ascenseur* and practically every movie she made.

Even as femme fatale, Moreau—perhaps because she lives in a different age, or because she hasn't the same dazzling and dangerous surface beauty of a Dietrich or a Louise Brooks—seems more the architect of her mystique. A prefeminist symbol of liberation and sexual freedom, she emerged in the late fifties and early sixties to represent something new that audiences were ready for, or almost: a wife who leaves husband, house, and children behind in Malle's other *amour fou* movie, *Les Amants*; the amoral magnet of desire in Truffaut's *Jules and Jim* and the instrument of revenge in his *The Bride Wore Black*; the listless and alienated wanderer in *La Notte* who reflects the anomie of Antonioni's modern landscape.

*Portions of this article were first published in *Film Comment*, March–April 1990, and *Mirabella*, January 1994. Copyright © 1994 by Molly Haskell.

One of the few French actresses who embody international stardom—
she could hold her own doing a road company strip tease with Bardot in
Viva Maria—Moreau wasn't a beauty in the conventional sense, and Louis
Malle had the temerity to shoot her in ways that didn't prettify her.
Dubbed the French Bette Davis, she actually began on the stage and was
more "real actress" than movie-created icon. Yet, like Davis, she won over
the camera and seduced audiences through a combination of will power,
self-possession, and eyes that could transfix you with the promise of
heedless passion.

She gravitated to the most interesting projects and directors, not only
Truffaut, Antonioni, and Malle, but Joseph Losey and Peter Brook as well.
As the signature star of the Nouvelle Vague, she was linked more with the
quality tradition within the movement than with its radical cutting edge.
Her ambivalent status is reflected in the fact that she was beloved of
Truffaut but detested by Godard, who reportedly said she was a slut and
the only role he'd ever cast her in was that of a waitress.

Goddess or slut? A playful enchantress who brings humor to the French
tradition of carnality or a *film noir* heroine whose outsize passions are a
destructive force? Both, of course, and nowhere more ambiguously than in
Jules and Jim. Truffaut once told an interviewer that he made the movie
because he hadn't liked Antonioni's excessively serious portrait of Moreau
in *La Notte* and wanted to show her lighter side. Yet despite its surface
gaiety, its reckless Keystone Kops silent-movie momentum, and its charm,
this is one of the darkest love stories ever made. Seen in a 1990 revival in
the shadow of Truffaut's untimely death, the morbidity pulls more than the
gaiety, and the heroine seems as monstrous as she is seductive. In 1961, I
was captivated by what I saw as an idyllic triangle with a woman embody-
ing free love, on *her* terms, at its center. On a recent viewing, I felt an
inward shrinking from this woman who is bound to wreck the very
happiness she creates. Moreau's Catherine, like Dietrich's Lola in *The Blue
Angel*, is a goddess of love whose uncompromising demand for fealty has
cruel consequences. In the end, Moreau drives off the cliff, taking one lover
with her and leaving a husband and child behind. In order to retain
audience sympathy for a renegade mother, however, Truffaut carefully
keeps the abandoned daughter out of the movie's last frame, when Oskar
Werner trudges away from the cemetery where the ashes of wife and best
friend are buried.

"Sa curieuse sourire qui m'avait tant plue"—"that curious smile that had so
tantalized me," she sang about herself, in that reedy, childlike voice, from

the man's point of view. In repose, her mouth, with its downturned edges, fell into a pout, her face a melancholy testament to disappointment. Then suddenly and swiftly, the corners would turn up. Deliciously, the sun breaking through stormy weather, the smile would ignite and dazzle; the prey, grateful for sunlight, was disarmed, ready to be swallowed whole.

When, in *La Femme Nikita*, it's time to turn Anne Parillaud from androgynous street punk into a professional hit-person and "real woman," la Moreau, Female Incarnate of French cinema, is brought in to supervise the makeover. Lurking within the transformation of Parillaud from sexless junkie into alluring femme fatale lies the fashionable idea that women are constructed, not born, and that being female is a matter of performing a role based on costume and gestures. Yet what the perennially fascinating Moreau really represents is something quite different—not the triumph of style in the form of cosmetics, or Saint Laurent couture, or great legs, or the artifices of the moment. Her radiance comes from within and, as she ages, from her willingness to let us see both the raptures and ravages of life on her glorious face.

The femme fatale is almost invariably a male-invented creation, the projection—and prisoner—of a director or writer's fears and fantasies, and probably a means of satisfying his own self-destructive urges. In return, she is flattered by being worshipped as a goddess and given godlike powers. One often feels that trapped inside the man-eating female is a cheerful, nonvoracious woman struggling to get out. Certainly in *Lumière*, the film Moreau herself directed, she saw herself in a less romantic, more realistic vein. As the actress heroine, she was not a temptress locked in a life-and-death passion but a working, if somewhat temperamental, woman, surrounded by friends, male and female, wrestling with the tensions of relationships and career.

In her latest picture, the charming little British comedy called *The Summer House*, her presence is a kind of joyous disturbance, a toxic wildflower among the tidy roses and zinnias offered by the Brits who surround her. She plays a half-British, half-Egyptian woman of the world named Lily. Into the dreary suburb of Croydon, 1959, she arrives to attend what she instantly realizes is an ill-matched wedding between an old friend's daughter and the twerp next door. (The young man is considered a dud even by his mother, played by the wonderful Joan Plowright.) Flashily dressed and bejeweled, with a no-regrets smile, and willing to drink everyone under the table, Lily appears like a very earthy goddess ex machina, privy to the mysteries, both spiritual and sexual, of an older world that haunts the genteel and conformist fifties milieu. She is an emissary from a world of pleasure, where everything is still possible, and *that* is always subversive.

"I wrote down some of Lily's funny remarks and pithy phrases," I tell her on the phone. I'm in New York, talking to her in Paris. "But I can't make out my notes. I thought if I could give you a word or two you might make sense of them. There was one about the British men wearing lace pants. Or the ironic lament 'princes went out with the war.'" We both giggle. "I don't think you need to think much about them," she says. "They just bubble up."

I tell her I was enchanted by the ending in which she manages to shock all the wedding guests and abort the nuptials in a wildly and comically carnal *coup de théâtre*. "But it's not just sexual liberation, it's spiritual, too," she reminds me. The girl had had an earlier mystical experience in Egypt, which had been buried. "She frees the young girl spiritually as well. She opens her way to God."

Yes, the two go together. That smile of carnal complicity is also that of a woman who has found inner peace.

Most Americans came to her via *Jules and Jim* and fell in love, as did the two men, with this irresistible but deadly free spirit. But she was carving out a new kind of restless modern woman before Truffaut decided to liberate her from the moody image she had been given by Malle and Antonioni.

In movies like *Moderato Cantabile*, *La Notte*, and Roger Vadim's *Les Liaisons Dangereuses*, she played bored, sexually unsatisfied women in roles that contain all the discontent soon to be given outlet and form as women's liberation.

In an unintentionally comical foreword to his 1959 *Les Liaisons Dangereuses*, Vadim appears onscreen to prepare us for Juliette, the sexually manipulative character played by Moreau, whom he seems both to condemn and exonerate. He talks of these vexing times in which, in their demand for "ayqualité of the sexes," certain women are "exploding lak overrap frut." He assures us that not all married women behave like Juliette, who wants to "prove huhself at any prahs," yet he notes, apparently in her defense, that when a man has many lovers he is known as a Don Juan, while a woman is known as a trollop. The character Moreau plays is punished in the end, but not before creating a far more interesting impression than all the blond bimbo Bardot wannabes that become her victims.

In fact, she and Bardot appeared at roughly the same moment, both heralding a new era, a new kind of woman who rejected bourgeois conventions and went after what she wanted. I can remember seeing *Les Amants* in Paris when it came out. Women both loved and were scandalized by the Moreau heroine, who runs off in the night with her lover, leaving husband, child, and chateau for an uncertain future with a man she hardly knows. She has been transformed in one magical (and for its time, wildly sexy) night of love with a virtual stranger (Jean-Marc Bory as the Harvey Keitel-like, at-one-with-nature man of his time, in opposition to the smooth but uptight husband) from a frivolous bored chatelaine into a passionate being who gives up everything for the woman she has discovered in herself.

In a sense, Moreau's characters are always avenging their sex for having to suffer the restricting conventions and no less crippling idealizations of men. In the minds of Jules and Jim, she is a statue come to life—the statue they saw in Greece and fell in love with, thus Woman rather than woman. Moreau's Catherine takes her revenge as a living Galatea might have taken revenge on the sculptor and the public who worshipped her, the perfect Other, an image safely and immutably preserved.

This year, as she turns sixty-six, Moreau has no fewer than three films coming out. *The Summer House* will be followed by *Call Me Victor*, in which she plays a woman who lost her lover and the use of her legs in an accident years ago. Next comes *A Foreign Field*, a British production in which she is sought out, on the fiftieth anniversary of VE-Day, by two old soldiers who loved her and who are astonished to find that she wasn't the woman they thought she was.

Meanwhile, Moreau has served for a year as president of the French commission that dispenses filmmaking subsidies, reading hundreds of scripts and deciding which deserve support in France's system of "avance sur recette." And she is getting ready to direct a picture with Carole Bouquet about a woman, once a concert pianist, who gave up her career to marry a rich and politically powerful man. When he is caught in a scandal, she becomes the focus of attention and is pursued by a strange young woman. In the alchemy of this short, intense relationship, the wife is inspired to go back to her music.

"It's taken me two years to adapt the script, because it was somebody else's original material. In the course of it, I came to understand how the husband felt, how *he* was trapped as well as the wife."

This idea of a woman suddenly finding her destiny reminds me of *Les*

Amants, and I tell her how explosive it was, this idea of a woman leaving not only her husband but her child. "Yes," Moreau says, "sometimes you have to give up something—it doesn't have to be children, but something that is part of you because a new self has to be born. It's very frightening, jumping into the void. In cinema, we are in danger all the time. Whatever people appear to be, however confident, there is fear of being judged."

"Even if you've been praised, adored, lionized?"

"Meaningless," she replies. "You forget everything. You are starting anew."

NEVER HAVING BEEN A glamor girl, or pinup, there is little of the faded star about her now. As she ages gracefully, talks intelligently, and continues to work and perform, we can look back at films like *l'Ascenseur* and *Jules and Jim* as at our own film-obsessed youth, at the moments when love and death seem inextricably linked, partly because of our wish, out of our own fear of aging, to see the beautiful woman die rather than grow old. From these black-and-white realms of darkness and light, her "*beau visage pale*" and "*voix si fatale*" haunt us more than ever. But the lesson that Moreau has to tell us is not how to die, or even how to stay fit or young or well-preserved, but how to live.

Goodness Has Nothing to Do with It

MAE WEST

M ae West, the blond, diamond-studded, wisecracking, sashaying vamp from Brooklyn who lit up the stage in the twenties and the screen in the thirties with a special brand of gender-bending sexuality, still defies categories and refuses to be conscripted into any one ideological army. The salty double entendres, delivered with the drawling voice and rolling hips, have been recycled by a thousand female impersonators, but she was already there. As early as 1934 she was being called (by a writer in *Vanity Fair*) "the greatest female impersonator of all time."

Her heart, soul, figure, and wardrobe belong to the Gay (18)90s, the decade in which she was born and which serves as the backdrop for many of her films, but in her roving eye and assertive sexuality she looks forward to the androgynous role-playing of a later era. Born one hundred years ago this week, on August 17, 1893, she might be said, on this year and month of her centennial, to span two decades and two zeitgeists a century apart: the Gay Nineties (hers) and the gay nineties (ours).

The late Parker Tyler, that pioneering and peerlessly witty chronicler of cinema's sexual—and homosexual—subtexts, claimed her as "the Mother Superior of the Faggots." Yet there is something straight, sweet, and womanly—even innocent—about West that escapes camp. Feminists have found her both liberating and awkward: her frank obsession with men as both lust objects and figures of identification have made her dubious as a "sister," but she's talking only to us when she says it's a man's game and she just "happen[s] to be smart enough to play it their way." Moreover, as the

*This article first appeared in *The New York Times*, Arts and Leisure Section, August 15, 1993. Copyright © 1993 by Molly Haskell.

writer and producer of her Broadway shows and the screenwriter (and uncredited *auteur*) of her films, she was a powerhouse who in 1934 knocked off the highest salary of any Hollywood star. And in blurring the lines between the biological and the culturally constructed woman, she stretches the ways in which we think about and define femininity and what it means to be a woman. As a self-parodying sex symbol, she's not a real siren, a turn-on, but she can brag about liking sex in a way that a more conventionally desirable woman couldn't. As such, she offers a fantasy, an imaginative projection of what a more sexually active and less romantically enslaved woman might be.

A transgressive, protean figure who both exposes and resolves the power struggle between male and female, she became a flashpoint for the moralists and guardians of public decency and is most famous now for having provoked the outrage that led to the enforcement of the Production Code, the censorship rules that governed Hollywood moviemaking until the sixties. Was it the words in *She Done Him Wrong* and *I'm No Angel*, or was it the fact that a *woman* was saying them? One can imagine Mary Pickford and William Randolph Hearst in hysterical telephone consternation over this woman who made bad seem good and refused to honor the dichotomy between virgin and whore.

"When I'm good I'm good . . . but when I'm bad, I'm better."

"It's not the men in your life . . . it's the life in your men."

Suitor: "If only I could trust you.

West: "You can . . . hundreds have."

She's a master of the triple dots. The wisecracks have a life of their own as does the West persona. Her image, complete with body language and voice, lifts buoyantly out of celluloid into space like the inflatable life preserver that was named after her in World War II. She's a pneumatic floozy presiding over an army of panting camp followers, a Catherine the Great from Brooklyn, a Salome who adds on the layers instead of shedding them, a Cleopatra whose infinite variety is debatable.

For years she fruitlessly pursued a movie project of *Catherine the Great*, in which she would offer a warmer and more sensual alternative to what she described as Dietrich's "hollow-cheeked doll." Although she finally succeeded in launching an unfunny Broadway play on the subject of the czarina, she was in fact playing a bawdy, carnivalesque version of Catherine, surrounded by an "honor guard" of admirers, for most of her career. See her, as the lion tamer in *I'm No Angel*, wearing a white spangled jumpsuit, entering atop an elephant. Looking at her now, we can't but applaud this middle-aged woman (she was forty when she made her first film), undisguisedly rotund, flaunting an unliposucted, unsiliconed body, and demanding her sexual privileges!

With unshakable confidence, she seems to have hungered for the spotlight from infancy, and when she got a chance to make her song-and-dance debut at the age of seven, she took it and never stopped showing off. She was the child of immigrants—a Bavarian mother (a "corset and fashion model," she tells us in her autobiography, *Goodness Had Nothing to Do with It*) and a pugilist Irish-English father who gave up boxing to become, successively, a livery stable owner and private detective. Until he became respectable, outfitting Mae and her mother in elegant horse-drawn carriages and fur-lined sleighs, he was known as "Battling Jack West, Champion of Brooklyn, New York." From him she may have inherited an extra dollop of testosterone; at any rate she found herself in the legal ring more than once. The first show she wrote, *Sex* (which couldn't be advertised in any New York newspaper because of the title), ran 375 performances before its author was arrested by the police, after pressure from the Society for the Suppression of Vice, and thrown into a cell (albeit a private, "celebrity" cell) on Welfare Island for eight days.

Corsets and boxing gloves; vaudeville and female impersonators; plump chorus girls and black dancers and singers. She drew on them all and brought her invented self to its apotheosis as Diamond Lil in the show of the same name that was a Broadway hit, then a Hollywood movie (her second) called *She Done Him Wrong*.

As the beauteous Lil, whose nude portrait presides over the the Gay Nineties saloon in the Bowery that is the film's setting, she makes the longest-delayed and most carefully anticipated entrance since Tartuffe, with every man in the bar testifying to her irresistibility before she arrives. Only Joan Crawford got away with such outrageously fawning, ego-feeding star buildups. In fact, entrances are what Mae West does best, and there are at least four in every film, each one, in a different and more lavish costume, outdazzling the one before. The fiction that a middle-aged woman is driving men wild is all in the intonation . . . and the imagination. When she enters, it's less as a real woman than a sexual landscape unfurling before our eyes, her hills and valleys set off by jewels and furs, feathers and diamonds; a large bow below the waist, concentric circles above, marking critical parts of her anatomy the way trees and shrubbery delineate the contours of the earth.

Her singing is nothing much, a cut-rate Sophie Tucker, but her real music is in her movement, part swagger, part slither, part come hither. In *I'm No Angel*, she virtually lists across the room into the arms of a dancing man and would-be lover. As a so-called sex goddess, she is as extreme as Monroe, her antipode: one as powerful and assertive as the other is needy and ripe for victimization. West makes it clear she isn't the marrying kind and doesn't need a protector, and it gives her freedom. She sizes up her prey like a military general—or a prizefighter—and says, as she does to Cary Grant in *She Done Him Wrong*, "You can be had."

Grant, her delicious leading man in two films (his first lead roles), is here the head of a mission (we think) looking to save souls. In this role reversal of the Don Juan story, she's the roué and he's the tasty virgin who challenges her jaded appetites. In *I'm No Angel*, he plays a patrician lawyer to her carnival performer—"Tira, the million-dollar beauty"—who's angling to better herself but not if it means compromising her heart. Preserving her Brooklyn accent ("It is kinda wearin' on the noives," she admits of her lion act), she is true to her outerborough roots, but she can become one of the swells when, through a typically sentimental ending, she gets Grant as a trophy husband. (In fact, her salty one-liners were often at variance with her behavior: "Marriage is a great institution—but I'm not ready for an institution." But then again, what woman wouldn't allow Cary Grant to put her behind bars!)

Not only does West cross gender lines, but in the unusual collaboration with blacks that marks her career, she crosses racial ones as well. In the 1920s, she saw the shimmy in a dark, all-"Negro" dive in Chicago and introduced it into her show. Some of her rhythm and inflections probably came out of the black side of show business.

The first time a black maid appears in *She Done Him Wrong*, we cringe, then immediately relax at the instant rapport between the "lady" and her black confidante. In *Belle of the Nineties* (1934), she stands on a balcony watching a black revival meeting, singing a blues song in counterpoint to their spiritual. In *I'm No Angel*, the film in which she utters the famous "Beulah, peel me a grape" line, there are three black maids who function as a Greek chorus, clucking and whooping with her about the ways of men, preparing her for her next sexual campaign. Her unique locution, lazy and mocking, matches theirs until we feel a bond of the powerless expressed in subversive speech patterns, the shuffling tempo and tone being a form of resistance to and rebellion against the ruling class—in this case men. Even in the end, as she embraces Grant, the cream of the jest has to be shared: "How'm I doin', Beulah?"

As a heroine, she has more in common with the powerful women of black culture—matriarchal, anti-romantic, less inhibited about multiple partners—than the classically vulnerable and virginal white heroines whose chastity was a sine qua non in the mating game.

"I always did like a man with masculine supremacy," she says to a suitor in *Belle of the Nineties* (pronouncing it "supreemacy"), but the trouble is, the supremacy is all hers, and it finally grows wearying. Leo McCarey directed this particular movie, and it is her most fluid, creating sympathy for other characters, showing her in a softer light; but that softness comes to seem incongruous. As the film's hoary plot unfolds, we are made doubly aware of the degree to which she insists on being smarter, tougher, handsomer than anyone around. Most of her movies, Victorian melodramas with mustachioed villains, are never far from tedium when she's not onstage, and they grow more tedious and desperate as the decade progresses.

Like many of the more sophisticated performers of the thirties—Garbo and Dietrich, Katharine Hepburn, even Astaire and Rogers—she was falling victim to changing tastes, heralded by small-town theater owners and the American public's increased resistance to highfalutin' airs and arrogance of stars who came to be tagged as box-office poison.

The thirties was a decade of romantic pairs, and after Grant (and Randolph Scott in *Go West, Young Man* in 1936), West never teamed up with anyone on her level. Her outing with W. C. Fields in *My Little Chickadee* in 1940 was a brilliant-sounding comic idea that went awry: in yet another confirmation of the double standard of emotional valence whereby the male layabout is more lovable than the successful female, the sardonic loser Fields plays is funnier and more sympathetic than West's eternal winner. Jean Harlow, platinum blond, wisecracking and lovably sluttish, and thus the thirties star who most resembled her, teamed up with the likes of Gable and Powell and proved herself against such stunning rivals as Mary Astor and Myrna Loy, while West, never one to share the stage with another female beauty, surrounded herself with increasingly numerous, and increasingly uninteresting, bevies of male musclemen. With no rivals and no visual competition male or female, with no plausibility on a realistic level, her films were too fragile as narrative conceits for the plainer appetites of the domestic audience. Maybe, like the great androgynous stars, she was des-tined never to find a co-star to equal her simply because she already was male and female, a composite, a gender-blender.

In the sixties, in what became a grotesque parody of a parody, she made *Myra Breckinridge* and *Sextette* at a time when she was too old—given society's aversion to aging female flesh—and her gay constituency had become more explicit and obtrusive. These unfortunate valedictory films may explain why she became more a figure of speech—in both senses of the word—than a beloved movie memory. And yet, with all her films now newly released on video cassette, it may be time to erase those later images and return with fresh eyes to see her in her prime. New viewers may well fall in love with that gusto and sexual braggadocio that came out of nowhere and did its work to chip away at the stereotypes of female looks and behavior. As for being on the receiving end of the male "gaze," an abject object in the parlance of deconstruction, she'd be offended if you *didn't* give her the appraising eye. As she herself said, "It's better to be looked over than to be overlooked."

The Other Side of the Legend

GLORIA SWANSON

T hose of us who first encountered Gloria Swanson in *Sunset Boulevard* can never quite separate her from the image of Norma Desmond, that fading, vainglorious movie star, buried alive like some Egyptian princess with the memories and memorabilia of her past. The lady herself admits that her alter ego is something of a problem: everybody, even her mother, expected her to throw a scenery-chewing tantrum when she failed to win the Oscar for *Sunset Boulevard*.

"When I first meet people," Gloria Swanson says, "they look at me with terror in their eyes, not knowing what I'll do."

She looks into mine. What she sees is not terror but wide-eyed wonder —wonder at this remarkable woman who looks younger in person, at eighty-one, than she did thirty years ago in *Sunset Boulevard*. No one—not even someone who's been drinking puree of green beans and zucchini and celery all her life—has a right to look this good at eighty-one. It has to be genes, and she concedes that's part of it. (But her mother and the rest of them—if they'd eaten properly and taken care of themselves, they would have lived longer. Her mother's life was cut short at eighty-six.)

Gloria Swanson is glowing, energetic, and impossibly stylish, a tiny person who wears clothes that only taller people are supposed to wear and colors that only younger people are supposed to wear and wears them better than they all do: black silk lounging pajamas—perfectly tailored, sensuous, just loose enough; a necklace of overlapping gold rings that is both bold and delicate; several inches of gold bracelets on her arms, linked

*This article first appeared in *Vogue*, December 1980. Copyright © 1980 by Molly Haskell.

together by the gadget that was used, on movie sets, to keep them from clanking.

The effect is precise, perfect. Nor is there anything vague in Gloria Swanson's conversation, no lapses of memory, no wavering of concentration. She is awesomely clear-eyed and in control.

This is a woman who doesn't look back. That's not to say she has shut out the past; far from it. Her ground-floor apartment off Fifth Avenue is filled with busts she has sculpted, portraits and photographs of herself, her children, her grandchildren, but the effect is more that of a living scrapbook than a mausoleum. Showing the apartment to me, she moves constantly, gracefully, almost prancing—like someone who is more comfortable on her feet than sitting down. I am the first one to head for the sofa with my glass of wine.

The apartment resembles Norma Desmond's mansion in that it is so completely an extension of its owner—no sign here of Bill Dufty, Gloria's husband number six. But this is no *Sunset Boulevard* set. A radio is playing, plants are everywhere, and it is surprisingly light for a ground-floor apartment. And the houseboy—a blond, lanky, slightly awkward young man who rushes in late to see about our drinks—is no Erich von Stroheim.

The only touch of the pampered and overprotected movie goddess has come earlier in the day, when a man identifying himself as Swanson's manager calls to make sure I am going to get a "fresh" angle and lures me into his office with mention of the "one thousand pages that didn't get into the book." Having just returned from a Venetian holiday where I spent a shocking amount of time in my hotel room reading the more than six hundred pages that *did* get into the book—her juicy autobiography, *Swanson on Swanson*—I am easily hooked. As it turns out, the purpose of this preliminary session is to interview me. In return for a few meager tidbits and off-the-record comments, I am screened for conversational impurities (topics to which Swanson is allergic: show business, her marriages) and simultaneously pumped up with enthusiasm. ("The theme, Molly, is survival, courage, compassion!") Some new angle.

The effect of all this is to make me think I'm walking on eggshells, when in fact the woman who greets me at the door seems quite capable of handling anything on two legs.

When aroused, she is ferocious. Remembering a doctor who was mistreating a friend: "I throttled him against the hospital wall." Of a private nurse who had endangered her mother's life by propping her up in bed: "You sat her up!" Swanson, replaying the scene, shrieks these words, causing me to jump out of my seat. "I turned into Norma Desmond, then," she continues, "and chased her down the stairs in the middle of the night."

Ahead of her times in so many ways, Swanson has a lifelong distrust of the medical profession that goes back a long way. At the age of twenty-five on the eve of her marriage to the Marquis de la Falaise, she had a botched abortion and almost died from the ensuing infection.

"And there was the time I almost committed murder," she tells me. "That didn't get into the book. My governess was deliberately trying to turn my children against me." She remembers details with such clarity that I wonder if it isn't partly the memory of such villainies that fuels her, keeps her going. There are many of them in the book: the studio executives who dictated her private life to protect their investment or who treated her like a queen as long as she belonged to them but then set out to destroy her when she became her own producer. And the husbands and lovers—at best, they were sponges; at worst, they took her affairs in hand and then left her almost destitute.

The book's pièce de résistance and chief selling point is, of course, her affair with Joseph P. Kennedy, the brash, charmingly know-it-all and infinitely ambitious Bostonian who was determined to make a success as a movie producer and almost took her down with him. But the others— Wallace Beery; director Mickey Neilan; Crancy Gartz, the millionaire Marxist playboy; Herbert Marshall; the Marquis—are juicy, lurid, funny, memorable. Stories that never got into *Screen Romance* are recounted vividly but with surprisingly little bitterness. Swanson, I suspect, is someone who got her anger out at the time; and the men in her life, having slipped from her orbit, are no longer quite real to her. She is mentally trim. There is no excess emotional baggage cluttering up this woman's life, no resentment or sentiment.

"I have always been a romantic where men are concerned," she says. Indeed, her story is a typical female one of looking over and over again for that illusory daddy figure and finding only disappointment. And yet when I look at this sparkling survivor sitting before me, I think those men were lucky to get out alive.

The girl who began her career in 1914 as an extra in Essanay films in Chicago did not march triumphantly into the eighties by subordinating herself to any one man, by allowing herself to be submerged in any one image. She seems to have had, from the beginning, a remarkably strong sense of her individuality.

When Mack Sennett, who gave her her first big job in Keystone comedies, tried to promote her into the leading lady of slapstick, he promised to make her another Mabel Normand. It was the wrong thing to say. Gloria Swanson didn't want to be another anybody. She went to Paramount and, under Cecil B. De Mille's direction, made the sophisticated and slightly risqué marital dramas that catapulted her to stardom. She was down-to-earth comical in Allan Dwan's *Manhandled* and *Stage Struck*. And she was both innocent and regal in the Joseph Kennedy–Erich von Stroheim commercial fiasco *Queen Kelly*. She played good women and slightly tarnished women; she played aristocrats and working girls. But always, she was independent. And always stylish. Her only failures were films in which she wore dowdy clothes. Her public insisted on seeing her in a certain number of new creations, and this was written into her contract.

How did she have the nerve to leave Paramount, and one of the juiciest contracts in Hollywood, to become her own producer? Or after that, to say goodbye to it altogether?

"Because I saw the way they treated you," she says. "They would give you the moon one minute, but as soon as they didn't need you anymore . . . " She makes a gesture of tossing away a used Kleenex.

"Also, I had my own life, my children. Women then were discouraged from having children. The studios didn't want you to take time out for childbearing. It didn't go with your image. We were supposed to be glamorous, free. There were never any children in movies."

It's true. It wasn't until the fifties that the winds of fashion changed and movies began pushing maternity as the feminine ideal and suburbia as a woman's sphere of operation. To someone raised on these narrowing horizons, the gay bachelor-girl spirit of Swanson's period seemed exhilarating indeed. "The world of 1916," she writes, "was a man's world." And so it probably was. But the twenties were on their way, with women's suffrage and a widening sense of opportunity for women who would seize it. Swanson, as always, was ahead of the pack.

"I'm an Aries," she offers, when I ask for an explanation. "We're born leaders."

While all the women I know are casting about in that search for the elusive "self," Gloria Swanson forges ahead with her projects, acting, for all the world, like someone who's got it and had it all along. She can play health advocate or housewife, glamor girl or grandmother, and all the identities are connected, like the bracelets, by a single link.

It's called style.

I have my own theory as to how she got it. It goes back to her childhood in Chicago, to the mother who made all of Gloria's clothes and, in defiance of family counsel, made them different. While schoolgirls then, as now, wanted only and desperately to look like each other, Gloria pranced in wearing hats and dresses and even shoes that were like nobody else's. And loved it.

The result was, and is, Gloria Swanson.

Swept Away on a Wave of Sexism

LINA WERTMULLER

L ina Wertmuller, in case you've been swept away on a Caribbean island, is the hottest thing in town, the newest media darling, the greatest woman director since . . . uh . . . well, let's say the woman director to put woman-directing on the map. She, of course, disdains such gender labels ("it's what gives women complexes") but is not eager to give away trade secrets to the Brownie filmmakers at her feet.

The celebrity of the hour, she is being courted and feted and interviewed and paid *hommage* to by *le tout New York*. I am to talk to her at five at the Pierre. The occasion is the almost simultaneous opening of two of her films. One, made before *Swept Away*, was called, to translate the Italian, *Everything's in Order but Nothing Works.*" It has been retitled *All Screwed Up* by its American distributor (who, according to Wertmuller, cut it badly) and hastily opened to cash in on the Wertmuller frenzy. An aggressively noisy pseudofarce about working class youth in Milan, it is a pastiche of social observation, caricature, mimicry, sex, and politics, but without the semblance of charm and emotional coherence that has been provided by Giancarlo Giannini in Wertmuller's other films, including the new and distinctly superior *Seven Beauties*.

*This combines a review of *Swept Away* (*The Village Voice*, September 29, 1975) and an interview in the *Voice*, January 26, 1976). The review, and the discussion of the resonance of the Giancarlo Giannini endings, was written *before* I saw *Seven Beauties* four months later—the film which exploited the sad-eyed Giannini look in a setting (the concentration camp) and for an effect far beyond anything in the preceding films. So in the interest of condensation, I have included that fourth film in the description of Giannini which preceded and uncannily foreshadowed it.

Wertmuller has stated that her purpose as a left-wing Italian filmmaker is to make movies with a political message that will appeal to the masses, i.e., the working classes. I don't know how her movies fare in poor Italian neighborhoods, but on New York's Upper East Side, which is hardly *Daily Worker* territory, they seem to have found an enthusiastic audience. Is this possibly because Miss Wertmuller does not pursue the correct Marxist or social-realist line to its constructive conclusion but ends with a more romantically pessimistic view wherein the individual is confounded by political realities?

In the four Wertmuller films with Giancarlo Giannini—*Love and Anarchy*, *The Seduction of Mimi*, *Swept Away by an Unusual Destiny in the Blue Sea of August*, and *Seven Beauties*—the most moving scenes are the four endings: Giannini as the whore-house pet and would-be assassin of Mussolini meeting his own death; Giannini, husband (of one woman) and lover (of another), selling out his political principles; Giannini, returned to civilization, waiting in vain for his tamed capitalist shrew (Mariangela Melato) to return to their island paradise. And finally Giannini as the concentration camp whore, the man who has devised a grotesque plan to save his neck, now looking at us, his eyes in giant close-up, with the expression of *uomo doloroso*. What matter if a man loseth his soul, what matter if he seduces the female commanding officer (Shirley Stoler), or, in *Swept Away*, brutalizes a woman into submission if, with his eyes, he showeth us he doth not mean it, that he is a poor, lost, vulnerable man, but a man withal!

For Wertmuller's dialectic of working class versus bourgeoisie is really a cover and alibi for a gender dialectic in which a man can be forgiven anything because he, being a working man, is the "oppressed."

Are these scenes moving because of the stray-dog quality of Giannini himself, a wire-haired terrier with straggly hair and huge, sad eyes that, like Al Pacino's, plead for martyrdom? Or because, in the throes of an emotional convulsion, political sympathies are swept away by the drama of the individual psyche, the only drama, as Wertmuller instinctively knows, that is truly "popular." The ending of *Swept Away*, with its aching sense of loss and regret, is as surefire romantic as that of *The Way We Were*, only it has much less to do with what has preceded it: a scantily clad Marxist allegory in which Thesis and Antithesis are stranded on a desert island. Thesis (rich capitalist bitch) is overthrown—abused, beaten, degraded, penetrated— by Antithesis (sexy Sicilian communist male), and in the reversal of the master-slave relationship, a temporary synthesis is struck. With woman's subjugation, love blossoms miraculously, in a manner closer to the Gloria Swanson movie version of *The Admirable Crichton* (retitled *Male and Female* lest small-town twenties moviegoers mistake it for a sea story!) than to James M. Barrie's witty play.

To begin with *Swept Away*: a private cruise ship lolls lazily in the Mediterranean, in waters just beyond human and chemical pollution. It is over ten years since *L'Avventura*, and the ruling class has roused itself from ennui and intramural bitchery to hurl epithets across the socioeconomic divide.

Raffaella (Mariangela Melato), an imperious blond lady, gives vent to reactionary sentiments in gusts of Italian invective, larded with the usual anti-Communist catchwords—Stalin, Siberia, etc. A fellow guest counterattacks with slogans from the male liberal catechism. But the real butt of Senora's increasingly personal vituperations is a crew member, the sad-eyed Gennarino (Giannini), who grumbles about the way upper-class men let their wives run loose. This "minus" character trait, like Raffaella's "plus" stands on abortion and ecology, is an attempt at a more equal distribution of sympathy. But why do I feel, even so, that Wertmuller endorses Gennarino's sexism and despises Raffaella's enlightenment?

When the two find themselves adrift on the high seas, Raffaella, unconcerned, keeps up her diatribe with an inappropriateness that is apparently deliberate. I say apparently, because it is never clear on precisely what level of unreality Wertmuller is operating. The artificiality of the basic situation —these two mouthpieces of the class struggle adrift, like the owl and the pussycat, in a beautiful yellow dinghy, against a backdrop that is dazzlingly and serenely real—establishes an incongruity that continues on the island, as metaphoric an island as ever there was, but photographed with the lush naturalism of a travel documentary.

And what are we meant to think when the roles are reversed, and political antagonism metamorphoses into desire? Gennarino turns sadist and, in the venerable tradition of man gratifying woman's sexual fantasies as envisioned by men ("understanding" her as she doesn't understand herself), he brutalizes her so that she can emerge in her true colors as the gold-plated whore. It would be easier to interpret this as ironic commentary, however unoriginal, if Wertmuller didn't orchestrate all that mood music, lighting and seminude scenes to convince us of the bliss of sexual surrender and the genuine passion of two lovers released at last to enjoy their "natural" roles.

Wertmuller's gallery of female grotesques—the whores in *Love and*

Anarchy, the huge fat woman in *The Seduction of Mimi* (the concentration camp commandante to come in *Seven Beauties*), and here, that arch-villainess cherished by Old Left and Macho Right alike, the frigid blond tease—are such that she can claim to have challenged the stereotype by exaggeration while indulging it with a relish she shares with male members of the audience. Anyone who doesn't appreciate the howling hilarity of these "parodies" is threatened with the label of humorless feminist.

Wertmuller's male chauvinism, her identification with the male sex, is more insidious. All of her women are treated as nonpersons, as types—the whore, the bitch, the devouring wife—while the man, most notably Giannini, is always treated as a person, a character who extends by virtue of his emotional complexity beyond the class or sexual function that defines the others. (Proof that her animus attaches to gender rather than class is that the upper-class men are not caricatures, while the lower-class women are.) The reason that Raffaella's original stridency doesn't disturb us, and neither does her conversion perplex us, is that we never see her as a real woman, while Gennarino is never less than a man, and an idealized one at that. (Earlier, he has expressed the puritanical disapproval of sex and drugs typical of his class, but later, when it comes to servicing his Lady Chatterley, he is thoroughly liberated in his attitude toward certain, shall we say, "advanced" sexual practices.) Her virtues, such as they are, are ridiculous, while his class defects are heroic, or at least winning. His ignorance is proof of his unwarped mind; yet he is cultivated enough to wipe his mouth fastidiously with a leaf after eating.

I don't buy the class-bound premise of *Swept Away*, where scheme precedes essence and feelings are parsed according to political categories. Another recent film, Alain Tanner's *The Middle of the World*, tried to establish an equation between sexual and economic politics, but the film owed its richness to the fact that the characters transcended and thwarted the scheme.

Lina Wertmuller is not afraid of grafting her sex and class dialectics onto grandiose hitching posts, and in *Seven Beauties* the hybrid role of female/bourgeoise is taken by the concentration camp commandante who lords it over and is finally seduced by the forlornly swaggering inmate in the role of the proletarian male.

The men in Wertmuller—the swinging fun-loving boys in *All Screwed Up*, for example—are dupes and foils, but never evil. The girls in that film are conniving, dreary-looking chippies who put the screws into the guys and are on their way to becoming petit-bourgeois housewives and tyrants, while the boys are corrupted by "natural" desires—lust, love, the will to please—and, if they are co-opted by the bourgeoisie, it is not out of ambition or materialism but out of pardonable human weakness.

Thus the ambiguous charisma of Giannini as Pasqualino in the film *Seven Beauties*, which is being hailed as a masterpiece even by those who were offended by the male chauvinist charade of *Swept Away*. The title (in Italian, *Pasqualino Settebellezze*) is the nickname of the protagonist, a braggadocio Neapolitan who lives off women, and goes to prison for a crime of "honor" having killed the pimp of one of the seven beauties under his "protection." Sent to an asylum, he commits rape; then, after serving time in the army, he winds up in a German concentration camp.

As the film, with its uneasy blend of comedy and horror, progresses, Pasqualino becomes the eyes through which we view a concentration camp, and then a testament to the dangers of "selling out." In an audacious scene, he strikes a bargain by which he saves his own life and by extension Italy's by blindly following the life instinct instead of dying for principle.

The contradiction at the heart of Wertmuller's films lies in her Garbo-like treatment of Giannini and her appeal, through him, to the romantic fantasies of a middle-class audience rather than the lower classes she presumably wants to reach. A fuzzy romanticism combines with social polemic to enable viewers to flagellate themselves, but never for too long and never without the emotional payoff of Giannini, who suffers for us all. Her films are like shaggy underdog stories in which every close-up of Giannini's spaniel eyes offer a silent punch line of balm.

Reviewers reach for superlatives. They describe as "subtle," "ambiguous," and "true to life" scenes I find riddled with confused thinking or false analogy. And while others delight in Wertmuller's "mixed moods" and operatic style, I say they are mixed metaphors and unmixed moods, thrown together by someone pumped up on speed.

With twelve films behind her, Wertmuller is probably one of the two or three most technically accomplished and experienced woman filmmakers working today and at the moment far and away the most successful. But lest we assume that the emergence of more women filmmakers will automatically "advance our cause," she is prime evidence of the contrary, being the one filmmaker who least identifies with the concerns and interests of the women's movement, from which she has repeatedly dissociated herself, proclaiming the "androgyny" of the artist.

I would like to think I agree with her on principle. Certainly I believe that no one is obliged to be a feminist, and the female artist, who has little enough encouragement from the world around her, must go, when she can muster the will and energy to go at all, where inspiration and temperament lead her. Nevertheless, I find myself with enormous reservations, both aesthetic and political, about her films, trying to sort out the two as I go into the Pierre.

I arrive at five and discover that things are running late, have been all day. Unperturbed and showing no sign of fatigue, she sits in her suite, talking, smiling, and intensely energetic in the midst of a mounting chaos with which she seems to be on the best of terms. During our interview, the phone will ring constantly, members of the entourage will appear and disappear into an adjoining room, flowers will arrive, urgent discussions in Italian will take place, and I will leave feeling not exhilarated but battered. I will have been, I realize, in a Lina Wertmuller movie.

But at the moment, I am ready to be charmed, to reconsider all my objections. (What approach shall I take, I wonder. Shall I admit that I am not among her most fervent admirers and ruin any chance for rapport; or shall I be polite and effusive and feel like a phony? I take the middle road, am respectful without gushing, and express my reservations in the questions I ask.)

I pay her a compliment—on her dress rather than her movies. It really is a magnificent creation, a scarlet ankle-length dashiki with a black border and scattered embroidered patches (from Madagascar, she tells me). It hangs loose, there is nothing binding anywhere, it is obviously warm in winter and cool in summer, the kind of thing all women ought to wear, we agree.

I pose a question. "Your attitude toward the Giannini character in *Seven Beauties* and the life force he represents is critical?"

"Oh, yes," she says. "He has learned nothing."

"But he does have a kind of beauty."

"Yes, the beauty of the forest."

Wertmuller, a socialist, is volubly concerned with the salvation of civilization. She believes that once the industrial revolution replaced the agricultural society, the people lost their roots, and they must somehow regain their footing. She talks constantly about finding a "solution," a new "structure," and explicitly opposes the notion of the "people" (whom she is for, and at whom she ostensibly directs her films) to the "petit bourgeois."

But what must happen to the "people," such as the proletarians played by Giancarlo Giannini, so that they don't either succumb to bourgeois values or live by blind instinct?

"They must reach a mental maturity, we must have a *mental* civilization. The possibility exists to save our civilization, if it is done with speed. Otherwise things will finish very soon . . . badly.

"There is a lot of alarm and anguish now, which is good. This polemical situation is much better than in the eighteenth century, when the concept of the bourgeoisie was triumphant. They had complete confidence in their property concept. Women were coming in, bringing tea, and sitting on their asses while under their chairs the blood was running from child workers, factory workers who worked seven days a week. We needn't be nostalgic about the past. One must constantly raise doubts. Leftist ideologies were crushed not because the left wasn't in the right (surely the future is with the left) but because they had to become something else. Russia is wrongly based because it lives off women. Incidentally, the Russians don't like my movies, they like Sophia Loren. Even the most beautiful experiment in the history of humanity will have to go through so many changes and revolutions before we'll find a structure that really respects the human right to live not *on* other people but with them."

I wonder how there can be one structure when, as she has pointed out, the class and economic levels are so different, and when people constantly want not equality but superiority . . . the innateness of competition, the elitist magic of star charisma, whether it be Sophia Loren or Giancarlo Giannini.

"The fact that people are different, that's why we may be able to find a structure. [She has the debater's way of turning questions to advantage.] If we weren't all different we would be finished already. In Italy there are the most differences—geographical, economic—but the most bitchy petit-bourgeois class of all. That's why the church has chosen to sit on Italy."

She is against most of the experiments, or what she understands as the experiments, of the young people of the sixties, because they were essentially petit bourgeois, and they rejected work and hence the working class. She has tremendous feeling for Pasolini and tells me he wrote a poem during the 1968 student riots in which he took up the cause of the policeman against the student.

"That was very much against the fashion at that time, but of course his analysis was correct," Wertmuller said. "He understood that the policeman came from the working class, while the students were the sons of capitalists." Like Pasolini, she sees television as the archvillain, responsible for false values and for violence, a phenomenon which, it seems, she avoids or glosses over in her films.

Somehow we cannot broach the issue of women without the subject immediately taking on broader political meanings. "I know," I say, "that you don't want to be categorized as a woman director, but—"

"No. I'm against all categories. That's what leads to racism. Women simply have to go ahead and enter society, do what they do well, earn money."

"Do you recognize, then, any such thing as a woman's point of view?"

"Sure," she said quickly. "I know a lot of men who have it."

The phone rings for the seventh time. Someone wants to know what time to arrange the dinner party that night and how many there will be. An animated discussion follows: Giancarlo Giannini is scheduled to have a dinner interview. With a female journalist. Wertmuller is quite insistent that his interview be rearranged so that he can come to dinner with them.

"They all want to get their hands on him," she says jokingly. The interview is rearranged.

At some point Giannini-in-person stops by. He is wearing blue jeans, but he doesn't look very proletarian.

"How have you managed to get financing? That seems to be a major problem with women directors."

"Oh, I don't know. Fantasies," she says. "Fortune."

I don't know what she means by fantasies, but by fortune I think she means luck rather than money. Nevertheless, she did have the luck to be born well off, in Rome. Her father was a successful lawyer, descended from a Swiss baron, hence the German-sounding name. Wertmuller first worked as a writer and director in theatre and television before becoming Fellini's assistant (on $8\frac{1}{2}$) and subsequently she wrote and directed her first film, *The Lizards*.

This film, about a group of small-town young men, is closest to Fellini in inspiration (specifically to *I Vittelloni*), but whereas Fellini's films are autobiographical and dreamlike, rooted in his own past, Wertmuller's are social and political, and outer-directed. That is, they seem not to emanate from the artist's personal vision but to address themselves to the working classes who are their models. Her films are, in a sense, an attempt to fuse Pasolini's proletarian parables with Fellini's lyricism; they also have a very specific feeling for locale and dialect which may be partially lost on a non-Italian speaking audience.

Men and women in her films, bound by traditional roles and often aspiring beyond or below their class, more often collide than connect. "You seem very pessimistic about the relations between the sexes," I suggest to her.

"Oh, no," she says. "I'm very optimistic. I believe in love. And I believe in the fifteen principles of sex. I only know four or five of them, but I believe in them all."

Everyone in the room—there are five or six now—laughs at this. I don't understand—does she mean "positions"?—but would rather die than ask.

"Do you believe in the family as such?"

"I believe the family is the social nucleus. But we have to find a new structure. The man can work at home, the woman can work at home, but there has to be somebody working at home. This is the problem and it is real."

"What about day-care centers?"

"That's a possibility," she shrugs her shoulders.

I ask her her attitude toward abortion (she says she's for it), because of her seemingly negative references in the films. In *All Screwed Up*, a young girl who has had seven children in two years goes to an abortion clinic but is so alarmed at their handling of a patient that she leaves in horror. Sidestepping the implications, Wertmuller then has her say that abortion clinics are assassination bureaus because of government prohibition. And in *Swept Away*, the most emancipated ideas on women come from the mouth of the most ridiculed and discredited character in the film, the aristocrat played by Mariangela Melato.

"But she's a symbol of bourgeois enlightenment," Wertmuller exclaims. "She represents bourgeois society, therefore she represents the man!"

Now that's what I call fancy footwork, I thought.

"That's what women don't understand," Wertmuller went on. "The Mariangela Melato character was really a man!" I confess that I was one of those befuddled females who thought Mariangela Melato was a woman.

"But looking at it on the sexual rather than the political level," I said "do you think women have this desire to be dominated? I really don't—"

"Eroticism," she replied, "is a painful argument. Instead of being funny, eroticism is always painful. Now, of all the things that provoke, many more men than we know about would love to be whipped in the ass and be raped and brutalized, would love to enjoy deeply their own femininity. At the same time, there are women who love to be whipped and who adore to live deeply their own masculinity.

"The main violence that women have submitted to is not erotic whipping or slapping, but psychological. They have been placed in the ghetto of the home, under the law of love and morality. That initiates a chain of violence more dangerous than the ass."

"But we are very sensitive here about rape, and the idea that women somehow want—"

"Listen," she interrupts yet again. "If you go out of this hotel and are assaulted by a father who wants money to feed his children . . . "

Somehow we've gone from rape to mugging, and from mugging to Jean Valjean. "Wait a minute," I say, "not food for his children, but [jabbing my inner arm] for his habit."

"All the more so," she quickly replies. "He has a false model he's gotten from television. Instead of the basic things of life, he wants the latest model of boots."

She points her finger at my boots. I wonder why. They are not fancy Italian boots, but plain rubber rain boots. Why doesn't she point to her own boots?

Does she put the finger on me because she thinks I am petit bourgeois? Does she conjure up visions of my being mugged outside her hotel because I am a "rich capitalist bitch"? Because I watch television? Because I am a woman? Or because I am going home to write what may be her only unfavorable review in New York?

Making Hash of the Blues

CAROL BURNETT

For the eleven-year run of her weekly comedy show, Carol Burnett was the funniest woman on television. Since being obstreperously funny still goes against the grain and social conditioning of most women, there is something both irritating and deeply exhilarating about the unregenerate slob in Burnett. When she browbeats two entire rows of spectators in a television studio into moving over so that she and Harvey Korman can sit together (a goal that could have been accomplished with a simple exchange of seats), then screeches, "That wasn't such a big deal, was it?," we shudder—with horror, with pleasure. She's every aggressive, uncivil harpy who ever tried to elbow her way in front of you at the checkout counter, and you want to clobber her, yet you can't help envying her sang-froid. She's impervious to what people will think. Here's a woman—you might say—who never learned to tidy her room as a little girl, and you'd be right. She never even *had* a room to *keep* tidy, but I'll get to that in a minute.

Though a quintessential television performer, she brings a non-McLuhanist heat to the cool medium. She's cerebral *and* physical, a meeting ground of the hip and the square. A figure of serpentine elegance and sharp repartee when she appears before the audience to open the show, she becomes, once it starts, déclassée with a vengeance: red fright wig, garish get-ups; the facial expressions are as loud as the voice, and the voice—paint-scraping, glass-shattering—is as loud as they come. The

*Portions of this article first appeared in the *New York Review of Books*, January 15, 1987, and as the essay "The Comic Genius of Carol Burnett" in the Museum of Television & Radio's exhibition catalogue *The Many Worlds of Carol Burnett*, 1988.

voice, in fact, is essential. She's less effective in pantomime—one of the things that separate her from the *Show of Shows* gang, who were superb mimes.

Burnett is also, perhaps essentially, our reigning genius of parody—parody not as simple mimicry or impersonation, but as a savage love poem, a tribute in the form of a broadside that plunges into the object parodied and comes out the other side but is always rooted in something real. Though they owed a great deal to a sharp and changing stable of writers, *The Carol Burnett Show*'s best skits come out of an intuitive, even uncanny affinity between performer and subject: Harvey Korman as Nigel Bruce's harrumphing Dr. Watson, befuddled by love and ratiocination; Burnett as Mildred Fierce; or her even more knowing rendering of Joan Crawford in "Torchy Song."

The best parody relies on an intimacy with the thing burlesqued, perhaps even an incestuous, addictive identification with the subject. Just how true this was in Burnett's case—and how remarkable under the circumstances—becomes clear in her autobiographical memoir.

WRITTEN IN THE FORM of a letter to her three daughters, the book takes us from her birth in San Antonio in 1933 to the years in New York leading up to *The Carol Burnett Show*, but the longest and most interesting section concerns her life as a girl in Hollywood.

Here she is at age eight, newly arrived in Los Angeles, a silent witness (and pawn) in round one of the ongoing battle between her grandmother, Mabel Eudora White ("Nanny"), and her mother, Ina Louise Burnett. Nanny, the vain, tyrannical virago, has been giving out-of-work, would-be writer Louise what for: what'n the world did she mean, sending for her and the little girl, and them coming all the way from San Antonio to California to live in a stinky one-room dump?

> "Who asked you? [Mama replies and Burnett records.] I *told* you, I *wrote* you! *I wrote you I was broke! You knew it*! You *knew* I didn't have a job yet. You *knew* I couldn't take care of you and Carol yet. I *begged* you to wait until I could get on my feet! But no! *You* were the one who wanted to come to Hollywood! It was *you*! Don't you blame me. You got just what you asked for, *goddammit*! Why can't you ever let up!"
>
> Then Nanny would say, "Why can't you get a job or a man?"

Mama would shriek, "Because I'm not like *you*! I'd never marry a man because he's a meal ticket."

Then Nanny would say, "Well, see then . . . I'm right! You *don't* love Carol!"

Everything in this passage—the inflections, repetitions, and emphases; the snarling exchange and devastating knockout punch line—could have come right from the Eunice family sketches, one of the funniest and most disconcerting features ever to run on network television. You can hear them and see them: Vicki Lawrence, shrewd and malicious as gray-haired battle-ax Mama, always knowing just where to insert the knife; Burnett as her grown daughter and perpetual wet blanket Eunice, shrilly masochistic, preferring to blame Mama rather than take control of her own thwarted life. At any moment, the door will open—the absent father made present, but barely—and Ed (Harvey Korman), wilted from a long day of failure at the hardware store, will come in and try in vain to scrape the blood off the flower wallpaper and stitch together the pieces of human flesh that lie strewn on the living room floor from this ritual mutual flagellation of mother and daughter. The center of the family portrait on *The Carol Burnett Show* is their fierce, greedy one-upmanship battle, each struggling to impose her own version of their shared history.

Their relationship is like three-dimensional chess compared with the relationship each shares—and exploits to the hilt—with Ed. From Mama he earns only withering dismissals (which do double duty as indictments of Eunice's lack of taste in men). There he goes, Mama says of him when they're all up rummaging in the attic, "on one of his almighty rushes to nowhere." This is the hilarious Fluffy-the-rabbit episode where Eunice, discovering a snapshot of her favorite childhood pet, reminisces about how devastated she was when he ran away; and Mama finally confesses that the smelly little animal didn't run away at all: she cooked him for dinner. Traumatized, Eunice declares that now she will have to review her whole life.

Ed and Eunice have two children to whom they are supremely indifferent and who are wisely kept forever in the wings, lest the already precarious balance between humor and horror tip over to the other side, into the pathology of child abuse. Because who could imagine that a child raised in this atmosphere of failure and spite could survive and flourish? Who could suspect that a girl subjected to such malice, not to mention poverty, alcoholism (a dual heritage), an ineffectual father, and an (apparently, to the child) unloving mother, would grow up to be Carol Burnett?

HOW DID IT HAPPEN? There's little pause for analysis or introspection in Burnett's disarmingly breezy, get-on-with-it memoir. With its forties slang, its letter-from-camp style, it spreads a transparent blanket of mystery as the most forthright statements often do. We are left to puzzle out just what kind of person it took to overcome such odds; whether, in fact, some concatenation of the sort of conditions that would send a social worker reeling, some mélange of love, loathing, showbiz, and junk food didn't actually produce a positive chemical reaction.

The details of the book, like the later skits, are vivid and grotesque—Dickensian squalor transformed by a swaggering Depression optimism, a story that would be appalling it it hadn't been converted into comedy. Nanny and Carol sharing a tiny room in a residential hotel on the corner of Yucca and Wilcox, its windows a foot away from those of the adjacent building. Nanny, smelling of Ben-Gay, Vicks, and gas, belching and farting, a Christian Scientist with a cabinet full of backup potions; a hypochondriac of operatic proportions who spends most of the day stretched out on the Murphy bed for fear of "heart attacks," with the windows closed for fear of "pneumonia," nevertheless rising from her "deathbed" (she will actually die at age eighty-two, leaving behind a forty-year-old boyfriend) to take Carol to the movies or drop by the drugstore, where she will pinch the occasional bit of silver to supplement the relief check.

Carol adores Nanny and, taking her death threats seriously, lives in constant fear for her granny's life. She recites her passages from Mary Baker Eddy's *Scientific Statement of Being*, sleeps on a sofa, hangs her tiny wardrobe on the shower rod, and when she actually attends classes (hardly daring to leave the perpetually dying grandmother), nods off after a breakfast of fried foods, pound cake, and Ovaltine. She spends most of the time listening to the radio and eavesdropping on the occupants of the neighboring building as they argue about booze and money, makes up her own radio show in order to outshout them, takes refuge in imaginary characters.

The father, a tall, lanky charmer and alcoholic, comes to call on the rare occasions when he's got a dollar or two in his pockets. Mother Louise lives down the hall, tries to cajole the fan magazines into giving her assignments, falls in love with a married man, has his child (Burnett's half-sister Christine), and sinks slowly into an alcoholic stupor, which doesn't prevent her from rising to the bait when Nanny puts out the battle scent.

It might be a George Price cartoon except that the two women, in Carol's account, are a little too proud to be slatterns and too talented to be mediocre—sometime-beauties with wide mouths, thin ankles, a history of romantic conquests, none of which has anything like the longevity or intensity of their ongoing feud This fierce love-hate war (or loving-to-hate war) seems to absorb all the Oedipal rivalry in the family and to leave Carol oddly outside, or perhaps deep inside, the eye of the hurricane.

Remaining a neutral party in their squabbles, a pawn rather than a participant, she nevertheless absorbs it all, to play it back not only in the Eunice and "Sis" skits but in her memorable duets with other female stars—Burnett and Julie Andrews as sparring prima donnas or catty violinists; she and Beverly Sills in competition for a starring musical role. Burnett gives dramatic form to many of the truths of relations between women: that sisterhood can be both mine field and sanctuary, that women bear one another a complicated ambivalence arising from the mother-daughter knot.

EVEN AS LOUISE BURNETT was languishing in her room—waiting for her lover to leave his wife, waiting for Cary Grant to agree to an interview—Carol was succeeding where her mother had failed. With the idea of doing articles on famous alumni for the high school paper, she obtained, and published, an interview with Joel McCrea. It can't have entirely delighted her mother, seeing her teenage daughter pick up the ball and run with it. But because she had already waived her emotional claim on Carol, the maternal ambivalence that can be crippling to daughters had little effect. The absence of an internalized maternal conscience may even have freed her from that taboo, so inhibiting to many writers, against exposing family skeletons. In any case, the grandmother who raised her was the shaping force in her life—a bond that is inevitably less intense, less fraught with the possibilities of guilt and betrayal. So that when it came time for Carol to leave—for college, then for New York—not all of Nanny's threats and tirades could keep her home.

In a story full of fabulous elements, such as money gifts by mysterious benefactors that enabled her to take flight, what is more astonishing than the fact of escape itself is that Burnett fled her monsters and the specter of failure only to re-create them in a New York studio. Her show *is* her autobiography and her early life a run-through for her skits, not in the usual figurative way of the child being father to the man but much more literally and directly. The images are all there, without disguise or trans-figuring: the char lady of logo and skit goes back to the time she and Nanny—out of spoons and relief money, no doubt—worked nights as cleaning women in the Warner executive offices. "Sis" was the kid sister Christine (born out of wedlock, like Eunice and Eunice's first child) whom Carol brought to live with her and her husband in New York.

Burnett and her family were show biz's stepchildren and poor relations, following the lives and footprints of the stars, living in a Hollywood every bit as seedy as the Palomar Arms, among people who, in Nathanael West's words, "had come to California to die." Burnett, however, was blessed not only with brains and energy but with an imaginative splitting, so that she was able to see the view from both sides of the barricade. She and Nanny would go to the star premieres and hang over the ropes, squeezed between the bleachers and the cops. On one particular night it was a Linda Darnell movie (Darnell, along with Betty Grable, was Burnett's favorite actress) at the Pantages. They were packed like sardines with the rest of the fans in a feeding frenzy out of *Day of the Locusts*. The star emerged from her lim-ousine and, somehow eluding her escort, walked right beside where Carol and Nanny were standing. Nanny grabbed her by the sleeve and began assaulting her with their life story ("Linda! We're from San Antonio, fellow Texans!") and asked for her autograph. As Burnett looked on, in a parox-ysm of admiration and mortification, she happened to notice that one of the star's nostrils was bigger than the other. She was shocked, but not disillusioned. She registered the flaw in all its grotesqueness but also saw it as a connecting link with her own awkwardness. It's this double vision—the ogling of the groupie alternating with the satirist's eye—that was to inspire her star impersonations.

Meanwhile, with the driving "personality" of the nonnarcissist and the light tread of someone whose past was meant to be left behind, Burnett pushed forward. She'd discovered at UCLA that she could hold a stage by making people laugh and had accepted the fact that she was a comic type. By her own account, she fell on her face only twice during her student theatrical career, and both times she had a "straight" part. The first time, reading a scene for the Theater Arts department from William Saroyan's *Hello Out There*, she "couldn't get up the nerve to go for the straight stuff." She was "embarrassed to let go and cry." On the second occasion, she was performing a torch song in fishnet stockings, slit skirt, and ankle-strap high heels. Having been forced to dress in the dark and grope her way onto the stage in a hurry, she found her spot and was settling into the song, feeling sultry and sexy, only to look down, to the sound of audience laughter, and see that the seams of her stockings were running up the front of her legs. The comic devil, the muse of parody, had taken over and was making hash of the blues.

When she found herself, along with all the other girls living at New York's Rehearsal Club (the all-women institution charmingly memorialized in *Stage Door*), pounding the pavements in a vicious cycle of no agent–no audition, she broke the cycle: she organized a talent show and made the agents come to her. What did she have to lose? She couldn't make a fool of herself if she played the fool.

The Burnett comic persona emerged in 1956, in the song that won her instant notoriety, "I Made a Fool of Myself over John Foster Dulles." This takeoff on the Elvis craze centering on the staid, noncharismatic Secretary of State, derives its humor from the comical fantasy coupling of Burnett the frumpy and Dulles the dour. It was the ultimate lament of the loser, the plain Jane who can't even develop a *crush* on a sexy man, much less attract one, and it had evolved naturally from her adolescent sense of herself: gawky, tall and gangly, all mouth, teeth, pimples, and stringy hair and, where boys are concerned, friend rather than femme fatale.

ON THE SPECTRUM OF comediennes, she stands midway between the gargoyles—Joan Rivers, Phyllis Diller, Martha Raye—and the pretty blondes—Carole Lombard, Lucille Ball, Judy Holliday. The latter trio could throw a custard pie, even screw up their faces in mock ugliness, but they were as soft and as sweet as a nursery all the same, destined for coupledom. Burnett, on the other hand, in the adolescent terms in which such feelings can be set for life, is too smart, too tall, too loud. By not being beautiful, she is sprung into the realm of the anarchists and the uglies—bag ladies, charladies, nonladies. Even her frilly or sexy women—the nympho-maniac bride, Charo of the pendulous bosoms and fierce prurience—are joyless and unsexy.

Burnett could identify with the downscale and frazzled ("queen of the laundromat" as one critic called her) and appeal to upscale audiences as well. Of the three greatest female comics of our television age—Burnett,

Ball, and Lily Tomlin—Burnett is the one, both chronologically and icono-
graphically, who bridges the gap between down-home shopping-mall
America and big-city bright-light know-it-alls. It wasn't so much that Ball
was square, as that the division hadn't been drawn and sides taken. She was
a universally beloved living room icon in a period when everybody still
watched the same shows and audiences felt themselves agreeably homoge-
neous. Tomlin, to the extent that she's associated with television at all, is
more a post-McLuhanist performer. Cool, ironic, disappearing behind her
blue-collar and white-collar and no-collar women, she's essentially a man-
darin figure playing to a coterie audience.

Burnett, on the other hand, is in the middle. As a fifties-style singer-
dancer-comedienne, she was already a bit of an anachronism when she
became a regular guest star on *The Garry Moore Show* in 1959. At that time,
comedy variety shows were not getting reviewed, and the big names like
Milton Berle and Sid Caesar were playing out the last days of their series.

In 1963, after she left *The Garry Moore Show*, she vowed she would never
do a television series. But with its relatively loose format (it had begun as a
daily show and had kept some of the laissez-faire spontaneity when it went
weekly) and family of team performers, the show had been the perfect
training ground for Burnett. She was able to use her musical comedy
background and the experience she had acquired in the major off-
Broadway hit *Once Upon a Mattress*, under George Abbott's direction.

Much of the credit for seeing where Burnett's genius lay and master-
minding her career at this stage must go to Joe Hamilton, the producer she
met on *The Garry Moore Show* and who had become her second husband. In
1967, after some notorious hits and misses (including one highly-publicized
"scandal"—Burnett's departure from the Broadway hit, *Fade Out—Fade
In*—and one resounding flop: her pairing with Bob Newhart for a TV series
called *The Entertainers*), Burnett, with Hamilton at the helm, signed a deal
with CBS, with whom she was already under contract, for a variety show.

It opened with its format, cast, and themes pretty much in place. On
the one hand, there was the show's solidly conventional, yet charming
feature: the boy-girl "flirtation" in which Burnett's easy way with men is
seen as she lusts up to stud-in-residence Lyle Waggoner by cooing over his
he-man diaphragm and muscles without turning into a latter-day Mae
West.

There was the projection of a cozy, all-in-the-family atmosphere when
she introduced Jim Nabors (with whom she would later do a straight

musical number) as the godfather of her baby girl. Then there were the more idiosyncratic features, sketches drawn from a less benign past, that would claim center stage and develop into the great comic dissonances of the show. For instance, the autobiographical older-sister/younger-sister relationship to Vicki Lawrence as Chris is a reworking of Carol's to her sister Chrissy, the Sophia Loren-like "looker," so precocious that Burnett said that when she "raised her, I was scared to take a bath in front of her." And there emerges that enduring Burnett theme, the opposition between the "feminine woman," a lusciously marriageable object, and the smart, sassy, aggressive tomboy whose only chance is camouflage or major re-modeling . . . or a man who goes for legs rather than faces. "You're supposed to be a girl, not King Kong," she tells Lawrence, ordering her to "be feminine, helpless, and slump!" In hunchback contortion, they go in to meet their men looking like two beasts of prey poised for attack. The idea of women twisting themselves out of shape to be desirable points the way to the challenging of sex roles that becomes one of the hallmarks of the show. Although *Saturday Night Live*, or even *The Show of Shows*, is usually considered more hip, *The Carol Burnett Show* is far more casually radical. Sketches that flirt with androgyny as performed by the inimitable quartet —Burnett, Lawrence, Harvey Korman, and Tim Conway—are downright Wildean in their daring, and, in fact, the four regulars are all—as the title of one skit had it—"Dr. Jekyll and Ms. Hyde."

Whatever else they are, her crazies are never pure victims. Some of her woman characters are straight wimps and melancholy woebegones, but the majority have a tough core and an exhilaratingly brutal, unlovable exterior. They are in the mold of Nanny: rude, chaotic, messy, smart, overbearing, protected as they ride roughshod over social niceties by a sheath of insen-sitivity against the virus of rejection. Mama, the unloving, with her balloon-ing, brook-no-nonsense bosom and a viciously puritanical smugness; Eu-nice, the unloved, screechy-voiced and scrawny in her bedspread-print dresses, an addict of haute trash; and sour oafish Ed: these are people to whom we should feel comfortably superior, yet somehow it doesn't work out that way. We see the consequences for those of us who "escape" our families and try to go home again in the devastating episode when Roddy McDowall, newly crowned literary lion, returns for a triumphant home-coming that is a total disaster. Having won a Nobel prize and a *Time* cover for a book about India, he arrives expecting at least a pat on the back, a look of familial pride. Instead, he is greeted with stunning indifference:

Eunice is buried in *TV Guide*, her sole reading matter, while Mama complains she hasn't got room on the shelf for *one more book*! They may be subliterate, but like all families they have total recall when it comes to remembrance of past wounds, slights, injustices, inequities, slurs, and unequal portions of dessert. And they are tactical geniuses, obsessed and indefatigable in knowing just when to lower the eyelids, or snicker, or drop the one apparently innocuous word of criticism that will drive another family member up the wall.

A deep vein of pessimism comes directly out of the humor, out of the sense of people freeze-dried in personality ruts. Far from the boosterish spirit of women's magazines, unattached women in the Burnett show don't make themselves over, Cosmo-girl style; they just sink further into misery, spreading hopelessness like cigarette smoke through singles bars. Ugly people are often ugly in spirit as well. There are problems that can't be solved, and as family members grow old, instead of rising to the eleventh hour reconciliations of patented family drama, they grow further apart, more rigid, more determined to have the last word before they go. Except for an occasional break in the hostilities, a rare moment of peace as they unite against the world, relations between Eunice and Mama deteriorate. Eunice grows more frenzied and desperate, finally winding up deranged, an automaton on an analyst's couch.

EVENTUALLY THE SKETCHES, LIKE the show itself, ran out of energy. People left, it became strained, as any long-running series will do. The touch was deserting it. Burnett herself decided to close shop and go off the air before CBS cancelled the show.

The movie roles she took reflected the actor's time-honored ambition to break new ground, but what her filmography—*Pete and Tillie*, *The Four Seasons*, *The Front Page*, *Annie*, *The Wedding*, and made-for-TV movies like *Friendly Fire*—most suggests is a sense of waste. The pathetic Molly Malloy in Billy Wilder's remake of *The Front Page* was the sort of woebegone floozy she would have kidded some life into on her show, but she played it straight, and her superior intelligence knocked holes in the thin fabric of the character. In *Friendly Fire* she captured the rigid, unlikable side of the mother whose son is missing in Vietnam, but there was no release in black humor. Instead of "stretching," she shrank. The ugly duckling turned into a dull swan.

Fresno, the send-up of prime-time soap operas, which featured Burnett as the matriarch of a shrinking raisin empire, sounded like a bright idea for her return to satire. But in her sub-Joan Collins portrait of a chicly aging vamp she seemed to have arrived at the point—the social climber's dream —where all traces of gaucheness have been erased. She was too comfortable in her *fab*ulous Hollywood couture, so much more inventive than the script or the acting. Gone was what was uniquely Burnett: the wild look in the eyes, the unpredictable gesture of a hit-and-run comedian, some lurking outrageous Nannyism that would burble out of her subconscious and sabotage any pretense at elegance.

One biographer, praising her figure, her glamor, her assurance as host on her show, chided her for the persistence of her inferiority complex, but her inferiority complex, like Chaplin's tramp, was her artistic soul. Becoming successful, and thus an insider at the banquet on which one has cast an outsider's skewering glance, is the Faustian dilemma no comic genius can avoid. Acceptance generally means losing one's comic edge, and Burnett was no exception. But before she lost her craziness, she was the best kind of pop crossover star—the hip and the culturally sophisticated could admire the precision of her work, while nonintellectuals responded to her warmth. There is, always, that extraordinary double perspective. Inside her most flamboyant creations there is someone straight—a normal, junior-high, PTA, church bake-off, folksy, prudish sort of person. When comedians as sharp as Burnett take on people beneath them, there's usually an ironic gap between performer and target that widens fatally into cruelty or camp. Burnett identifies too closely with her screechy harridans and soggy failures for contempt to creep in, and she's too straight for camp. The savagery, or what passes for cruelty, is constantly being redeemed by complicity.

I can say the most terrible things about these people, she seems to be saying, because they're my *family*. And she's right. They are.

Lucy et al.

Here's Lucille Ball, the queen of domestic comedy and of comic domesticity, on the *I Love Lucy* show: comfortably fortyish, schlepping around in kerchiefs and housecoats, smocks ample enough to conceal a frying pan and a garbage can lid (her "bullet-proof vest" when she thinks Ricky is going to kill her), or, in another episode, a stolen cuckoo clock. Yet even in tent couture, she has the aura of glamor of the Goldwyn Girl she played in her second movie (*Roman Scandals*, with Eddie Cantor, in 1933). Performing the classic commercial for "Vitameatavegamin," she's as regal as a model—which she *was* (dashingly high-fashioned, third from the right in the Astaire-Rogers musical *Roberta*). But she can let the model's carriage go slack, sag and wither like a deflating balloon, her Donald Duck eyelids at half mast, as she begins to feel the alcoholic effects of her "health" drink.

No wonder Hollywood didn't know quite what to do with her. Being a clown with impeccable timing and a beauty with impeccable legs is a contradiction. Beauties aren't supposed to be witty, or to mug—it contorts their lovely features, carves permanent lines in their faces. Glamorous redheads aren't supposed to disclose their beauty secrets, as Lucy does at every opportunity:

Ricky's Cuban uncle, meeting her for the first time: "Where did you get your beautiful red hair?"

Lucy: "I get it every two weeks—(gasp) oops!"

She catches herself not because she's keeping the henna treatments a secret, but because it's not the thing to say to the pompous paterfamilias who still thinks Ricky should have married a Cuban.

*The essay "Lucy et al." was first published in the Museum of Television & Radio's exhibition catalogue *Lucille Ball: First Lady of Comedy*, 1985.

As the Lucy persona evolves, putting her foot in it is one of her specialties, but she usually manages to take a few sacred cows and chauvinist bulls down with her. Trying to say thank you to the aforementioned uncle and garbling her Spanish, she calls him a fat pig ("Macho grasso") before accidentally (?) shredding his foot-long hand-rolled cigar. Lucy—and Lucille—would disavow any connection with feminism, but she cuts a wide swath through the preserves of maledom. Driving through the inflated egos that fall prey to her, she begins with her sweet sitting-duck babalu husband and ends by smothering such icons as Richard Widmark, John Wayne, and William Holden with her lethal adoration.

Like other fair-haired comediennes—Carole Lombard, Judy Holliday—she carries with her an air of perpetual innocence, an angelic Who me? She is starting life again each moment, without memory, without morality—she lies shamelessly, but, like a child, she does it with chocolate all over her face. This innocence is a quality particularly well suited to the weekly series, where life begins anew with each show. She doesn't remember that last week she drove Ricky crazy, wild with fear, to the point of breakdown, which is just as well, because the dumb blonde's cultivated amnesia is her one great weapon. She and Ethel operate in a sexually divided world in which men still have the power, the pursestrings, and the privileges: Ricky and Fred can go to the fights alone, but she and Ethel can't go to the Copa without dates. Dates?! Where . . . ?? A plot is hatched. And thus did Eve, when Adam threatened to go off and play touch football with a coconut, develop her wiles.

The sheer mass-market popularity and availability of the show has given us a take-it-for-granted attitude towards her that has obscured both the genius of Ball's contribution and the movie career, the undeservedly neglected other life, that preceded it.

In *Follow the Fleet* she was briefly seen as an elegant golddigger. In RKO's Annabel films she played a zany actress who with her agent (Jack Oakie) was always getting into scrapes. The slapstick is closer to the later Ball, but she was still a dish. She played a variety of brassy-earthy showgirl-actress types, but her most memorable movies were *Stage Door*, with Katharine Hepburn, and Dorothy Arzner's *Dance, Girl, Dance*, with Maureen O'Hara. In both she was a glittering and robust counterpoint, a ballast-like foil to the artier pretensions of the other two. Later, as Lucy, one of her funniest routines is an audition for an Italian director in which she does a parody of Hepburn's Calla-lily scene.

In *Dance, Girl, Dance*, she plays Bubbles, the burlesque queen, whose lascivious bumps and grinds make a lecherous audience all the more impatient with O'Hara's willowy pirouettes.

Her career, spanning six decades, is extraordinary, even by the tough-girl standards of durability set by Bette Davis and Joan Crawford. A workhorse, she was born in upstate New York of a telephone linesman who died when she was four, and a mother who encouraged her to work and fight her way into show business. She took tony jobs when she could, menial when she couldn't; fought back from a crippling two-year bout of rheumatoid arthritis. All of this accounts not only for her toughness and resilience but the instinctual empathy she shares with low-life characters. Of her performance in the Damon Runyon movie *The Big Street* (1941), in which she played a crippled nightclub queen to Henry Fonda's smitten busboy, James Agee wrote that she was "born for the parts Ginger Rogers sweats over [and] tackles her 'emotional' role as if it were sirloin and she didn't care who was looking."

When, in the first of the *I Love Lucy* Connecticut episodes, she disguises herself as a gum-chewing moll to horrify the owners of the house and sour the deal, she is Her Highness all over again. Even throwaway lines are funny, but she gets off a gem that is side-splitting. In the same scene, referring to Ricky ("the Brain") she says to sidekick Fred, "Watch out or you'll step on the Brain's toes, Fingers."

Her great comedy writers—Jess Oppenheimer, Madelyn Pugh, Bob Carroll, Jr.—went with her from radio to television and helped shape the Lucy persona. Ball never added or altered a word, though she wrapped herself around the lines till they were all hers. But she worked for hours on the business, and what business it was! With the help of the great German cinematographer Karl Freund, she developed gags that were richer and more complex than anything on television. You have to go back to silent comedy to find the equivalent of the assembly line scene in the chocolate factory, in which her hands pull and dance through the liquid chocolate like two independent creatures. There's a similarly gooey sensuality and weird beauty to the Italian wine vat routine, in which she stomps and sinks and flaps her wings, then (capturing always the rhythm of a mounting "high" followed by a sinking "low") gets into a love-hate war-dance with the Italian *signora* who is her hapless co-worker.

Ball traces her roots backwards to vaudeville and the silent comedians. She shared offices with Keaton, does a Chaplin impersonation; one of her funniest sketches is with Harpo Marx—doing the mirror scene with herself as the reflection. And she looks forward, as an influence, to the moderns, to Carol Burnett, to the "wild and crazy" style of the *Saturday Night Live* crowd and even to Monty Python. (The episode with the cuckoo clock is as nuttily off-the-wall as any of their dead-pan riffs.)

She risks not being lovable: there's a klutzy, unappealing, low-brow, ugly-American side to her women on the move. And though the gags are so exquisitely worked out they are saved from coarseness, there are shades of Rupert Pupkin in her aggressive groupie, lusting for a pound of Star flesh.

The catch here is that, like Chaplin, she is a hugely successful star playing a creep, an outsider. Why is Lucille Ball, star of TV's hottest show, on a tour bus ogling the houses of the "greats" instead of being ogled herself? Yet she *is* ordinary—a back-fence gossip, an onlooker—in a way Chaplin wasn't.

Whether the lewd and the sexy were domesticated out of her by television and the nice-girl values of the fifties, or whether that's where she was headed all along, she becomes a champion, an angel of ordinariness, a woman of blinkered credulity capable of flights of comic beauty. She meets her equal, in one of the most hilarious one-hour shows ever filmed, when she locks horns with Tallulah: it's middle-America versus Camp, the girl-next-door versus vamp, fighting it out in suburbia. Lucy, furious, mimics Tallulah. "Ye-e-es, da-ah-hling," she says with as much spite as she can muster. "If you don't watch out," Tallu replies, "I'll pull your pink hair out by its black roots." It's a match made in comic heaven.

For all her tussles with men, Lucy's best moments are with women, with women rivals and with her great woman pal, Ethel, the sweet, slow-on-the-uptake neighbor played by Vivian Vance. As Vance says in an interview included in a splendid compilation film, *Lucille Ball: The First 25 Years*, they were two grown women living out childhood fantasies.

Their childlike natures mesh intuitively in one of the funniest and—to my thinking—most beautiful episode of *The Lucy Show* (the series that followed *I Love Lucy*). Practically wordless, it has them trying to repair a shower from the inside when the shower door sticks. The water begins rising till they are all but submerged. Struggling, their tennis shoes flapping, they are like two tadpoles in an aquarium, or two babes in amniotic fluid.

Lucille Ball takes us back to our roots, both comic and cosmic—the hairline beneath the henna, the universal womb where humor and life are born.

Still Here

SHIRLEY MACLAINE

W hile other stars have flashed through the Hollywood orbit with more fire and dazzle, Shirley MacLaine has crept up on us as one of the most enduring of them all. A forty-year run of good and very good movies in an industry that no longer nurtures and sustains careers would be a major achievement by anyone, but for a woman to have such staying power is phenomenal.

The image that kept her out of the glamor category—closer to perky indominatrix than *femme fatale*—has been the latter-day blessing of her career. There is no breathtakingly beautiful early MacLaine with whom her aging self must bear unfavorable comparison. We might conjecture that sometime long ago, in the divvying up of shares in the sibling talent pool, she ceded the role of seducer to bro' Warren, became the turtle to his relentlessly sexy rabbit (though with her graceful dancer's buoyancy and striking, candy store good looks, she is a turtle only metaphorically and comparatively).

There are further reasons, I think, that MacLaine has been one of the less appreciated and written-about of major stars. One is that she herself has done the job for us, having been for years her own most articulate critic and apologist. On talk shows and in books she has kept up a running monologue, candid, intelligent, rueful, about life, love, movies. Add to this a screen persona that defies categories, a talent that can go either way, into comedy or melodrama, uptown or downtown, Broadway, Las Vegas, or movies, and you have precisely the sort of star that Hollywood—and, let's

*This article was first published in *Film Comment*, May–June 1995. Copyright © 1995 by Molly Haskell.

face it, critics—are uncomfortable with. She's never been enough of a heartthrob to inspire male mash notes and tone poems. On the other hand, with her peculiar repertory of kooks and hookers and mistresses, and, more recently, suffering mothers, she doesn't exactly qualify as a candidate for feminist canonization.

But isn't this precisely the sort of woman we should be praising to the skies, an actress who, being offbeat and eccentric, makes original things possible? Her long career can be looked at as one that continually liberated the screen from habit and custom, from simple black and white.

She hasn't sought our love and has often forfeited sympathy on the altar of what passes for rebelliousness in Hollywood: leading her own life, making up her own rules, wanting to push the envelope further than most of her directors were willing to go.

In those hookers and mistresses, wallflowers and lesbians, kooks and lovers, and finally dames who refuse to retire gracefully into the night of oblivion, we find the staying power of the nonnarcissist, the girl who can't take the world's adoration for granted and so has developed character and moxie. As elevator operator Fran Kubelik in Billy Wilder's *The Apartment* she had and kept the sort of cloddish joke of a name that other actresses and woman characters dropped, with the pounds and the bushy eyebrows and any hint of ethnicity, on the Damascus Road to stardom: Carole Lombard's Mildred Plotke to Lily Garland in *Twentieth Century*; and Garland herself (ex-Frances Gumm, for goodness sake!)—Esther Blodgett to Vicki Lester in *A Star Is Born*.

MacLaine (b. Shirley Maclean Beaty), already dancing by the age of two, was perhaps closer to being a star born than most of her Hollywood contemporaries. She somehow managed to survive or was driven forward by not only the upstaging brother but a deeply conservative birthplace in a nationally conservative era. I can guarantee that Richmond, Virginia, in the forties and fifties was not a place that encouraged little girls and young women to strut their stuff in public, an act wholly inimical to their future vocation as clubwomen and wives.

It was on to New York, where she found herself in a real-life version of that perennial Broadway-to-Hollywood fairy tale, the chorus girl who replaces the ailing star and goes on to make showbiz history—as did Shirley MacLaine, substituting for Carol Haney in *The Pajama Game*.

Making her film debut in Hitchcock's uncharacteristically playful *The Trouble with Harry* in 1955, the red-haired newcomer held her own with the vibrant New England fall coloring. From there she went from one good director to another and from one wildly different project to another. She played the first of her cheerful losers as the hooker in Vincente Minnelli's *Some Came Running* (1958), then the woebegone working-girl romantic in Billy Wilder's *The Apartment* (1960). Her more professional "poules," in *Irma la Douce* (1963) and *Sweet Charity* (1968), based on *Nights of Cabiria* but set in New York, are too American and sanitized for their European settings. If she could have taken them into Fellini-like lower depths, developed the earthier and grimmer aspects of their lives, as she claimed in a recent television interview she wanted to do, they would have been different films altogether—certainly not the ones their directors were out to make or America was ready for.

For example, with Fosse she broached the subject of wanting to get at the underbelly of prostitution, but the director of *Sweet Charity* said he didn't like American prostitutes and so made her into a dance hall girl. She could play disturbed and disturbing though she didn't often get the opportunity. Her idea for Martha in *The Children's Hour* was to make her lesbianism explicit; the audience would grasp it before she did, and the child's accusation would then strike home instead of simply turning into some kind of gratuitous bad-seed meanness as it does in Wyler's version of the Hellman play. As it stands, MacLaine's performance is the best thing in the movie—quiet, anxious, stubborn, conveying at least some of the misplaced yearning that is never articulated in the screenplay.

Her seriousness can be dull—in *The Turning Point* (1977) she has to make the case for motherhood over career, a case which emerges as sourly triumphant since we catch her when her rival, Anne Bancroft, is at the bitter end of her life as a professional dancer. In the TV interview, recalling the scene in the bar when Bancroft throws a highball at her, she offered some insight into her acting methods. Apparently, unbeknownst to MacLaine, Herbert Ross had put Bancroft up to it, wanting to catch a spontaneous rise out of her. MacLaine blew up all right, and without blowing the scene, but the emotion was hers, not the character's. She was furious at Bancroft and Ross, and that was the emotion he got. She was deliberate in her preparation and didn't like surprises.

She is probably best known nowadays for her Oscar-winning Aurora Greenway, the sweet-but-spiky mother of cancer-victim Debra Winger in *Terms of Endearment* (for James Brooks, 1983). Less well known among her eccentric roles are some lovely little sleepers in between—Joseph McGrath's *The Bliss of Mrs. Blossom* (1968) and Don Siegel's *Two Mules for Sister Sara* (1970). The whimsicality of *Mrs. Blossom* obscures a penetrating insight into what marriage is all about. A wife enjoys the attentions of a kooky male messenger (James Booth) she hides in the attic while her more conventional husband (Richard Attenborough) works to bring home the bacon, thus suggesting that marriage is less about physical attraction than what people do all day. Women want security, but they also want to have fun.

A bleaker sort of humanity irradiates one of her most impressive and atypical performances, that of the cat-bitten wife engulfed by urban angst in Frank Gilroy's grimly absorbing *Desperate Characters* (1970, adapted from the novel by Paula Fox). From the vulnerable fortress of their Brooklyn townhouse, she and husband Kenneth Mars shoulder through a weekend of horrors, beginning with a bite from the stray cat, a metaphor for all the homeless, foodless, loveless urban riff-raff who pose an eternal challenge to our principles and generosity, and ending with the vandalism of their summer home, probably by resentful locals entrusted with guarding it. Too close to home, too depressing: the film's failure is no more of a mystery today than it was then. In fact, it looks even bleaker now: nothing has changed and we're all getting older. But MacLaine manages to give an extraordinarily *un*depressing portrait of depression. Her middle-aged Sophie is intelligent, sensitive, yet sinking as she finds herself alienated from all the people who constituted her lifelines—her husband, her ex-lover, friends who can barely lend an ear before retreating into their islands of self-absorption. MacLaine's ability to maintain a kind of unembittered grace through this urban-marital hell is astonishing and makes us wonder how much more she could have given us in an intelligent, realistic vein if she'd been offered the chance.

She belongs to the middle period of movies, after glamor and before grunge. Films about intelligent, nonmalignant, non gun-toting people were still being made, and women were no longer obliged to be either very likable or unlikable with nothing in between.

She also occupies a midway zone between comedy and melodrama. The downside of her charm and eccentricity is that she doesn't have the emotional intensity for heavy drama. She can be emotional but can't suffer grandly in the manner of the great women's film stars, nor is she sexy or seductive enough for most romantic comedy. As the hooker in *Some Came Running*, she was less sexual than her rival for Sinatra's love, Martha Hyer's prim schoolteacher, thus pointing up an underlying paradox in the American spin on the virgin-whore split. In our domestic Garden of Eden, the whore, with her heart of gold, is really the mother, while the Nice Girl—

beneath her cool facade and perfect syntax—is really a slut. One of the more excruciating scenes in the movie is the interview between MacLaine's musical-comedy tart and Hyer's stiff fifties nice girl, each somehow pointing up the artificiality of the archetypes they are forced to play. But MacLaine's embarrassingly doggy devotion to Sinatra and her kewpie doll vulgarity are at last redeemed in the film's sublime finale, when MacLaine's mothering whore, finally married to Sinatra, flings herself on his fallen body and takes the bullet meant for him, hitting the sort of high note in death that her character had been denied in life—and was rarely struck in MacLaine's career.

There was something so sane even in her eccentricity, so much more inclined to fun than to passion. In the same television interview she commented on the happy times she had with the Rat Pack, getting to know Sinatra and Martin—waking them in the morning, getting them coffee, playing gin rummy, and in general playing the nonsexual roles of pal and nursemaid and good sport. The perfect buddy/wife for life rather than the imperfect—and obsolescent—temptress.

And in truth she gave us her motto in *Postcards from the Edge* (Mike Nichols, 1990): "I'm still here," she sings, sitting on the piano in a scarlet dress, serving notice to actress-singer daughter Meryl Streep that she's not moving aside yet. The daughter's career and life, blotted by drugs and Oedipal rivalry, are on hold, but the old dame just won't get down from the piano or leave her daughter's boyfriends alone. Now finally flowering into the role of seducer, the broad as diva is getting her revenge on the younger ones, the daughters, the little brothers. Similarly, in *Guarding Tess* (Hugh Wilson, 1994), as the widow of a former President, she makes life hell for every member of her federally mandated retinue and especially her personal Secret Service agent (Nicholas Cage). She fuels her anger at being old and infirm and ignored into a livid display of icy contempt and intractability toward the very one she likes and needs most. She's all the sick, once-proud women who've outlived their usefulness as wives and mothers, worn out their welcome with ungrateful children, and at least have the gumption (and the wherewithal) to set off a few firecrackers and disturb the peace. Watching this intergenerational screwball romance, you realize how few movies deal with mothers and sons, the relationship being too charged with intimations of male humiliation and dependency. Instead, Hollywood prefers (and has always preferred) the safer thrills of all-male bonding in whatever form—buddies, surrogate fathers and sons, real fathers and sons—a rivalry that promises, if one or the other *has* to lose or surrender, that at least it will be to another man. Yet the fear of woman—powerful woman, mother of the nursery—is as nothing compared with the fear of the Old Woman, shared by both sexes.

That's why one of MacLaine's gutsiest moments comes in *Postcards from the Edge*, in one of that underrated film's many irresistible tough-love encounters between mother and daughter (MacLaine and Streep standing in, you will remember, for Debbie Reynolds and Carrie Fisher—professional rivalry only taking the normal competitiveness and mutual narcissism of mother and daughter to a grandiose pitch). Having survived a drunk-driving accident, MacLaine lies propped up in a hospital bed, bald, unmade up, and without even eyebrows and eyelashes, as raw as a newborn infant and twice as vulnerable. She's allowing herself to be the "crone" that Germaine Greer exhorts post-menopausal women to be; in one terrifying, exhilarating moment she abandons the spotlight, the struggle, stardom, all the panoply of seductive arts to move aside, to make way for the next generation. Not offscreen or offstage, mind you, just . . . over!

Beeban Kidron's *Used People* (1992) begins by having everyone in an ethnic Queens family screeching at each other so they can undergo one of those eleventh-hour sit-com transformations in which mutually detesting blood relations (sisters Kathy Bates and Marcia Gay Harden) and mother and daughter MacLaine and Bates are magically redeemed by love. In the midst of the contrivances, MacLaine has an aria-like moment in which she disgorges for the benefit of the horizontally challenged daughter who is abandoning her for California, all the years of pent-up spite, resentment, and self-sacrifice. It's a juicy moment and a neat trick—holding the spotlight in revenge for having been shunted out of it. For heaven's sake let's keep her there!

Two Protofeminist Heroines

H O W A R D   H A W K S

His Girl Friday

The marvel of *His Girl Friday* is that a newspaper comedy about two men—the big-city editor trying to hold onto his suburbia-bound ace reporter—could with so little alteration be turned into a divorced-lover comedy about a male editor and a female reporter, played respectively and unforgettably by Cary Grant and Rosalind Russell. The play, Ben Hecht and Charles MacArthur's *The Front Page*, had already been made into one film (1931; directed by Lewis Milestone) when Howard Hawks got hold of it. Supposedly the idea came to the director when, in a reading of the play, he had his female secretary take the part of Hildy. But the male buddy story is already a love story of the screwball variety—antagonism as a cover for attraction; they can't admit how much they need each other—so it was not so much a stretch as a natural step into the open expression of sexual attraction, complicated and enhanced by the conflict between marriage and work for the professional woman.

Indeed, *His Girl Friday* has become the classic version of that conflict, copied and emulated in films like *Broadcast News* and *I Love Trouble*, or Jennifer Jason-Leigh's pseudo Ros Russell–Katharine Hepburn brash suit-wearing reporter in *The Hudsucker Proxy*. But this conundrum was peculiarly suited to the male-female cosmology of Howard Hawks, where the best woman was often an honorary male and the highest accolade was that, in performing some task, she was "good"! Russell, quick-witted, resourceful, and articulate, is repeatedly referred to as a great "newspaperman."

*"His Girl Friday" was first published in *Scenario*, Fall 1995. Copyright © 1995 by Molly Haskell.

Whatever defects the Hawksian worldview may be held to have in its compensatory overvaluation of male heroics, its adolescent hierarchical rating of manliness, stoicism, professionalism, Hawks has given us some of the most exhilaratingly rambunctious and assertive heroines in cinema. They have outlasted more pliant female characters, becoming prophetic representatives of a species of women who yearn for something beyond settling down and nesting, with or without marriage and family.

In one of the great opening scenes in all of cinema, Russell's Hildy sweeps through the old familiar newsroom like a ship in full sail, waving the new engagement ring which she will display triumphantly to her ex, editor Walter Burns. Like two prizefighters used to each other's moves but relishing the unexpected, their encounter is a veritable compendium of virtuoso acting, editing, and mise-en-scene, in which two "old pros" play two old pros. The rhythm and timing of their moves and countermoves brings their past relationship into focus and, in a series of gestural and verbal jabs, thrusts and parries, launches them afresh into battle.

As Hildy gets sucked into the maelstrom of her work and falls prey to Walter's killer charms, none of Hawks' heroines speaks more gallantly to the conflict in certain women between a zeal for work on the one hand and the socially conditioned yearning to be taken care of. Or between two kinds of husbands: the charismatic heel and the dull safe bet.

Hawks of course tips the scales outrageously, making poor Ralph Bellamy's insurance salesman not such a safe bet after all, but a Momma's boy wimp who doesn't know enough to come out of the rain. Rubbers and all, he is a sitting duck for the skewering by the utterly unscrupulous Grant. Replaying in more brutal terms the rivalry they acted out in *The Awful Truth*, Grant and Bellamy represent more than a simple contrast in type, or urban vs. suburban. They prove conclusively that no marriage will give a woman everything, so it's best not to count on it for the ultimate fulfillment. Grant will never reform: the famously interrupted honeymoon will always be a honeymoon interruptus; the fire, explosion, earthquake, scoop will always come first. No time out for smooching, pregnancy, garden club meetings, "normal" life.

The script is by Charles Lederer (with uncredited work by Ben Hecht), a buddy of Hecht's who contributed dialogue to the 1931 *The Front Page*. Using most of the dialogue from the original, the script gains the rich layer of a romance while losing none of the play's savagery and cynicism. The love story is played out against a prison backdrop and the lugubrious Earl Wilson–Molly Malloy melodrama and so is itself tainted by the specter of corrupt news-gathering.

With Hecht's *Nothing Sacred*, it's one of the few movies to really take on the greed of journalism and the shameless hunger for catastrophe. Hecht and MacArthur began their careers as reporters in Chicago, an experience that furnished them with the material for this and other collaborations. The first film of *The Front Page* starred Adolphe Menjou as Walter Burns, in the part Osgood Perkins had played on the stage, and Pat O'Brien as Hildy (Lee Tracy on the stage). An interesting sidenote: Gable and Cagney were available and eager to do the film, but producer Howard Hughes turned them down! (In all fairness, neither was a star at the time.) Then, in 1974, Billy Wilder made one of his less successful comedies in a superannuated version of *The Front Page* with Walter Matthau and Jack Lemmon.

Hawks, in 1940, shows himself very much in sync with Hecht's vision, with the ambivalence towards the ruthless professionalism of doing a job well. The hectic pace and the uncompromising ruthlessness of Grant are very much at the heart of the film's meaning: it's wild, fun, breathlessly involving, but it also prevents you from ever stopping to wonder if what you're doing is right or ethical. Hawks's version is the least sentimental, refusing either to condemn Grant's behavior or modify it. And Hildy herself, running after him in the film's "happy ending," bags in hand, accepts both the unreliable and the unethical side of Grant (though she is seen as in some sense a benign influence) in return for the obvious highs of work and marriage.

Hildy is a heroine who *thinks* she wants what she calls "a halfway normal life" only to discover she is something other than what she thought, so that what she wants as a mate must suit this other self. Thus *His Girl Friday*'s most modern and contemporary aspect is that it imagines this new kind of marriage, one of mutuality, one in which the turn-on is work, one in which male and female do not occupy separate spheres but lose themselves (and their romantic self-consciousness) in a unifying, energizing, and eternally engaging profession.

The "halfway normal life" that a conventional love story might offer is limned in the glimpse we get of the engaged couple's courtship. When Hildy leaves Bruce at the door, he looks at her adoringly and simpers, "Even ten minutes is a long time to be away from you."

Having been roughed up in her relationship with the unchivalrous Grant, she beams at this bit of lap dog-courtliness, replying, "I can stand to be spoiled." She is seen in close-up and in soft-focus, and we are given to understand this is what her idea of being a woman is—spoiled and petted and flattered, the feminine object of masculine adulation. In the course of the film, she learns not that she has to be more of a man—indeed, her significant contribution to the hardbitten world of reporters is to inject a healthy dose of "female" consideration, conscience, and humanity—but that she has to expand her definition of what it means to be a woman. Home is what she wants, but "home" is not a house in suburbia with a white picket fence and complete coverage. Instead it is "at home" on the road with a guy who doesn't offer much in the way of assurance or insurance: running down a story, holed up in some hotel room, lucky if they can sit still long enough to get room service. Being a journalist and being a woman may require some juggling but they aren't incompatible.

Such are the vagaries of casting and moviemaking that if Hawks had gotten either of his first two choices for the role of Hildy—Jean Arthur and Irene Dunne—*His Girl Friday* would probably not have become the protofeminist classic it is. Arthur and Dunne, enchanting as they are, are unimaginable as "newspapermen." One would always feel with them the pull of domesticity, the appeal of traditional womanliness. They don't have the size and heft, literally, to battle Grant on his turf on anything like equal terms.

Russell, however, tall, dashing (physically and figuratively) in her stylish but occasionally cumbersome suit and hat ensemble (reportedly based on the look of newspaperwoman Adela Rogers St. John), is tailor-made for the part that she tailor-makes her own. There is a tomboyish lack of narcissism in her moves as she rushes into the street, lifting her straight skirt awkwardly.

She was a "doll-faced hick" when Grant first plucked her from obscurity, became her mentor and taught her the trade—in other words, she had enough sex appeal to get his attention but not so much that it interferes with her doing the job . . . and becoming very much an aggressive reporter in her own right. Despite the sexist implications in a title implying the subordination of the female, *His Girl Friday* is one of the few Hollywood movies of any era to celebrate the equality of the sexes.

Man's Favorite Sport?

American films, especially the action and thriller genres, flourish to an unusually large degree on an unconscious level. As you might expect, the signals sent up from this sub-textual region are mostly sexual, id impulses unsettling the straight-arrow conventions of a masculine genre or chaste adventure story. The earrings of *Madame de* resonate quite explicitly with accumulated meanings—the transience and perversity of desire, the conflict between decorum and passion, whereas the underlying pathology of a Hitchcock character covertly addresses the darker side of our natures.

Critics will spend hours with divining rods over the hermetic mindscape of Bergman, Antonioni, etc., giving them the benefit of every passing doubt. But they will scorn similar excursions into the rich, cryptic, and more innocent-seeming terrain of home-grown talents.

I recently watched for the second time Howard Hawks's *Man's Favorite Sport?*, a film which was universally ridiculed when it appeared in 1964, and which I myself hadn't much liked. I wanted to watch it again just to make sure—it is almost impossible for a great director to make a worthless film, and a few years in a film's life and ours can change one's perspective. This time I was both delighted and deeply moved by the film—delighted by the grace and real humor with which the story is told, and moved by the reverberations of a whole substratum of meaning, of sexual antagonism, desire, and despair.

The two layers, narrative and allegorical, interweave in such a way that the cruelty is constantly tempered by compassion and the ridiculous is redeemed by risk and anguish. As a result, the intrigue is not only richer, but the humor is funnier. In describing the substratum, I don't mean to suggest that Hawks is an unconscious artist. He is far more deliberate and articulate in his vision of the American male than, say, John Cassavetes, who in *Husbands* arrives at truths almost (but not quite) accidentally. The control and precision, the economy and follow-through of a Hawks film is assurance that he *knows* where he is going in a way that is more than intuitive but short of theoretical.

In a Hawks film, men and women are on their own, starting out in, and

**"Man's Favorite Sport" first appeared in *The Village Voice*, January 21, 1971. Copyright © 1978 by Molly Haskell.*

trying to fill, a vacuum. In *Man's Favorite Sport?* he gives us Rock Hudson
and Paula Prentiss as primordial man and woman, Adam and Eve in the
lush, hazardous Eden of a hunting and fishing resort. But an Adam and Eve
saddled with a bitter, comical heritage of sexual distrust, bravado, and fear,
archetypes that are infinitely closer to the American experience than such
articulate *angst*-mongers as Jeanne and Monica and Marcello and Max and
Harriet and Jean-Paul (Sartre or Belmondo).

Rock Hudson works as a salesman in the sporting goods department of
Abercrombie and Fitch. He has written an authoritative book on fishing,
although he has never gone fishing in his life and finds the idea repugnant.
His professional standing, therefore, is a hoax. Or, in the vocabulary of the
sexual allegory to which the film implicitly alludes, Hudson is a virgin, who
has written a "How to" book on sex while harboring a deep, fastidious
horror of it. His masculinity is a lie. (Interestingly, he is engaged, but has
never told his fiancée he can't "fish.")

Paula Prentiss, an aggressive, outdoorsy girl with a soupçon of butch
(the female equivalent of a man's man), arrives on the scene to browbeat
Hudson into entering a fishing competition at the lodge where she works.
(They first collide in a parking lot, in a scene which has been cut from the
print now shown on television.)

But certain modifying characteristics emerge. Although Paula Prentiss
seems strident and overbearing in her action, there is something in the way
Hawks directs her behavior—her soft, nervous gestures and the odd
rhythm of delivery—which suggests vulnerability. And although Rock
Hudson seems inoffensive and gentle—just a man trying to mind his own
business and have peace—there is something flaccid and unresponsive
about him, a self-satisfaction which is untested and therefore undeserved.
Paula Prentiss, in a remarkable performance, is the girl we knew at college,
smart and good at everything but terrified of (and therefore hostile to)
men. She spends all her time in the smoker while other girls come and go;
she has a shell of genial sarcasm to protect her from the humiliation of
desire and rejection.

But she is competent—even sexually, in the film's metaphor—and it is
she who must take the initiative in Hudson's sexual initiation, for which the
fishing exploit is metaphor. Fish are phallic symbols, of course, and there is
even a scene in which a loose fish thrashes around inside Hudson's pants,
causing him to jump and jerk uncontrollably.

Hawksian comedy, as Peter Wollen and other critics have pointed out, is the underside of, and compensation for, the action drama. Heroism and danger are replaced by adolescence and sexual failure, the way falling in a dream compensates for our overweening aspirations. The progression, in drama, from life to death, giving birth to an ideal, becomes, in the comedy, a progression from death (Hudson's inertia) to life, with the burial of a false ideal. Alongside Hudson's false-hero there is even a phony Indian—a cynic, European-style, who poses as an Indian for the tourists and continually tries to blackmail Hudson. (He is finally disarmed by the very naïveté of Hudson; the sleeping bag episode suggests that, whereas Europeans cheat romantically without ever being caught, Americans don't do anything and are immediately suspect.)

Without giving a play-by-play analysis, I will mention several of the loveliest and most complex images:

In a small clearing—his own Garden of Eden—Hudson tries unsuccessfully to pitch his (pink) tent, while Paula Prentiss and her girlfriend, serpents in frog suits, hide behind the bushes laughing, and finally intrude upon his privacy. The tent collapses, wrapping the inept Hudson in swaddling clothes. (This sequence is reversed in the end of the film, in which Hudson, now the aggressor, comes to Prentiss's tent, in a well-constructed, firelit campsite.)

When Hudson finally learns to "fish" it is not by reading his book of instructions, not by the rules, but by accidents of nature . . . or, instinct. (Before he learns, there is a "men in groups" scene at the lodge bar, where Hudson gives the men "tips"—an approximation of the locker room ritual of sexual tall tales.) But when Hudson wins the tournament, he has the confidence (or virility) to tell the truth.

An incident that disturbs many people occurs when Rock Hudson has given her the long-awaited kiss, and Paula Prentiss cries, "That was terrible," and runs off. But how eloquently this expresses her desperate resistance at being overwhelmed; her defensiveness over the kiss she has longed for and for which, when it comes, she is totally unprepared.

The head-on collision of trains in the film-within-a-film—the explosion, the electricity—is one side of the Hudson-Prentiss relationship; their drifting in peace and communion along the river of mutual fulfillment is the other. For both Hudson and Prentiss there is embarrassment and humiliation, and they are finally closer to each other than to those graceful members of society who establish rapports more easily.

Hawks's conception of woman, as a creature both equal and threatening

to man, can be seen as adolescent and anthropomorphic, but never idealizing or domesticating. He may not penetrate the secrets of a woman's heart
and her unique dilemma the way the so-called "woman's directors" do. But
at the same time he never excludes them from the action, never even
implicitly suggests that a woman occupies a fixed place—the home,
society—or that she is man's subordinate. Instinctively, he strikes a very
modern note in the image of a couple united not by the attraction of
opposites but the unanimity of similarities. The male-female polarity is
reconciled by the struggle to assert oneself in life, in the crazy American
scene, in which man and woman can be—as much as man and man—
natural allies.

Guys

. . . .

Lights . . . Camera . . . Daddy!

B ack in the old days, when mommies were mommies and daddies were
daddies, the one who Knew Best came home from the office a mite gruff
and tired, perhaps, and was withdrawn at the dinner table, but we knew he'd
been working for us and loved us. He didn't need to prove it by "speaking our
language" (God forbid!) or giving us "quality time" or babbling and blubber-
ing over past crimes and future promises. Today, being a male parent is a full-
time job (there are rumors that certain California universities are giving
degrees in it). And men, if we are to believe Hollywood movies, are doing so
well at it that mothers may soon become obsolete.

In an endless procession of what the British critic Raymond Durgnat has
dubbed "male weepies"—*Kramer vs. Kramer, Author! Author!, Tribute, Ordinary
People, The Great Santini, On Golden Pond, The Champ, Table for Five, Man, Woman
and Child, Six Weeks*—men are discovering how *good* they are at loving their
children. In juicily androgynous roles, actors like Al Pacino, Dustin Hoffman,
and Jon Voight compete for the Mother of the Year Award.

From these man-child paradises women are either relegated to the
wings or expelled altogether. In *Kramer vs. Kramer*, the villain is a watered-
down feminism: Meryl Streep abandons her family to pursue the will-o'-
the-wisp of self-realization. In *Author! Author!*, playwright Israel Horovitz's
fantasy of fame, fortune, and fatherhood, promiscuous longings over which
she has no control prompt Tuesday Weld to desert. In *Table for Five*, the
mother dies halfway through the film—one of the more dignified exits
provided for a woman. The final image in these films is usually of father and

*This article was first published in *The Nation*, May 28, 1983. Copyright © 1983 by
Molly Haskell.

child together—on a doorstep (Donald Sutherland and Timothy Hutton in *Ordinary People*), on the tearful brink of separation (Martin Sheen and his bastard son in *Man, Woman and Child*), playing touch football in the yard (Robert Duvall and his stepson in *Tender Mercies*), in a backstage huddle (Pacino and his oldest son in *Author! Author!*). In an odd permutation, *Table for Five* fades out on father and *father*. Voight, a former golf pro and flop of a father, having learned about love and parental responsibility on a Greek island cruise with his kids, wants to keep them when Mom—his ex-wife— dies. But so does their stepfather (Richard Crenna, who not only loves the kids but pays the orthodontic bills). Solution: Love Daddy and Money Daddy reach some sort of mystical and never-explained compromise and waltz off together into the Grecian sunset.

The open misogyny of these films goes beyond the censoriousness of those earlier Hollywood fables in which women were penalized or shown as unfeminine for neglecting their maternal duties. When Joan Crawford or Rosalind Russell got uppity, they had to be brought down a peg, but at heart was the preservation of the American family. There was always a male bias: in *Woman of the Year*, Katharine Hepburn's cosmopolitan reporter was ridiculed for being unable to fry an egg, while Spencer Tracy was not only a regular guy of the meat-and-potatoes school but a better parent to their adopted child. Mothers could never get it quite right, being either too remiss or too self-sacrificing. Still, the basic impulse was to housebreak the woman rather than to banish her, reflecting the collective thinking of moguls who, however hypocritically, were family men, believers in purity, honor, motherhood, and romance.

In recent years the sanctity of the family has gone from being a joke, courtesy of the Me Decade, to being a subject for nostalgia, with men resurrecting it according to their specifications. Hollywood is now in the hands of a new breed of producers, directors, and screenwriters, most of whom have been divorced at least once and are governed by a different set of conscious and unconscious motives, which inevitably find their way into movies: the guilt of divorced (or workaholic) fathers for having placed their happiness over that of their children; anger at their own neglectful or undemonstrative fathers, which leads them to try to right old wrongs, either by making Dad over *(Tribute, On Golden Pond)* or by showing how loving *they* can be; vengeance toward ex-wives and feminists for withdrawing all those emotional and domestic props.

Last, but by no means least, is the issue of custody. Mothers, as we know, are no longer automatically awarded custody in divorce cases. The vast majority of fathers do not sue for custody of their children, but for those who do the odds of getting it are very good: according to recent statistics, men win one-half to two-thirds of court battles. In view of this development, movies testifying to men's superior qualifications for parenthood take on a slightly sinister tone.

In an interview in *American Film* magazine, Dustin Hoffman put the case succinctly. Discussing his preparations for *Tootsie*—in which he plays the first mainstream middle-aged feminist heroine of our era—he credited the character to his work in *Kramer vs. Kramer*: "We improvised a lot in that movie—we improvised a courtroom scene and at one point I had a good emotional thing going. The judge said, 'Why should you have the child?' I said, 'Because I'm his mother.' And I didn't know I said it and I couldn't get Bob Benton and Stanley Jaffe to use it in the cut—they thought it was gilding the lily."

In most of the father-child valentines what begins as a stopgap measure —Dad lurching into the breach when Mom makes her exit—ends as a paean to the emotional and domestic virtuosity of the male. By the end of *Kramer*, Hoffman has not only figured out what grade his son is in at school, he has mastered the art of making French toast. Jon Voight learns the names of his children's teachers, Al Pacino the correct proportion of bleach to detergent for white-as-snow laundry. Their accomplishments, it should be noted, stop short of potty training and diaper changing, the messier and harsher realities of child rearing—their children are all at an "interesting" age, marginally self-sufficient and adorable. In the fantasy world of many of these films, father and son regress into an ideal world of all-male permissiveness. As fathers and their children form a mutual admiration society, an interesting exchange takes place. Men find in their kiddies' loving eyes the hero worship once provided by their wives. And conversely, simply by taking on the job of child rearing, men give it a dignity and status it never has when women do it. It's known as the men-upgrade-the-neighborhood-women-ruin-property-values phenomenon. In contrast to recent findings about just how much (i.e., how *little*) housework men actually do, movie heroes plunge in and take over and bask in a self-congratulatory glow besides, all without losing their status as Real Men.

As befits a world in which parenthood is up for grabs, sometimes the nurturing father is a father surrogate. Judd Hirsch, for example, brings ethnic "soul" to the psychoanalyst-as-nurturing-parent in *Ordinary People* and the detective-as-nurturing-parent in *Without a Trace*. (The latter, incidentally, was directed by *Kramer* producer—and divorced father—Stanley

Jaffe.) Against the frigid mother (Mary Tyler Moore) of *Ordinary People* and the stoic, over-educated mother (Kate Nelligan) of *Without a Trace*, Hirsch counterposes *mensch* directness and feeling.

The Nelligan mother is an arresting figure—she's modern, complex and, unlike the Moore mother, no villain. Her refusal to "let go" after her son is kidnapped is the source of the movie's emotional power, but at the same time we are made to feel that her reserve is somehow unnatural, not quite "womanly." She's an infinitely more vital and capable parent than the father (David Dukes), who's hopeless on every level—but then it was her outstripping him professionally that "unmanned" him and destroyed their marriage.

Nostalgia for the old-fashioned wife is the spark that ignites *Tender Mercies*, a beautiful, ballad-like film, conservative to the core. Robert Duvall's dissolute country singer is redeemed by the love of a "good" (i.e., simple, unchallenging) woman after the wreckage wrought by his hard-driving, country-singing, and competitive former wife.

But then (what's a girl to do?) in *Man, Woman and Child*, a preposterous fantasy from the pen of Erich never-having-to-say-you're-sorry Segal, the "good," faithful wife (Blythe Danner) winds up with egg on her face, while the independent, libidinous Frenchie who gives Martin Sheen his son represents the ideal: she's self-employed; she doesn't want to marry; she wants You and only You to create a beautiful baby in her womb, after which you will be free to depart, no strings; and she dies young and far away, your name on her lips but in love, not reproach.

Run these fantasies through the data processor and what do we get? The best woman is a dead woman, especially a dead independent woman! Next best is one who pulls a disappearing act in a manner that reflects badly on her character rather than the husband's. Third preference (where the woman is *determined* to hang in there and stay married) is an all-forgiving mother-wife, who looks the other way at her mate's peccadilloes and even embraces the fruit of his waywardness afterward. Although the women's magazines like to tell us we can "have it all," the message of these movies is that we can't have much of anything. The irony is that most male weepies are merchandised as women's pictures and cater to female audiences.

The mother is dead. Long live the mother. And his name is . . . fill in the blank with your favorite bankable male star. Presumably a great many women are paying good money to choke back the tears over a doting Dudley Moore or a fumbling Al Pacino or a misty-eyed Jon Voight. We ought instead to be laughing these male mothers off the screen.

Rape: The 2,000-Year-Old Misunderstanding

Some time ago, on the if-I-don't-do-it-they'll-get-somebody-worse the-ory, I agreed to appear on an ABC late-night special on rape. My segment was devoted to its portrayal on film: clips of the rape scenes from *Two Women* and *Straw Dogs* were shown, followed by a discussion between myself and moderator David Frost. The sequence from *Two Women* was the scene in which Sophia Loren and her daughter were gang-raped by Moor-ish soldiers. Rape is regarded as an outrage against nature and an outgrowth of war, and is treated, in the neorealistic language of Vittorio de Sica's film, as ugly, brutal, and harsh. Although the violation of the sensual earth mother played by Sophia Loren has, inevitably, a certain erotic appeal for a male audience, rape is seen from a woman's point of view: that is, in its true colors, as an act of territorial aggression, sexual possession, and hostility, to which the only possible response is horror and fear.

At the other extreme is that *pièce de résistance* and titillation from Sam Peckinpah's *Straw Dogs*, in which the sluttish Susan George finally "gets hers" from the town hoods whom she has been provoking, and, in the course of the rape, begins to respond. We know the signs well enough: the little white hand, at first pressing furiously against the burly shoulder, suddenly relaxes, goes limp, then clutches passionately at that same shoul-der, converting an act of unilateral aggression into one of mutual lust, thereby confirming afresh the old adage: "She wanted it all along."

Expressing my indignation over the scene, I mentioned to Frost that one (male) critic had heralded this scene as "a woman's fantasy," whereas it obviously represented—as the critic's own response testified—a man's fantasy of a woman's fantasy.

"But what about women's rape fantasies?" inquired Frost. "Surely they have them. Where are the movies that portray them?"

"What rape fantasies?" I said. "I don't have them, and I don't know any women who do. At least not in the sense of a stranger holding a knife at your throat in a dark alley."

But there, I realized, was the rub. What other sense can rape fantasy have if rape itself—as we have at last come to understand it—is not a sexual act, but an act of pure, violent aggression, an act of battery carried out with sexual equipment. For a woman to fantasize rape in the correct sense of the term would be to fantasize not love or lust but mutilation, and no sane women—and very few insane ones—express such a desire, even unconsciously.

But when I began an informal poll of friends and acquaintances, the extent of the confusion, the tangle of meanings, came home to me.

"A rape fantasy," said Lois Gould, "has nothing to do with the *Daily News* rape, with the physical pain of ripping your vagina open. The fantasy takes you up to the point of physical interaction. It's very sensual, very exciting, but it's also tender and loving."

"A rape fantasy," said another friend, "has nothing to do with having a couple of teeth knocked out. It's when Robert Redford won't take no for an answer. It's a tribute to the woman's desirability, and the man acts for your pleasure."

But these fantasies, containing neither violence nor unpleasantness, are something quite different from rape itself. In fantasies of sexual domination, a partner, chosen by a woman, fulfills her needs without having to assume the responsibility or bear the guilt. They are the product of—and antidote to—a social situation in which a woman is not supposed to take the sexual initiative or direct love play for her own pleasure. The male lead is not some seedy delivery boy with a knife lurking in a doorway, but Clark Gable or Robert Redford in the setting of her choice; he acts not out of hostility but out of desire; and the fantasy ends in euphoria rather than in night court.

The fantasies generally stop short of penetration, but even when they don't, consummation is not really the point—the emphasis is on the prelude, and an aura of sensuality, a sort of generalized voluptuousness in which the woman's needs and desirability are the controlling motifs. In an essay in *Crazy Salad*, Nora Ephron describes with mock contrition the lingering pubescent fantasy of being "dominated by faceless males who rip my clothes off." But that's as far as the fantasy goes—at least as far as Ephron tells it—and the all-important element is that the men "go mad with desire."

Incorrectly grouped under the misnomer of "rape fantasy," these disparate fantasies have come to be linked to a brutal and impersonal, criminal and nonsensual act of violence committed by one human being against another, inviting the widespread belief that women are turned on by violence, and from there that they want and invite rape. When fantasies do involve violence, it is of a very special kind—an expression of fear rather than desire, for instance, or the reworking of sexual traumas. In either case, they have nothing to do with real rape. Nor are they—it is here that the term "wish fulfillment" has led us astray—blueprints for reality; rather, they have a full and complete life of their own, in a realm of existence quite separate from reality.

The world of difference between "rape fantasy" and rape can be expressed in one word: control. The point of a fantasy is that a woman—or any fantasizer—orders the reality within it, ordains its terms, and censors it according to her needs; the point of rape is that a woman is violated against her will. In one, there is sheer helplessness; in the other, helplessness is one of the conditions controlled by the fantasizer.

Isn't this the appeal of fantasy: an entire season of plays in which one is always the star, the playwright, the director? A realm of existence that is purer than reality, that is poetically ordered and resolved by the authority of one vision? The "zipless fuck" fantasized by the heroine of Erica Jong's *Fear of Flying* has been interpreted (and criticized) by many men as projecting onto the female the less admirable aspects of male sexuality. But the essence of the fantasy—which is, in a sense, a parody of male womanizing—is its appeal not to the libido but to the head: it is the woman who chooses the who, when, and where, rather than waiting to be chosen.

The problem with the transactions of sex in real life is that two individuals approach each other from different backgrounds and with different expectations. They jockey for position and the least insecure gains the upper hand. Here I would qualify the grim and monochromatic portrait of male villainy and female victimization Susan Brownmiller presents in *Against Our Will: Men, Women and Rape*, for there are gray areas of social intercourse. The power in a relationship is not invariably on the side of the male—the distinction between coercion and collusion is a fine one, and in our sexual tastes more than in any other aspect of our lives we are at the mercy of reflexes formed by early experiences and emotions prompted by a tangle of needs that are inaccessible to logic.

This is one reason why sex is so difficult to generalize about, or to politicize into male/female polarities. The minute you describe a sexual experience to another person, it is transformed by the listener or reader into something else, in accordance with his or her fantasy life. I have become aware, in the process of telling someone of my being "felt up" in a movie theater or rubbed against in a subway, of that person's excitement. The odor and ugliness, the hostility of the actual experience, disappear in the retelling; the episode is filtered through the imagination of my listener and turned into a sexual fantasy. To describe a sexual act is to launch a balloon whose destiny one can't control.

This principle accounts, I think, for the violently differing reactions of women to Lina Wertmuller's *Swept Away*. While many (myself included) see it as an offensive rehash of the old chestnut that the "rich bitch" wants to be brutalized into submission, other women perceive that the "vulnerable" lower-class male really doesn't *mean* the violence (it's proof of his desire and the retaliation he's been driven to out of sexual and class humiliation). He may be bruising her with his hands, but with his hurt, hangdog eyes he is telling us that he is about to fall in love.

Brute force, as the first principle and last refuge of male supremacy, occupies a crucial place in our sexual consciousness. In a technological world where the exercise of physical strength is of a largely nonessential nature, the reassuring stereotypes of male physical superiority are more in demand than ever. The myth of the rapist-as-sexual-superman is one of these. It flourishes largely through a powerful unconscious resistance to the more accurate picture of the rapist as a sniveling, impotent, petty criminal.

"The fantasy is sustained," one man admitted to me, "by newspaper accounts. In these, there are no pictures, only words, and it is not a realistic presentation, but actually a sort of exercise in pornography. There is little about the physical savagery and the ugliness of it, or the age of the victim (even if it is mentioned, we don't see her), so that the reader is permitted, even encouraged, to fantasize an act of mastery—an erect penis (contrary to the facts of most cases) and an orgasm. Also we get this image of women as victims because those are the only cases reported. But we never hear about the thousands of occasions when a man makes advances to a woman and she says no and walks away. Consequently the account that appears in public print is a very one-sided one, and very conducive to the stereotypes of masochistic women and masterful men."

It is against such powerful and highly differentiated fantasy machinery that reality itself must contend and accounts of rape and molestation seek to be understood for what they are. Yet within this generally cloudy area, misunderstandings over the term "rape fantasy" seem to divide the sexes rather more clearly than any other issue. I think it is safe to say that women have been using the term to mean one thing, and men have been using it to mean another, yet we have been conversing as if we meant the same thing. We have read the same books and we have seen the same movies, and we have received altogether different messages. Say, for example, we go to see *Gone with the Wind*. An impressionable male will see Clark Gable as the personification of the male image: cool, superior, using force at the right moment to win the woman, who secretly wants to be raped. The female spectator, on the other hand, will see the drama as belonging specifically to the characters Clark Gable/Rhett Butler and Vivien Leigh/Scarlett O'Hara, and she will see Rhett's taking of Scarlett not as rape, not as instruction in what a Man should do to win a Woman, but as an expression of mutual love between two equals in the only language strong enough to dissolve the barriers raised by pride. Where a man will see territorial conquest in Gable's action, a woman will see uncontrollable longing. That we have been so often at cross-purposes goes back, perhaps, to the cultural impasse that nearly divides the sexes and prefigures their antagonism: woman's personal quest for a great love, and man's impersonal quest for a good lay.

The male version of a woman's "rape fantasy," which has prevailed in popular culture, psychiatric literature, and courts of law, and therefore served in some way as a justification of rape, is based on the assumption that women are masochistic and want to be taken by force. Resistance— the woman's signal that she is virtuous and therefore worthy of conquest —is also interpreted as a facade, a lid on the carnal bombshell waiting to explode. What enables an otherwise sane man to sustain this "rape fantasy" and side with the rapist against the victim—who might have been his own wife or daughter—is the rationale that women are lying: they say no and mean yes. Women—Archetypal Women, not Sadie or Beth or Mom—are entrappers; beneath their virginal pose they crave the sex that society forbids them to seek actively. They are consequently forced into devious and neurotic behavior, inviting a man to overwhelm them, then turning on him. The duplicity inherent in this dual nature imputed to woman is perhaps nothing less than a projection onto the female of the male's own chronic split—between love and lust, between Mother and the Whore.

But what about those conscious female fantasies that do involve violence and the submission of woman to brute power: Sylvia Plath's "Women love the boot in the face," or the Black Gunman fantasy that is the controlling metaphor of Lois Gould's *A Sea-Change*? Both are largely symbolic, archetypal rather than individual: an acknowledgment and visceral rendering of the reality of male power in its most graphically phallic form—the boot and the gun. In the sexual imagery of a patriarchal society, male power is eroticized, as is female passivity. Internalizing notions of eroticism, we feel ourselves as desirable—desired by men—when we are passive and compliant. It is only recently that women have begun to define themselves apart from the putative norm of male sexuality and male desire.

One of the first casualties should be the theory of the "rape fantasy" and the misconceptions surrounding it bequeathed us by its chief architect, Helene Deutsch, a disciple of Freud. Her two-volume study, *The Psychology of Women* (1944), is the textual underpinning of much of the social mythology concerning female masochism. Deutsch gave "rape fantasy" a pivotal place in the female psyche, while allowing it to stand indiscriminately for daydreams and night dreams; wish fulfillments and fears; adolescent and adult fantasies; the fantasies of a borderline psychotic and those of a relatively normal, functioning woman.

Helene Deutsch thus paved the way for the diverse associations of a term that was problematic enough to begin with to become politicized as general sexual rule for women. No one assumed that because men had castration anxieties—i.e., fantasies—they wanted to be castrated. Also, fantasy has long been credited by psychiatrists with the function of enabling us to become acquainted with our fears. We fantasize rape, or the death of our parents, in order to face the intolerable. By envisioning such horrors we have seen the worst; by envisioning and eroticizing rape, we have gained a psychological ascendancy over it.

Deutsch's analysis of female behavior is based on her hypothesis that prehistoric woman was torn by male force away from her own natural rhythm and made to adapt to man's sexual nature. But instead of seeing in the peculiarities of women's fantasies a continued resistance to such a tyranny, she is determined to see women as actively embracing their sexual oppression. Having posited male sexuality as the absolute, she is blind to alternative interpretations. In her analysis of the King Kong myth, for example, she realizes that brutal possession by "the ape with his powerful arms, or the bear" is often an act of *rescue* rather than sexual assault. He "saves the girl from a threatening disaster that is mostly of a sexual nature—and the threat comes from someone else, not from the rescuer." But then, adopting the interpretation that will confirm her theories, she sees the metamorphosis as satisfying the "masochistic longings" of the girl's dreams, "which reproduce the situation of the primitive conquered woman." In other words, she sees as end point and *goal* what might more sensibly be interpreted as beginning and *given*!—the brute conquest from which the girl wants to escape rather than the fate she actively seeks.

I remember some years ago reacting with similar dismay to a Jungian analysis of a young woman's dream (included in the anthology *Man and His Symbols*). The woman, who was now married and planning to have children eventually ("because it was expected of her," according to the psychiatrist), had been an intellectually gifted college student. She got along well with husband and friends, except for occasional angry outbursts which alienated men. This overreaction bothered her.

In the dream, for which she has sought psychiatric help because it seemed so important, she is standing in a line of women, each of whom is being decapitated. She patiently awaits her turn.

The analyst explained that this meant she must give up the habit of "living in her head," so that she could assume her natural biological role in motherhood. But obviously—to me, not to him—it was precisely this "natural biological role" that filled her with terror, since it signified the final annihilation of that intellectual identity symbolized by the head. No wonder she was angry in the presence of men who were free to pursue their intellectual interests which she, as a prospective mother, was expected to forsake!

Similarly, Deutsch doesn't go far enough in understanding the subversive significance of the King Kong figure, who is not only the endangered female's savior but also a being with whom she enjoys an odd sort of equality. A mutual bargain is struck—his strength for her beauty, his ugliness for her helplessness. He has no masculine "image" to uphold, since he is unarguably stronger than the most threatening male. Because he is not *macho*, but sexually secure, he can afford to be gentle and loving, protective and monogamous.

Perhaps the "rape fantasy" myth had its purest expression in the Southern variant with which I grew up: "All White Women fantasize being raped by Negroes." The notion was expressed as a warning: what I or some other uppity girl (one who wouldn't "put out") really needed was to get raped in a dark alley. The dark alley was a figurative rendering of the black man, and the threat has its modern analogue in the thigh-slapper that "what those feminists really need is a good fuck."

But the dictum, uttered half-facetiously, was only partially a revenge fantasy on the part of the luckless male. It also carried a connotation of promise to the female, of wish-fulfilling bliss. This, went the unspoken message, was what the prima donna, the virgin princess, had wanted and needed to become a "real" woman.

It was possibly a sense of class guilt—rather than sexual masochism—that made me and other Southern women accept even superficially the idea that we wanted to be raped by our social inferiors. In the "rape fantasy," the slave becomes the master and social injustice is avenged. But the truth is that the myth corresponded to no emotion I'd ever felt or image I had ever invoked. Eventually I came to trust my own intuition. I knew as well as I knew anything on earth that I didn't want to be raped by any man, black or white.

Most recent psychological studies support my intuition. Among psychiatrists who dispute the theory of rape fantasy, Dr. Robert Seidenberg, author of *Marriage Between Equals* and *Corporate Wives–Corporate Casualties*, believes that "the rape fantasy has been completely misinterpreted as a desire rather than a woman's way of expressing what has been going on with her all of her life. My colleagues," Seidenberg told me, "interpret, as part of a woman's basic masochism, that she needs punishment or pain."

"What about the idea," I asked him, "that she's conditioned to need them?"

"That's not even true," he said. "It's superimposed on the woman. The concept of masochism, that it is woman's normal state, comes from Freud. 'They must be masochistic,' goes the thinking, 'because they don't complain. Women must therefore need pain and we therefore shouldn't feel guilty about supplying it.' It's a little like the idea that 'darkies really enjoy work and being told what to do—they're like children—therefore we should treat them that way.'"

The rape fantasy as psychoanalytic theory and popular myth served the same purpose as the theory of penis envy—or rather, had the same effect, since both are less a matter of conspiracy than a natural masculine bias, reinforcing a system of values in which the phallic principle of male sexuality was the norm and the ideal, and women's needs and fantasies were the weak counterpart. Just as female sexuality was an emasculated version of the real thing, fantasy itself was a pallid imitation of, a sick substitute for, real life.

Not only was fantasy seen by Freud as an obstruction to life rather than the salvation of an obstructed person, but its identification with neurosis had the effect of discrediting it as an outlet for the creative and healthy adult. Fantasy was considered an improper and shameful—or at best adolescent—indulgence.

But like fairy tales and the conventions of romance that have been given new life in recent books by Bruno Bettelheim and Northrop Frye, fantasies are making a comeback. Bettelheim and Frye have shown how rich and primal are the archetypal story patterns of genres discredited by recent intellectual fashions, by literary realism, or, in the case of fairy tales, by parental ideas about nonviolence. The need for violence in our fairy tales and for happy endings in our fables goes deeper than social conditioning or surface sentimentality; narrative conventions correspond to deep needs and anxieties within us, just as fantasies offer not just an escape from but a reentry into life, a reconciliation on more than one level of the conflicting drives within us.

Women, denied access to so many avenues of real-life activity, have lived as much if not more in their imaginations than men, and consequently have developed a rich and varied fantasy life. Novels by women writers testify to this and to a corresponding evolution in the social status of women. For instance, that same equalization of the sexes that was accomplished in the King Kong fantasy was brought about in Charlotte Brontë's *Jane Eyre* when the powerful Rochester is reduced to a cripple, dependent on the heroine. This process of equalization appears to be a major objective in the fantasies of women who have felt themselves most circumscribed— as they were in pre-twentieth-century society or, within the individual life, in prepuberty.

The principle of compensation acts in a diametrically different way in the fantasies of women who feel relatively in control of their lives, who feel sexually and/or professionally fulfilled. These women often fantasize bondage or domination by groups of men and enjoy the passivity they have relinquished in their working lives.

A feminist admitted to me that she had what some might call a "rape fantasy" and that she was in fact not happy about it. "I disapprove of this heartily, but I allow myself to enjoy it. I have other women friends who say, 'When I have a fantasy like this, I stop myself.'"

I asked her what it involved.

"It's really what I would call a domination fantasy. A car comes down the street, one man leans out and asks me what time it is, other men get me into the car. There is no fear or terror, by the way. Then they force me to have sex with them. It's not a very nice fantasy for a feminist, but I know a lot of women who have that kind of fantasy."

I tell her that I think that, on the contrary, the fantasy is directly related to her feminism, and ask her when she first began having it.

"About 1967. The year I become involved in feminism. But," she quickly added, "there's no connection."

I tell her I think there is, since the Women's Movement brought women to the point where they could acknowledge their sexual natures and fantasize yearnings that had long been suppressed. Moreover, fantasies of domination provided a release from the new burdens of independence without one's having to actually compromise that independence. Strong women, if the rape/domination fictions of Ayn Rand's *The Fountainhead* and Marilyn Durham's *The Man Who Loved Cat Dancing* are any indication, often need to envision an even stronger man. A recent article in *Psychology Today* concludes that passivity in a fantasy is in no way a reflection of a woman's actual behavior, or her role in marriage. The most assertive, creative, independent wives were the most likely to fantasize.

Those militants who declare that "real feminists do not have 'rape fantasies'" are simply falling into the same old trap of (1) identifying fantasy as a neurosis (here ideological rather than psychological) to be combatted, and (2) misinterpreting fantasy as something a woman wants to happen in real life.

As part of the same myopic approach, analysts—both lay and professional—have seized upon the broad outlines of fantasies, the ways they conformed to dominant archetypes and prefabricated meanings, without appreciating the variations provided by emotional undertones (for example, the lack of pain or fear), and the specific variations on a theme worked by, or for, the female imagination.

One woman offered this analysis of Pauline Réage's *The Story of O*: "The heroine is not into pain for pleasure, but she is submitting to what the dominant person wants out of devotion to that person. It's the definition of masochism that fits into all male-female relationships."

Whereas I would agree with the first part of her statement, I would challenge the latter. I think it is precisely those women who are not confined to subordinate or masochistic roles who enjoy fantasizing the opposite—the road not taken or transcended. In another sense, we are always returning to, reclaiming, redeeming our history. Those of us in our thirties or older are compelled to return, in fantasy form, to the male-worshipping world of our former selves, a patriarchy that is social as well as oedipal. We cannot so easily discard the past; we cannot turn a man's world into a man-woman world, and make up new rules for love and marriage, without an emotional upheaval. Fantasy provides the perfect vehicle for this return, a never-never land of the imagination where we can rearrange and transmute our earlier lives and sexual selves. Because of their subtle and contradictory nature—what seems masochistic being often its antithesis—fantasies cannot be judged by the criteria by which we judge our actions. Their essence is paradox, and their charm is that they do not have a moral or politically correct dimension.

We should never censor these fantasies in the name of civic virtue. They are our own private property, and men are not expected to act upon them as if they were in the public domain. That is *their* fantasy, not ours.

Unmourned Losses, Unsettled Claims

TRUMAN CAPOTE

"Holly Golightly, *c'est moi*," Truman Capote might well have said, echoing the words of Flaubert. A number of dashing women about town claimed to be the model for the heroine of *Breakfast at Tiffany's*, but to a marked degree she took her shape and essence and angst and humming-bird existence from the author himself. Flaubert, Capote's literary idol, only entered the mind of Emma Bovary, whereas Capote *was* his provincial waif. In this 1950 novel, the future avatar of "new journalism" was already recording the arc of his life. He had come to the big city from Monroeville, Alabama; he charmed and wrote his way into the literary limelight and seduced the rich and famous. He would waver at the top where drugs, alcohol, and the "mean reds"—the free-floating anxiety that ambushed the deeply insecure—would get the best of him, and he would spiral down in a sordid exit that lacked the grace and brevity of Holly's.

Moreover, when it came time to do the movie of *Breakfast at Tiffany's* he saw Holly not as Audrey Hepburn but as Marilyn Monroe. In a tantalizing aside in Gerald Clarke's enthralling, novel-like biography, we learn that Capote actually argued Monroe's case (in vain, fortunately) with the producers. In her blithe elegance, Audrey Hepburn was a perfect emblem for the "swans"—"Babe" Paley, Gloria Guinness, "Slim" Keith—to whom Capote would be attracted as courtier and confidant, but the more vulnerable Monroe was his mirror image, another yellow-haired love-starved country bumpkin with a little girl's voice who never quite filled the void in her heart and who finally overdosed on love's substitutes, drugs and celebrity.

*This article first appeared in *The New York Times Book Review*, June 12, 1988. Copyright © by Molly Haskell.

138

We tend to look at such careers as tragic foreshortenings—Monroe's sudden suicide, Capote's slow motion crash-landing (except for occasional stories and some brilliant fragments in *Answered Prayers*, he wrote himself out with *In Cold Blood*, almost twenty years before his death in 1984). But looked at from another angle, Capote's was a triumph over the sort of background that turns disturbed people into ax murderers—the cold-blooded killers that Capote encountered when he went to Holcomb, Kansas, to write of the murder of the Clutter family and met Perry Smith and Dick Hickok; the killer that Capote himself became—far more efficiently than Perry and Dick—when, in poisonous prose and on talk shows, he laid to waste his friends and skewered his competitors with malice as pure as the air in an oxygen tent.

How Capote went from an enchanter, the startlingly fresh voice of his debut novel *Other Voices, Other Rooms*, to someone you wanted to hold away from you with a pair of tongs is an amazing story, as disturbing as anything Capote ever wrote. In this work of prodigious research gracefully presented, Clarke, who had his subject's confidence during the last years, gives Capote what the writer himself, in a last grand, gutsy gesture, declared he wanted: a book in which nothing, nothing at all was left out. Clarke, a former senior writer at *Time* magazine, makes us take a longer look at Capote than I, for one, ever thought I wanted to take, and the result is mesmerizing, a fine-tuned balance—unusual for an author so immersed in his subject—of empathy and dispassion. The book reads as if it were written alongside the life, rather than after it, like a car following a train, the driver picking up passengers as they alight, always catching the right people at the right time. He pulls together the pieces of the puzzle and makes us see a terrible inevitability in the journey from the fetching little fellow with an uncanny talent ("a specific gift for writing," said one early observer, "like a musician's for music") to the blocked and bloated self-parody whose most severe lacerations were self-inflicted.

Capote was born Truman Streckfus Persons in a New Orleans hotel in 1924, of parents who were alike only in their frightening inadequacy as parents. Lillie Mae Faulk realized she had made a mistake hours after marrying Arch Persons, and they more or less went their separate ways thereafter, leaving Truman to be raised by an eccentric family of maiden aunts and a bachelor uncle. Lillie Mae was that most treacherous of mothers, a discontented small-town beauty who would appear in his life for a day or two, wafting the perfume of motherhood over him, then disappear.

Arch was a likable, no-account con man, but it was Arch who, in prevent-
ing Lillie Mae from having the abortion she had desperately wanted, saved
Truman's life. And it was Arch whom Truman had to thank for his literary
talent: the Personses were great letter writers, and samples of Arch's
wheedling money-grubbing epistles are comic masterpieces, marvels of
double-talk and self-deception.

With his father's instinct for charming people and articulating their
wants before they quite knew them, Truman was a born seducer and spell-
binder, a "pocket Merlin," Harper Lee called him in the fictional portrait of
her childhood companion that appears in *To Kill a Mockingbird*—a "curiosity
. . . [whose] hair was snow white and stuck to his head like duck fluff. . . .
[and] whose head teemed with eccentric plans, strange longings and quaint
fancies." Odd little elf that he soon recognized himself to be, he saw the
advantage of using his oddness to get the attention he craved. He felt his
effeminacy early on and came to terms with it. Until he was nine, Clarke
tells us, "he found being a boy so demanding and burdensome that he
actually wanted to be a girl." The mannerisms of his homosexuality—the
whiny lisp, the feyness, the mischievous needling, all exaggerated for
effect—were also the budding performer's way of flaunting his difference
and upstaging the competition.

Meanwhile, Lillie Mae had moved to New York, successfully remarried
(Joe Capote, a Cuban businessman), and gained custody of Truman, and
she was wild with alarm over her son's sissy mannerisms. Ever sensitive to
public opinion—she changed her name from the yokelish Lillie Mae to
Nina in preparation for her ascendancy to the suburban *haute bourgeoisie*—
she began hauling him to shrinks, sending him to military schools, and
moaning to friends and neighbors that she would have preferred a dumb,
football-playing, insurance-salesman son to the one she had. And from that
time on, through the decline of Joe Capote's fortunes and her growing
misery and drunkenness, she was unrelenting in her refusal to forgive his
homosexuality or accept compensation in the form of his growing literary
achievement. She had her bouts of affection, too, as such mothers do, and
mother and son—the son waiting (as children do) for the sudden sunbursts
—were locked into a lifelong love-hate relationship, sharing apartments
and bottles, evenings and battles until she died, a suicide, in 1954. Like
Narcissus, Capote was enraptured by his own reflection. He was a genius at
self promotion, and those indelible photographs became inseparable from
the prose itself: the flirtatious changeling in the humid, sultry picture on

the jacket of *Other Voices* wafts up from every page of the book, and Harold Halma's portrait of the supine seducer clung to him for years.

Yet paradoxically, Capote's freakishness was a kind of camouflage that allowed him to disappear, become a fly on the wall. His size and mascot-like appearance put people off guard. The number of animal references that crop up in Clarke's book is almost comical: "lion cub," "pony," "chipmunk," "koala bear," "alley cat," "bunny," "bantam rooster," "ant of genius," "frog," and Jacqueline Susann's famous retaliatory "capon" (after he said she looked "like a truck driver in drag") are a few of the zoological images, some more benign than others, that spring to the minds of witnesses.

Coupled with his disarming appearance was his shrewd conversational tactic of offering people juicy tidbits of his own past, whereupon they, according to the tacit trade-off on which gossip and fellowship are based, would disgorge volumes of their own. In a long, drunken dinner in a Hong Kong hotel room, the fiercely reticent Marlon Brando found himself pouring out the story of his own mother's alcoholism that would turn up in Capote's famous *New Yorker* profile, "A Duke in His Domain."

The cast of characters with whom he fell in and out of love, collaborated, yachted, and partied is enormous, swelling through four decades, shrinking in one, an eclectic collection of highbrow and lowlife, a geographical stretch from Peggy Guggenheim's palazzo to the flesh-pots of 42nd Street.

They were also a voluble and bitchy lot, and much of the brightness of the book comes from the aptness of the observations Clarke has tracked down or got first hand. A very funny description of Capote's brief tenure as a copy boy at the *New Yorker*, where his behavior and appearance caused havoc among the normally phlegmatic staff ("Two of the elevator men were so confused that they bet a dollar on his gender," reports Clarke, and "one of the women was so vividly impressed by him that she dreamed that his veins were filled with milk—whole or skimmed, she did not say") is interspersed with the curmudgeonly voices of E. B. White and Harold Ross ("For God's sake!" Ross cried when he saw the tiny employee, "what's that?"). Neither the uproar he caused nor the alliances he formed—most notably with Daise Terry, the notoriously difficult office manager—nor the stories he submitted induced anyone to lift the *New Yorker*'s traditional barrier against copy boys becoming writers, which was, Clarke ventures, a stroke of good fortune. Trying to write the genteel, made-to-order story then in vogue would have stifled the quirkily original gifts Capote was able to develop in the more adventurous pages of *Harper's Bazaar* and *Mademoiselle* under the literary tutelage of editors like George Davis and Mary Louise Aswell.

His love affairs, mostly with older men of a conservative stamp, are amply documented. Among the most fascinating was his long, weekends-only relationship with Newton Arvin, the conservative Smith professor and Melville scholar, whom he met at Yaddo and with whom he served a sort of literary apprenticeship. Capote had never gone to college, and he had the autodidact's fanatical favorites and unaccountable gaps. He went to the movie of *Great Expectations* and became more and more agitated: "They've stolen my plot!" he screamed furiously.

Capote's stories arise out of nowhere, self-made, innocent, and all-knowing; the prose is exquisite, limpid with bright sharp images in a shallow field. Yet it's the shallowness that gives his characters their eerie and essentially two-dimensional sense of isolation. The tableau-like vignettes he creates in *In Cold Blood* are as stark as an Edward Hopper painting: those representatives of the two Americas—the well-rounded, God-fearing Clutters on the one hand and the scum-of-the-earth Hickok and Smith on the other—are equally solitary figures in an American landscape that is chilling even in 100-degree heat.

The absence of other writing voices in his literary bloodstream, enriching and harmonizing with his own, may have had a diminishing effect, but it also enabled him to preserve what was unique in his own sensibility: that thin air of receptivity, a listening void, a recording apparatus for human voices he encountered and registered so acutely. He was a strange sort of ventriloquist, taking into his confidence Kansas housewives and FBI agents and filling station owners and murderers and monomaniacal sheriffs, getting inside them and speaking with their voices. His best sustained acts of metempsychosis were with society's subsidiary characters, small, unofficial character players that nobody else listened to: older women, gigolos, fashion plates, waifs, arrivistes, outsiders, all those whose satellite status gave them special poignancy.

He was especially good with women. Jennifer Jones was never more relaxed than as the playful aggressor to Humphrey Bogart's cynic in *Beat the Devil*, the John Huston melodrama in which Capote's mischievous screenplay offered a sly counterpoint to Huston's sourly masculine worldview.

But most of all, he was a child who enticed us into becoming children again and who, with his bathroom and boudoir privileges, turned us all into diminutive voyeurs.

Even Capote's grandiosity—his invocations of Proust, the formal innovations claimed for In Cold Blood, and his fury at being passed over by the literary establishment for the awards and credit he thought were his due—had something of the child's pique. Although In Cold Blood deserved to be considered a pioneering work in the sort of idiosyncratic, personal, fiction-like journalism that would enliven the sixties and seventies, Capote's insistance in giving it the pretentiously exalted—and meaningless—title of "non-fiction novel" did him more harm than good. This literary coup was followed by that no-less-grandiose social "coup," the mammoth black-and-white ball at the Plaza Hotel for Katharine Graham and five hundred close friends—a child's fantasy that was intended to overwhelm as much as entertain and that was as important for who was left out as for who was included.

It was in 1966, the year of these two triumphs—when black and white, positive and negative, were precariously balanced—that things began to unravel. With the spectacular success of In Cold Blood, Capote's favorite quotation, St. Teresa of Avila's "More tears are shed over answered prayers than unanswered ones," was on its way to becoming his epitaph. He had spent over five years on the book, living it, conducting hundreds of interviews, writing it, involved in a story that was moving slowly, inexorably toward the hanging of two people with whom he had become intimate. Gradually, and just as inexorably, something happened to him: the voices of the past, the grudges, the unaccepted and unmourned losses and unsettled claims rose up to haunt him. And in Perry, Clarke suggests, he seemed to come face to face with the demons of failure, the dark side of his own unloved self he had been fleeing all his life.

Perry, the half-Cherokee psychopath with the dreamy eyes and the literary ambitions, the stocky little guy whose feet didn't touch the floor when he sat in a chair, the lost soul who'd been betrayed by an alcoholic mother and spurned by a loved and hated father; the pretentiously self-educated "writer" who'd never gone beyond the third grade but nurtured a murderous grudge against anybody who had—it all came too close for comfort. Capote's dark doppelganger faced him from behind bars, waiting to be executed, howling with self-pity, and infuriating Capote with that trait from which he himself was remarkably free but which he had recognized and hated in his own father. How could he not have felt shadowed by

Perry's feelings, Perry's fate? A writer who had a notoriously difficult time with endings, those soundings of the depths that are advance notices of mortality, he simply sidestepped this one altogether: he reported Dick Hickok's last words and actions, but he left a hole where Perry should have been.

As his sense of himself began slipping, so did his female alter egos, his Galateas. In the fifties, the stylishly rich women who obsessed him did so as much for their stories as for their beauty. Gloria Guinness, Slim Hayward (later Lady Keith), Pamela Churchill, Marella Agnelli—many of them, says Clarke, "had struggled, schemed and fought to be where they were. They had created themselves as he himself had done. Each was an artist, he said, 'whose sole creation was her perishable self.'" What Clarke calls Capote's "Pygmalion complex" was limited to a kind of creative empathy with women who were already highly evolved: he drew them out, filled in the gaps (for example, instructing Babe Paley in literature while she polished and tutored his taste in decor, the fine arts, and other refinements of the good life). However, his later more ambitious projects—to make Lee Radziwell an actress, Joanne Carson a toast of Los Angeles society—were dismal failures. The drugs and alcohol he'd successfully avoided for so much of his life he now turned to with a vengeance, and the writing became more difficult as he grew disenchanted and even repelled by the jet-set nobs he'd panted after.

The task he had assigned himself—a Proustian masterwork chronicling the excesses, the charms, the conversations of the "beau monde" he knew so well—was turning into a work of unrelieved if brilliant venom and was finally sabotaged with the publication of the "Cote Basque" episode in *Esquire*. His friends dropped him; he was stunned, or pretended to be.

Capote hadn't played by the rules, hadn't understood that his status among the rich was that of a petted and tolerated outsider. He was meant to celebrate, not expose them. Isolated, he lashed back, and his social and sexual habits grew ever more labyrinthine and degenerate. In an attempt to complete the broken triangle of his childhood, he had made a specialty of attaching himself to couples. But, as with the Paleys, with whom he formed the major, glorious triangle of his life, he was then compelled to drive a wedge between the partners and try to destroy them by seducing one (if only emotionally), then the other.

His love affairs took a pathological turn as well. Between reunions with Jack Dunphy, the writer with whom he had lived for many years, he took up with heterosexual nonentities—bartenders, air conditioner salesmen—whose only appeal was their utter averageness. They were, as Clarke points out, pale reincarnations of the all-American type preferred by his mother and of the military school boys who had once mocked him. He prided himself on having seduced these rather weak specimens of heterosexuality away from women, although one notable art critic suggested he had simply grown too fat and ugly and undesirable to attract a homosexual. But as social embarrassments, these preposterous lovers may have had another, more deviously self-destructive, purpose: that of dissolving Capote's few remaining friendships.

Capote's take on the world, the sexual picaresque of *Answered Prayers* with its writer/gigolo hero, is a throwback to Tobias Smollett, that cheerfully conscienceless and sexually frank Scotsman who chronicled the vice and disorder of eighteenth-century England, and of whom George Orwell said, "Many of his best passages would be ruined by any intrusion of the moral sense." What made Smollett worth reading, wrote Orwell, is that he is funny, and that he "often attains a truthfulness that more serious novelists have missed [because] he is willing to mention things which do happen in real life but are almost invariably kept out of fiction." There is nothing funnier or more outlandish than the description, in *Answered Prayers*, of Miss Victoria Self, proprietor of the Self Service—a "Teutonized Marianne Moore" who plies her sex trade as if it were an employment office for Vassar graduates; or the story of a Tennessee Williams-like client at the Plaza Hotel with a monstrously messy English bulldog; or the party at which Dorothy Parker, Tallulah Bankhead, and Montgomery Clift outdo each other in wild, drunken incoherence.

To writers, to all of us, Capote became a morbidly fascinating spectacle. In his ad hominem writing and his mincing, swaggering knock-out punches on talk shows, he revealed more about the literary and jet-set worlds, and their insidious interminglings, than we wanted to know. Sometimes his nastiness was refreshing, an antidote to the preening and liberal-minded attitudinizing of most media darlings.

But in exposing the secrets of real people in private situations, in his willingness to betray all confidences, all conversations, Capote transgressed limits which even the most cavalierly confessional writers have accepted, if only in the interest of self-preservation. Cruelty has a way of boomeranging. If the people Capote had once loved were now loathsome and worthless, how did he escape the taint of that worthlessness? And if they're larger than he was? He wrote exquisitely mean things about Sartre, de Beauvoir, Camus, but they're still standing tall (or at least two of them are) and he isn't.

P. D. Jones, his alter ego in *Answered Prayers*, argues the superiority of truth over fiction, claiming *Remembrance of Things Past* would have been "better" (though less convincing) if it had been more factual, less disguised. This strikes me as a desperate alibi for Capote himself, whose last stories were more shapelessly journalistic than his earlier ones, lacking the transfiguring quality of art and the richer promptings of the unconscious.

If Proust's characters diminished before his disenchanted eyes, there was still something behind and beyond them that wasn't small: God, and if not God, then love, and if not love, then culture itself. Capote wasn't in search of time past but of an escape into an eternal present. There was no madeleine for Capote, no magic lantern. Only emptiness.

Finally the toxicity of the venom, fueled by self-hatred, became all-corroding. And the beauty, what beauty there was, was hollow and unreal. Though I find myself generally concurring with Clarke's appraisals of Capote's work, when he speculates that Kate McCloud, the central figure of *Answered Prayers*, might have become "the most remarkable of his heroines," I can't agree. The red-haired, green-eyed heiress is as idealized as a fairy princess. She's not Capote at all, not "tres fou" as Holly might have said. Although P. D. Jones is rapt in his admiration, we never quite fall for this paragon or believe in her fervently maternal mission: she is out to recapture her child from her tycoon husband who has threatened to kill her if she tries.

Perhaps Capote could never believe in such a woman, a mother who would risk her money and her life to keep her son. In any case, he was now too far gone in darkness to find redemption in Kate McCloud. What the mirror on the wall reflected back was the mother who hadn't wanted her child in the first place and the child whose nature, so much like her own, she had never accepted.

What Makes John Wayne Larger than Life?

W e're on the set of *The Shootist* in its next-to-last day of shooting at Burbank Studios. The scene is the interior of a barber shop in the Western town of Culver City, Nevada, 1900. John Wayne, lying ornery and full of life in the barber's chair, plays John Bernard Books, a legendary gunfighter dying of cancer. There are certain reverberations, since the sixty-nine-year-old Wayne himself had cancer in 1964, and has been living on one lung and borrowed time ever since. He had pneumonia before filming began, and my own interview, along with the shooting had already been delayed once for two weeks while Wayne and director Don Siegel were out with the flu.

While the barber cranks Wayne to an upright position, John Carradine saunters in. As Beckum, the town undertaker, Carradine has a proposition: the finest funeral Culver City can offer, featuring a casket befitting the dying gunfighter's status, a Carrara marble headstone, a funeral with a minimum of two mourners and guaranteed plot maintenance . . . all for nothing! Wayne knows what Carradine is up to. The undertaker will place him on display and charge admission to spectators; then, when interest peters out, he'll wrap him in a gunny sack and dump him into a hole. Somehow Wayne manages to turn the tables on Carradine so that the offer is not only rejected, but the undertaker comes out promising Wayne a decent, dignified burial—and $50 to boot.

Carradine is about to depart when Wayne reminds him of the $50.

*This article combines excerpts from three articles that first appeared in *Ladies' Home Journal*, July 1976; *The Village Voice*, August 16, 1976; and *Rocky Mountain Magazine*, May/June 1980. Copyright © 1976, 1980 by Molly Haskell.

"Books, you're a hard man to deal with," says Carradine.

Pause. Then, in that rich, familiar baritone: "I'm alive."

The way Wayne says it, the low, husky drawl rising ruefully at the end, says it all. It's a comic moment. Wayne, talking to me a few moments later, will insist on its humor. But if it's so funny, why do I have tears in my eyes?

The two words, the way they are said, are more than a simple assertion of fact. They express the knowledge of a lifetime, filtered through the awareness of a man who sees precisely what the whole sorry world is all about but won't surrender an inch of its space or a moment of its precious time without a struggle. They say, "I'm here because I want to be here, make no mistake. I've survived in a rough business not by luck, don't kid youself, fella, but by outguessing the other guy as well as outdrawing him. Yeah, I'm a little bitter, but less than I've a right to be, since people I expected a hell of a lot more from than you have let me down. Don't misunderstand me, I'm not asking for any favors. But if you don't mind, I'll just hang around a little longer, keep the buzzards at bay till I'm ready. And when I'm ready, it won't be a two-bit chiseler like you that gets the last word."

I'm alive. Not dead. It is one of those Bazinian moments when life and art intersect, when the literal miracle of the real John Wayne's survival merges with that of the character he plays. The audience will be led to the association by an opening montage of scenes from early John Wayne movies, bringing him chronologically and filmographically up to date, which begin the film and set its obituary theme. Although rumors that it would be his last film have been scotched by the Duke himself, *The Shootist* virtually asks to be taken as John Wayne's epitaph.

The screenplay, adapted from Glendon Swarthout's novel by his son Miles Hood Swarthout and Scott Hale, marches with biblical solemnity through the final days of John Bernard Books, from the time he arrives in Culver City, Nevada, on the day of Queen Victoria's death in January 1901, until he dies eight days later in a saloon gunfight that he himself has arranged. It's his parting gift to a town that has offered him relatively little in the way of hospitality, being too busy with its strivings toward a middle-class respectability that his presence threatens. Among his allies are Jimmy Stewart as the town doctor who confirms the grim diagnosis and Lauren Bacall, who lets him a room in her boarding house. There he wishes only to pass his final days in dignity but is called upon to repulse various and sundry opportunists, like Carradine and an eager reporter, who want to cash in on his newsworthy demise.

What a lot of legend there is to mine. I think back to Ringo Kid of

Stagecoach, in 1939, the John Ford film that made Wayne a star . . . and took the Western from pulp status into one of the great American movie genres. Both had been consigned to B-movie territory, until Pappy Ford gave them a new moral and stylistic seriousness that would attract some of the greatest actors and directors of American cinema.

Meanwhile Wayne evolved into the sometimes benign, sometimes difficult Indian fighter of *Fort Apache*, the passionate Irish-American suitor of *The Quiet Man*, the peacemaker of *She Wore a Yellow Ribbon*, the wounded family man of *Rio Grande*, and the grounded flier of *The Wings of Eagles* through the obsessed heroes of *Red River* and *The Searchers* to the laconic ex-gunfighter of *The Man Who Shot Liberty Valence* and the paternal cowboy of *Rio Bravo* and the increasingly retired old-timers of his late period. There were genial, less memorable roles in the non-Ford and non-Hawks movies, commanding officers of submarines, settling down heroes, men who'd lived long enough to learn there was more to life than battles. Longevity and durability allowed him to play both Achilles-like warrior and Odyssean survivor. That is, he evolved from the fighter-in-his-prime archetype, Achilles- or Ajax-like, who are the last of a dying breed (they must bow to the ascendant values of civilization: the democratic polis of Athens or the new Western city) to savvy, homeward-bound Odysseus. Watching him, seeing the long line of wily gunfighters, straightshooters, and patriarchs that have brought him to where he is now, I am filled with an emotion that surprises me by its force.

I am here because I consider Wayne one of the great movie actors of all time—a view not universally held among my fellow film critics and the folks back east. At least, that's why I think I am here. But I never expected the sight of him to wipe me out.

I first met him the previous day. He came off the set wearing the Western outfit that is as timelessly a part of him as his eyes or voice. Most movie actors are disappointments in the flesh, diminished shadows of their voluptuous screen images, but John Wayne is larger than life in real life, too. It is not just a matter of size but of magnetism, of an authority that he wears as easily as his Western outfit.

I ask him how he feels.

"Good," he says. "Actually I feel good today for the first time in a year."

We chat. "Molly," he muses as he walks back to his trailer. "That was my mother's name. Finest girl I ever knew."

His huge bulk disappears into the makeshift dressing room, where a running chess game is in progress with a photographer on the film. The publicist tells me I will just have to grab Wayne whenever I can. I'm not very good at that, particularly when I discover I am awestruck and tongue-tied at the mere sight of him. In his presence, I feel like I am twelve years old. Once or twice, he simply walks up to me and hugs me, then walks off without saying anything. We have what amounts to a subverbal rapport, but how will I convert it into words? Wayne is wary of interviews, and he doesn't trust critics, particularly those who represent what he sneeringly refers to as the "Eastern Liberal Establishment." When we first met, he was guarded and as prickly as a cactus. He assumed I was one of "them." And why shouldn't he, after the sneering abuse he's taken from them?

I've seen otherwise dispassionate and civilized intellectuals go red in the face at the mere mention of Wayne's name. True, his politics are unpalatable and little given to nuance. As a flag waver and Republican fund raiser, he is to the right of Ronald Reagan, but other Hollywood right-wingers had spouted jingoistic rhetoric—the aforementioned president and Bob Hope, for example—without getting under their enemies' skin quite the way Wayne did. There's also a feeling among his detractors that the high ground of the superpatriot to which he lays claim is a bit slippery. The brief against him is that the movie hero who in the minds of many of his countrymen slew the Japanese army singlehandedly never served in World War II. (He was in his thirties during the war, and the rumor is that when they wouldn't take him as an officer, he refused to enlist as a private.)

He earned the undying hatred of many of the blacklisted, including Lionel Stander, for his excessive zeal on the "Americanism" committees in Hollywood during the forties and fifties. (He went much further, for example, than his right-wing friend and director, John Ford.)

But however wrongheaded Wayne's ideas, he seems never to have acted for ulterior or opportunistic reasons. . . . or even if he did, isn't it too late now to get at anything so elusive as an unvarnished truth? Myth has overtaken reality; it just depends, as a character in Liberty Valence might have said, on which myth you print.

LITTLE BY LITTLE WE become friends, or as close an approximation as is possible between takes, visitors, lung treatments, chess games, and the constant pressure to finish a film that has gone on too long and almost done everybody in. It's Siegel, now, who looks pale and beaten-down, whether because he has never recovered from his own bout with the flu or because he has never emerged with a clear victory in his running battle with Wayne over who's directing the picture. Wayne, though he's coughing constantly and spitting phlegm, looks terrific, and he doesn't hesitate to tell me what he thinks of Siegel's direction (too rigid, he blocks out scenes instead of letting them flow). It's no secret on the set that the two locked horns in a fierce power struggle during the early days of filming. (Was it because, after working with the greats, Wayne had become accustomed to "house directors" like Andrew McLaglen whom he could push around? Did Siegel hold it over Wayne that he had wanted and failed to get him for the lead in *Dirty Harry*—to Clint Eastwood's everlasting satisfaction and Wayne's supposed regret?) Because everyone's anxious to get the picture behind them, they seem to have patched over their differences now, but it's clear Wayne has gotten used to being boss.

He doesn't wait to be called for a scene but seems to sense when his presence is required. He ambles over to where they're setting up the scene, considers what is going on, offers suggestions, and occasionally produces irritation in the crew because, as one member put it, "he's almost too damn knowledgeable." He knows as much or more about their craft than every crew member. He began his movie career as a prop man (in 1926) and he has always been acutely aware of the contribution props can make toward the atmosphere of a scene.

After failing to become an overnight sensation in his first starring role (in Raoul Walsh's *The Big Trail* in 1930), he worked for a lean, unglamorous, but ultimately rewarding decade in action serials. There he learned an indispensable lesson: how to give dramatic interest to the kind of expository dialogue that characterizes B films. He also got in the habit of doing all of his own stunts, and it was he who developed the technique for throwing a punch so that nobody got hit.

The face—tired, grinning or snarling, tan under the tan makeup (he has always used, and believes in using, makeup)—and the rich, reassuring voice evoke four decades of movie roles, mingling, passing in review, eternally present in the here and now of memory.

There, in the slightly tarnished hero of *Stagecoach* (1939), played by a thirty-three-year-old Wayne, is a man with the face of an angel but one who has already put some miles between himself and heaven. He looks clean-cut, strong, all-American, like the football player he was (he played guard for the University of Southern California Trojans his freshman year), yet there is something else: an ethereal quality that dates back to the dreamy youth of the Iowa boy.

In that role as the Ringo Kid, Wayne hasn't the smooth narcissistic beauty of Cooper nor the glib, easy charm of Gable. Awkward with women, he becomes a character lead rather than a romantic one. He is closer to Fonda and Stewart in type and in the movie terrain he will come to occupy, yet he differs markedly from them, too. Less naive to begin with, he paradoxically retains true innocence longer. All three have an interestingly neurotic side—Fonda closed off, rigid (his squaring off against the more straightforward and flexible Wayne in *Fort Apache* is one of the great character duels of cinema); Stewart, prone to passivity and martyrdom; and Wayne with a barely concealed rage and bent for revenge that threatens to annihilate everything in its path.

He has played heroes who were fallible in different ways: sometimes wrongheaded, sometimes puritanical, sometimes ruthless, sometimes drunken, sometimes shy, sometimes earthy, sometimes crotchety, but rarely mean-spirited and never petty. Not for Wayne the pusillanimous rogue or the shaggy antihero in the modern tradition. While it is nonsense to say, as many have, that he "always plays John Wayne," he makes no bones about wanting to play men with whom audiences can identify.

"They have got to have vitality," he says of the parts he chooses. "I don't like to play prissy, pure people. Before I went into Westerns, the hero wore white gloves and a white hat and he never got dirty.

"I went in with a good pair of boots and a good hat, and what was in between didn't matter. The heavy threw a table at me, and I turned around and hit him, knocked him out. He said, 'What are you doing?' and I said, 'My dad told me if I got in a fight, to win.'"

It was an oft told tale, and, in fact, he had done yeoman's work as a stuntman in apprenticeship and continued to do the stunts and dirty work. Some of the aphorisms he used to spin about his legend are less reliable. In the sixties and seventies Wayne was famous for grousing in public that in the old Westerns the good guy and bad guy shot each other to death, whereas in the new, adult Westerns they talked each other to death. In fact, as Andrew Sarris pointed out, the real joke was that the laconic Wayne was the creation of Ford's movies and his brilliantly pared down dialogue, whereas it was when Wayne directed himself that the movies became a "tedious talkfest" full of patriotic speeches.

Wayne comes out of a classical tradition of Hollywood acting built on type: stars using their faces and personalities as basic texts on which to build characterizations. Unlike most modern actors, these stars didn't want to, or have to, invent themselves anew with each role. Wayne is all of a piece; at any given moment, he is the sum of his past performances and experiences.

For some time he has had the power to choose and alter properties in accordance with his tastes. The original script of *The Shootist* was not to his liking. It was, he says, "dirty," which turns out to mean not just its language but its vision of life: nasty (or in modern terms, "realistic"), cynical *and* clinical, brutal and unfunny. The script is now funny, less clinical, and decidedly less cynical. For example, the young boy who becomes Wayne's surrogate son (played by Ron Howard, of the TV series *Happy Days*), was originally an unscrupulous brat who couldn't wait to see the old gunfighter bite the dust. The script has been changed to make the boy more honorable and to give Wayne's death a redeeming power for him.

They are doing a scene together in a woodshed. A terrible misunderstanding has occurred. The boy Gillum, who is like a son to Books, has discovered the old man is dying and investigated selling his horse. Books is deeply wounded.

"Gillum," Wayne says sadly, "I never thought you were a horse thief."

He is so powerful, so quietly commanding, that it is a miracle he doesn't wipe everybody else off the screen.

I tell him this.

He doesn't hesitate to acknowledge the possibility. "Hawks used to worry about that," he says, "and so he would give other actors things to do, to build up their parts."

What about the chinks in my knight's armor? He talks a lot about patriotism, but there have been rumors about "special treatment" accorded him by the I.R.S. He can't stand "dirty" talk on the screen, but his own conversation is packed with expletives. But somehow, when he says them, it's different. You laugh or you quake. I'd just as soon not have been in the shoes of the clumsy crew-member who walked between Wayne and a light as he was trying to read the script. "Will you get the **** out of the light?" he roared.

I suggest that certain of the new freedoms of expression in films have been beneficial, or that at least the Production Code wasn't an entirely happy affair. But there's no arguing with him. And he's dead right about the ingenuity with which good directors circumvented the taboos.

"I'll give you an example," he said. "In *The Quiet Man*, Ford wanted Maureen O'Hara to come into the confessional and say that she hadn't slept with her husband. 'You can't show that on the screen,' the producer told him. This irritated Ford into a good scene. He has the confession take place in the open air, down by the river. It's half in Irish and half in English, and you understand everything she is saying to him by his answers. Ford was forced to use more imagination. The loss of illusion has hurt the artistry of the business."

A woman arrives with a cookbook of recipes contributed by the stars. Wayne has one in it, a cheese souffle, which he swears is his very own. We talk about food, about the time he had an ulcer and had to swear off booze and cigarettes for six months and could have only milk and baby food. I allow as to how I think milk would be worse than baby food.

An expression of distaste. "I don't like it either," he says, "except with toast."

"With toast?"

"Yeah, in the morning for breakfast, you put a piece of toast in milk. Then an egg on top of that. Then sugar on top of that." (I make a face.) He thinks for a moment. "It's a cake—unassembled."

We talk about women. About his mother ("She was the first women's libber. She used to smoke when women didn't smoke—I caught her when I was seven or eight. She was a campaign manager for a local politician, she kept him on the straight and narrow"). And about Marlene Dietrich.

"She was great, just a German *Hausfrau*. She used to cook pressurized beef to make beef bouillon for everybody. It may have been an act, but it brought her a great deal of enjoyment. 'Course [he stops and reflects] maybe one reason she enjoyed it so much was she didn't have to do it all the time."

This is what I always suspected about Dietrich's famous domesticity— just one more costume, one more endearing role for the fans—but how interesting that Wayne remembered it, enjoyed it, and, upon reflection, saw through it. And he saw through that to the difference between the home virtues as practiced by stars and the same "virtues"—known as chores—as endured daily by those who have no choice.

It would be a mistake to take as sum of the man this stereotype, drawn from Wayne's politics and movies like *Green Berets* and the war pictures rather than the great Ford and Hawks films. Consider the xeno-phobic, violently anti-Indian Ethan Edwards of *The Searchers*, the arrogant and obtuse cattle driver of *Red River*, the prudish male chauvinist of *The Quiet Man*, the fanatic Spig Wead, Naval commander, in *The Wings of Eagles*.

Wayne was not a lusty sort in the fanny-pinching tradition, not one to carouse with the boys or leer at women. There was none of the compul-sive womanizing of the male chauvinist or, on a subtler level, the sexual indifference that is as much a part of the macho pose as swagger. Wayne had his own mission, his own promises to keep—to a woman, to a battalion, to a dead friend. The fact that it was a private sort of mission, one he wouldn't blab about, means that he would not fit in with the current notion, supposedly a by-product of the Women's Movement—that men should drop the stoical pose and open up their souls and their tear ducts.

The New Man pats himself on the back for his parenting skills, showing that he can change diapers and spend quality time with his kid. But in one of Wayne's loveliest scenes, in *Operation Pacific* (1951), he commands a submarine where his company has rescued several nuns who have come aboard with infants orphaned by war, including a newborn. The men are all thumbs, baffled at what to do with the tiny passenger, but Wayne fills a rubber glove with milk, checks the temperature carefully with sidekick Ward Bond, then feeds the baby the milk using the glove's fingers as teats. It's a charming scene, made even more so when Wayne later muses briefly about the vagaries of life and death, marveling at how "this gutsy little guy came into the world" to stay, then grows silent—it turns out his shore-bound wife Patricia Neal had given birth to their own little boy, but Wayne was on a farflung mission when the child was born and on another when he died six months later. The quiet stoicism, the willingness to subordinate his private anguish into the struggle for the common good is so out of fashion now as to seem either quaint or incomprehensible.

Wayne's relationships with women were secondary to the action but no less profound for that. In *They Were Expendable*, Ford's great World War II movie, he and Robert Montgomery are captains of torpedo boats in the Philippines that are being sent on sacrifice missions. He calls Donna Reed, the nurse in one of the mountain hospitals with whom he has fallen in love, to say good-bye. He has only a few minutes to talk: neither will acknowledge the parting is probably forever, they speak of love and hope, and then, amidst the noise of war maneuvers which won't even give them peace or privacy, the phone goes dead. It is a moment of great emotional depth, painful, charged with the interplay of frustration, loss, acceptance. They'll never see each other again, but their mute courage in love is a chord that vibrates through the rest of the film.

If he thought he was better off on his own, it was not from the narcissism of the compulsive loner but because he hadn't yet come to understand what he eventually *would* understand: that men and women could be not only lovers but friends. One of the loveliest aspects of *The Shootist* is the December-December relationship with Bacall, a friendship which is never compelled to blossom into romance.

Wayne had more than one adult love affair on film—with Katharine Hepburn in *Rooster Cogburn*, with Angie Dickinson in *Rio Bravo*, with Colleen Dewhurst in *McQ*, and perhaps most gloriously with Patricia Neal in *In Harm's Way*. How many other maturing male stars have allowed themselves to be paired with women who were roughly their contemporaries, instead of dropping back one generation, then another?

THE HEROES OF HIS later films acknowledge their mortality by leaning on others: on James Caan in *El Dorado*, on the young girls in *Rio Lobo*, on Kim Darby in *True Grit*, and on Katharine Hepburn in *Rooster Cogburn*, with a vulnerability that has made him all the more appealing, especially to women. I discovered this when I talked to people about my interview. "Wayne!" The men seem surprised. "What is there left to say about him? He's creaking in the saddle." Could it be that men see in him a reflection of their own mortality and approaching old age? Are they made uncomfortable by the sight of a man who refuses to give up? Whereas women, less demanding of physical perfection, see that youth has nothing to do with virility and respond to him more passionately than ever, and on many levels.

Wayne makes his co-stars look good because he is secure enough that he doesn't preen sexually, doesn't need sweet young things to bolster his ego. To me, *macho* is Paul Newman in *The Drowning Pool* with an endless supply of nubile nymphets—whom he can take pleasure in rejecting! That sort of thing is not Wayne's style at all, and yet—

"They tag you with the image of the male chauvinist," I said to him, "whereas to me it's the 'effete Easterners' who have to strut to prove themselves."

"It's true," he replied. "I've never done those things. I've avoided them because I'm quite sensitive to them. Everybody thinks of me with a machine gun [here he mimes the gesture], mowing down a patrol of Japanese. But I never did that. The real swashbuckling guy was John Garfield. He was the one with the virility thing. But sooner or later, I got tagged with it. Finally you just let them say what they want.

"Yesterday these two fellas come in here [two British journalists] and all they can talk about is politics. So finally I just give them an answer that will fit their preconceptions. I just accommodate them quickly, it saves time.

"They say I'm a conservative, too, but I think I'm a moderate. I listen to people. I've given money for three Democrats and three Republicans."

There is more than one reason why this ambling mountain of taciturnity and implacable maleness appeals to a blabbermouth feminist like me. As a film enthusiast I was more sympathetic to westerns than most women I know—most men, for that matter. As a transplanted southerner, I could embrace, through Wayne, certain conservative values I had theoretically rejected in leaving the South. He stood for a civilization in which men were men and women were women, in which chivalric ideals still had meaning and physical action had authority. I could love in Wayne a surrogate for my own dead father, a traditionalist who would have disapproved of many of the attitudes and activities of my adult life. If only in fantasy and up on the screen, our differences could be expressed, then reconciled. In his struggles with representatives of the new order, with young whippersnappers of both sexes, he gave expression to tensions between father and daughter, father and son, between old values and the confusing modern world. In so doing, he became that part of us that we must reject to become ourselves but that we can never bury completely without losing ourselves.

I remind him of the time he went to Harvard. The kids, who came to jeer someone they regarded as the Godzilla of American imperialism, stayed to cheer the man.

"Yeah," he laughed, "they went from one extreme to the other. They thought I was a horse's ass, but when they saw I was as honest about what I thought as they were about their beliefs, they came around. Then they went too far the other way. We stayed up all night drinking. I guess I was the father they never had."

Or the father we had but lost, which is, I suppose, what he is to me. *The Searchers* is perhaps his greatest film. And its most heartrending moment occurs when the vengeful Ethan Edwards, played by Wayne, has finally found the niece (Natalie Wood), who has been brought up and assimilated by the despised Indians. As he stands there looking at her, all the hardness of heart and hatred that had stiffened him for the search melt out of him, and he picks her up in his arms in one of the most beautiful scenes of Christian reconciliation in art.

For me, an even more devastating moment occurs in *The Wings of Eagles*, the film based on the life of Naval Commander Spig Wead—not an entirely sympathetic character, devoted to the Navy first and only secondly to his wife and family. When he is on one of his brief visits home, he falls on a child's toy and winds up in a wheelchair. The film was made in 1957, the year my own father died as the result of the progressively crippling Lou Gehrig's disease which he had contracted three years earlier. He was a handsome man and a man of integrity, made even more extraordinary by a daughter's idealizing memories. Perhaps I would have begun to qualify my adulation and its corollary, my secret self-loathing (the phenomenon so acutely described by Freud in *Mourning and Melancholia*), if he had been around longer, but he died before the struggles could begin. It was even harder at such an age to watch someone who was the very image of the male ideal deteriorate physically and humiliatingly into a helplessly bedridden and often angry shadow of what he'd been.

When I saw *The Wings of Eagles* for the first time in the late sixties and watched John Wayne succumb to a similar fate, and with the same mixture of good and bad grace, it was almost more than I could bear.

Is that why, when I see him, I desperately want him to take me in his arms and tell me that everything is going to be all right? That it was all a big mistake—my father's disease, Wayne's cancer, us both going our separate ways, never to meet again.

If, in real life, our fathers were not just authority figures but adventurers in the world with whom we identified, so our loyalty to Wayne, as moviegoers, takes us back (some of us, anyway) to when we were tree-climbing adolescents, identifying with the hero rather than with the hero's schoolteacher girlfriend, or saloon girl "pal." We rode the range instead of tending the hearth or the boudoir until the sexual highway forked and rites of adolescence planted us more firmly on the path to femininity.

I ask him about working with Katharine Hepburn. "I heard that Hepburn said you were the person who reminded her most of Spencer Tracy since his death."

"I don't know. I don't know. She's some woman. A strong feminist, and yet, you know, she worshipped her father. He was a kind of god."

"But he was the only one."

"The only one except Tracy. He was like her father to her, a god. He really—" Wayne searches for words, then makes his arms into a circle— "enclosed her."

Wayne is the father figure (my own was also named John) who made the world safe for us so that we could explore it on our own terms. In the current mood of the women's movement, father figures are the un-acknowledged eminences in the struggle for independence. Movies have always been full of fathers, real and surrogate, who served to nurture and protect heroines of the most spirited kind. (Movies were less generous to mothers.) The fathers and father surrogates watched over and guided them and, in a rite of passage similar to that served by the "older woman" for the young man in other countries and less puritanical cinemas, allowed them to become themselves more fully.

Wayne represents to me those true conservative values—personal honor and integrity, individualism with responsibility—that have long ago been abandoned by the party that pretends to honor them. He represents the West as an imaginary land, a place of hope compromised by death but undiluted by vulgarity. Monument Valley is our inverted Olympus, a place from which sprang forth the gods and goddesses appropriate to our psychic landscape. His West, as carved out of the films of Ford and Hawks, gave us myths built out of contradictory urges—the urge to settle down and the urge to move on; the need to be alone and the need to save; the love of woman and the love of man; strength and vulnerability. And it is Wayne who stands on all borders, reconciling the warring ambiguities of which his political persona is a crude distortion.

Standing at the crossroads of our mythic universe, Wayne couldn't help becoming a magical figure, loathed intensely and intensely loved. He was a dinosaur, a hero who survived into an antiheroic era. He was the star of a genre, the western, that was our *Iliad*, set in the past of the imagination and that was almost extinct. But the western was the only form that could have created and accommodated Wayne's own legend.

John Wayne didn't win an Oscar for the Ringo Kid of *Stagecoach* or the heroes who struggled with their pride and learned humility in *They Were Expendable*, *The Quiet Man*, or *The Searchers*. His Academy Award—and considering the fate of Chaplin, Garbo, Grant, we should be grateful he got one at all—was for *True Grit*, in which he played a self-mocking old geezer to Kim Darby's tomboy. He'd been standing tall on the cinematic horizon as long as anyone could remember, with just that touch of a slouch to put him within talking and spittin' distance of everyone else. Yet his last appearance was as a shrunken Wayne on a shrunken screen. When he was dying of cancer in 1979 he graced the Oscars to receive a special award, and permitted us to see the once-majestic frame withered by lung cancer and to hear the once-resonant voice (the cigarette raspiness now all that was left) hardly able to get out a few well-known names. Though painful at the time, it was, in retrospect, perhaps his most heroic performance.

Now he has been dead these many years, no longer a fit subject for satire or demonization. In the obituaries that followed his death of cancer in 1979, media pundits and the eastern press who once fell sideways out of their chairs sneering at the Duke suddenly went teary-eyed over the passing of the Last Old-fashioned Hero. Apparently Wayne's heroic show-down with the Big C wiped the slate clean of his previous confrontation with that other Big C, Communism.

Yet beneath the eulogies there was an audible sigh of relief. His presence had been too large . . . too embarrassing—and, I might hazard, too much charged with our own ambivalent yearning for some kind of straightfor-ward symbol of virility. His hawkish, flag-waving Green Beret movie was fresh in everyone's mind, and most of his assailants among the media and liberal establishment had never been fans of the western or seen the great Ford and Hawks movies which defined his persona. Very few people, fans or otherwise, had appreciated his genius as a performer, his knowing how to be still and let somene else dominate a scene without himself disappear-ing. Like a father whose memory has at last been laid to rest.

Literary Heroines

. . . .

Against the Grain of Womanhood

THE BOSTONIANS

Olive Chancellor, the feminist heroine of Henry James's 1886 novel *The Bostonians*, was a thorn in the side of her own times and a hot potato thrust into the future, the very image of what men of a later age would point to and denounce as the epitome of a movement composed of bra-burners and man-haters. She may even prove embarrassing to those contemporary feminists who place ideology above art—and thus general and positive "role models" over specific fictional creations; or look for glamorous Hollywood stars to play them in movement movies. You will have to scour literature to find a heroine who goes as much against the grain of womanhood—and the literary conception of womanhood—as Olive Chancellor. Not among the wasted rebels of Chekhov, nor among rural independents of George Eliot, nor among the workers and wanderers of Charlotte Brontë or Doris Lessing, nor among the actual feminists of Virginia Woolf, Ford Madox Ford, and others, nor among the sexual activists and mad housewives of contemporary women writers is there a heroine who observes so little of the biological and cultural destiny commonly assigned to women. With Henry James's fierce and tragic nineteenth-century suffragette there is not a scent of femininity, a secret hope of matrimony, an ounce of the nurturing or nesting instinct waiting in the wings to be brought to fruition by a man. Indeed, the final image of Olive Chancellor is of her standing alone on a stage in Boston's Music Hall, where she must confront a hostile audience with the news that their long-awaited guest lecturer, the "inspirational" speaker Verena Tarrant, will not be able to appear. Verena, Olive's protégée and the love of

*This review first appeared in *The Village Voice*, July 25, 1974. Copyright © 1974 by Molly Haskell.

her life, has succumbed to her "woman's" fate and fled in the arms of Basil Ransom, Olive's southern cousin and archenemy. All of the minor frustrations and disappointments Olive has endured, and for which she has suffered disproportionately, pale beside the compound agony, the loss, terror, and abject humiliation, of this moment. I see her towering, in a low angle shot similar to the one of Rosalind Russell at the end of Dorothy Arzner's film of *Craig's Wife*. She stands there deserted, defeated, punished beyond the call of poetic justice, and yet awesome in her loneliness and her capacity to suffer such a fate and to feel pain—a capacity denied her more "normal" and adjusted adversaries.

Olive's feminism and lesbianism are not the causes of her wretchedness, nor are they "sicknesses" in themselves, but rather symptoms of a soul divided against itself, with a need for mortification as deep as her lust for power. The movement is the river into which her hatred—of self, of men—pours itself, and the young and impressionable Verena the vessel for her ambitions. Olive is misguided, even evil in her desire to possess another human being, but how rare her refusal to ask for pity or sympathy. Her ideology is warped by suppressed sexuality and in that sense is not disinterested, yet how free her love is from envy and pettiness and vanity.

Unlike the spinster heroines of the last few decades, creations of more "liberated" writers in an age dominated by what Virginia Woolf called, as early as 1926, a "sex consciousness," whose insufficiencies were traceable at least by implication to sexual privation (and were therefore curable by a steady diet of Vitamin Stud), Olive's character cannot be reduced to the clinical description of a sexual aberration . . . nor can we imagine her finding satisfaction in what we, in our enlightenment, call an "alternative life style." (Perhaps terminology, rather than biology, is destiny. How fortunate James was to be writing before the proliferation of liberated labels, tags generously offered to us on which to hang our identities, and ourselves.)

Basil Ransom and Olive Chancellor are not James's deepest characters, but in some ways, partly because they are not deep but bold, they are his most vivid, poised on separate peaks of the American social consciousness, fighting for the soul of Verena Tarrant, the "uncommitted bloc," like the battle for the "discontented housewife" that rages today between feminists and traditionalists. There is something archetypal in the struggle between the Mississippi gentleman and the Boston puritan. The spectacle, too, has something of the Biblical, Jacob and the Angel wrestling till dawn. Basil Ransom's triumph—an apparent victory for the traditional marriage—is shot through with foreboding. Verena's tears for Olive, for the road not taken, will, James intimates, flow freely at every collision with her husband.

In the time-honored tradition of what Shaw contemptuously called the "womanly woman," she has allowed herself to be swept up by a man who will then bear the brunt for every moment of her discontent in a marriage for which she can now hold him forever responsible.

To find for Olive Chancellor such an opponent as Basil Ransom was a brilliant strategy on James's part. A connoisseur of the fair sex, Ransom, with his wit and courtliness and charm, offers to feminism its most potent antagonist because in him the traditional separation of the sexes assumes its most attractive form. He is no misogynist. Nor is he a mamma's boy whose fear of women's emancipation betrays his own insecurity (in the prospective loss of the doting mother figure). Nor is he a male fellow traveler who without being particularly interested in women, supports feminism because it is politically correct. He adores women, prefers their company, is open, curious, confident, with an easy virility, his sunny and sun-blessed nature clouded only by a becoming melancholy, the residue of the southern defeat. If anything can puncture the feminist balloon it will not be the logic of argument but the magic of Basil's charm.

It is through the satirical gleam in his eyes that we first see the luminaries of the women's movement and its satellites as James has created and planted them in a New England drawing room: Miss Birdseye, a dotty little fanatic and "humanitarian hack" who has grafted her abolitionist sympathies onto the women's movement; Mrs. Farrinder, the sophisticated New Yorker and grande dame of the cause who knows which way the wind is blowing at every moment; the no-nonsense Dr. Prance, who has "made it" without the movement and has no use for it; and Verena Tarrant, the gaudy, malleable beauty, who at this point is but an electrifying mouthpiece for her father's ventriloquist act.

Basil's skepticism, like his philosophy of not taking things too seriously, is feminism's deadliest but most seductive enemy. He is beautiful and Olive ugly to such a degree that were their story adapted to the screen and cast with any fidelity, the imbalance would be too great.* His weaknesses are easily translated into virtues, so much so that he has often been interpreted

---

*In fact, in the 1984 James Ivory film, Christopher Reeve's relative weakness in the role—dashing enough to look at, but with none of the weight and irony of James's character—simply turned Basil Ransom into a stick figure, while Vanessa Redgrave's Olive Chancellor, though a commanding presence, was strangely uninvolving. With the exception of Reeve, the movie boasted a stellar cast and the usual Merchant-Ivory polish and fidelity to period, yet it remained lifeless—instead of the passionate film about repression that might have been made, a repressed film about repression.

as James's point-of-view character, and in such a possibility James has bequeathed us his finest sexual insight. That we are likely to forgive Basil everything and Olive nothing should suggest to us the roots of a male chauvinism that is as instinctual as it is universal.

James does not spare his feminists their grotesqueness, but in the minute details with which he observes them there is more love than in the broad brushstroke portraits of more "positive" women, and they glow from an inner light made visible through externals. The moment in which James allows Olive's heart to go out to Miss Birdseye, transfiguring them both in the process, even in the mist of martyrdom, is one of the most beautiful passages in James and, in the light of the rest of the book, heartbreaking:

> Olive Chancellor looked at her with love, remembered that she had never, in her long, unrewarded, weary life had a thought or an impulse for herself. She had been consumed by the passion of sympathy; it had crumbled her into as many creases as an old glazed, distended glove. She had been laughed at, but she never knew it; she was treated as a bore, but she never cared. She had nothing in the world but the clothes on her back, and when she should go down into the grave she would leave nothing behind her but her grotesque, undistinguished, pathetic little name. And yet people said that women were vain, that they were personal, that they were interested!

Olive then reaches over and fastens a loose brooch on Miss Birdseye's collar.

To his St. Theresa James is hardly as indulgent as George Eliot in *Middlemarch* is to hers, and, although our contemporary martyrs would do well to be treated so compassionately, James is more accurate than Eliot in perceiving the roots of the impulse to martyrdom and the mutually disfiguring effect of person and cause.

If Basil Ransom's ideal of a resurgent masculinity and the venerable relationship between man and wife as master and servant/goddess is as obsolete as the feudal South he has quit to seek his fortune, the "cause" is no less deluded in its utopian promise and perhaps, to James, more of an anathema in that it refuses to acknowledge loss, pain, imperfection—the mutations that must occur if it is to succeed on its own terms. James's indictment is of reformism as an American compulsion, an extremism in which differences and the need of one sex or one class for another are not acknowledged. Implicit in every portrait in a book that offers no solutions and no vision of a sexual norm is that whatever sex we are born into, we have lost something in not being born into the other, and we should begin our conversation not with assertions of independence but with the confession of mutual incompleteness. It is a loss, a loneliness that we must live with, like the prospect of death, redeemable—and then only temporarily —by the imaginative process of which art and love are the highest expressions. For any sex or political movement to claim self-sufficiency is an act of disrespect to the mystery and importance of what it is *not*. There are many things James was not, but it was his greatness to have felt their loss and made the imaginative leap to encompass them in his art. He was the man of reflection who appreciated—regretted, distrusted—the man of action. He was alternately American and European. He was a kindred soul to his New England spinsters with their suffering and rectitude, and yet he gave the liveliest benefit of the doubt to the vulgar and energetic classless American beauties, the Verena Tarrants and Daisy Millers, who confounded the aristocrats and made the intellectuals suffer. They were born for each other, the creatures of instinct being the demi-gods against whose powers women (and men) of finer intellect discovered the limits of their own.

Female in the Purest State

COLETTE

I n these days of professional and sexual angst, Colette's attitude toward herself and her literary vocation seems comically cavalier. She wrote largely out of economic necessity; she probably enjoyed her intermittent career as a mime and (sometimes topless) music hall performer more than writing; and when at age sixty she opened a cosmetics business, she transferred her gift to writing promotional copy without a qualm. And always, always, she looked for love, heedless of the warming issued by her mother in *La Naissance du Jour*, and quoted by Margaret Crosland in her new biography that "a woman in love gives the man all her 'most precious gifts.'" When, early in her marriage to Willy, he threw back her first schoolgirl scribblings, telling her "it's no good at all," Colette felt "liberated." She could go back to her dream, her cat, and her friends. Given the priorities of women today, her idea of liberation is ironic—the antithesis, in fact, of our current conception of the term. And yet the dialectic on which it is based, the dramatic conflict between the urge to achieve and the desire to be "just a woman," remains.

Colette went on, of course, to write and publish some fifty books of short stories, novels, journalism, and nonfictional reminiscences; to become president of the Academie Goncourt and a scandal to the Catholic Church (which refused to officiate at her state funeral); to become, as Crosland observes, the first great French woman writer to emerge from the middle class. Once she recovered from the shambles of her marriage to Willy, she came to appreciate her independence, but never, perhaps, without some

*This review first appeared in *The Village Voice*, December 13, 1973. Copyright © 1973 by Molly Haskell.

sense that it was a sacrilege, a violation of her feminine destiny. Despite her intense, amorous relationships with members of her own sex (the principal of which was with the Marquise de Morny, known as "Missy"), she saw herself, like many another extraordinary woman, as wanting only that happiness due an ordinary woman, culminating in the love of a man. If her life was a quest for this elusive ideal, her male characters were the palest approximations of it, and her writings were really celebrations of almost every other aspect of life: nature, childhood, family, animals, colors, smells, and, above all, women.

She wrote brilliantly of women, of their peculiarly intimate yet competitive relationships with one another, of their—and her—anguish at growing old. She portrayed every kind of woman—tough, warm, sensual, pragmatic—all of them ignited, in some obscure way, by the eternal flame of love that burned between Colette and her mother. For Sido, as Crosland points out, was the great love of her life, the mother she left behind to marry Willy and later rejoined, not in person but in the voluminous correspondence through which she escaped the misery of her marriage and recreated the idyll of her childhood.

Colette, with her glinting eyes and triangular face, was an animal, a bird perhaps or, as one friend described her, half cat and half dog, but as remote from any kind of common "political" identity with women today as she was from the political issues of her own time. She was quintessentially French in her acute response to sensory stimuli and most un-French (some would say most womanly) in her refusal to translate sensory impressions into an idea, into psychology. Even her love of words was more tactile than ideational. This comes through clearly in the articles written for the newspaper *Le Matin*, in the collection *The Thousand and One Mornings* that has just been translated into English. In an account of three speakers in the Chambre des Deputés, she gives no indication of their political affiliation or the substance of their addresses, only vivid descriptions of their voices, their gestures, and whatever glimpses of character can be deduced through these externals.

There is no grand social importance, nothing instructive or edifying in her writing, and it is this, I think, rather than the sensationalism of her life or her work, as Miss Crosland maintains, that has kept her from being mandatory reading in most schools. She, not Zola, is the true naturalist, the observer who approaches nature without preconceived notions, who is a part of that nature, hence as refreshing as a rain and as cruel and impartial as an earthquake. And there is enough of the Protestant or Cartesian ethic in all of us that we resist surrendering to this genuinely pantheistic spirit that knows none of the tortures or pleasures of guilt. Where the heterosexual apotheosis of *Lady Chatterley's Lover* is willed, that of *Le Blé en Herbe* is not, yet one is as foreign to most of us as the other.

Crosland, a British translator of Colette, is a knowledgeable biographer: reserved, quiet, eminently readable, yet curiously lacking in passion and treading as gently as an angel where an occasional foolhardy conjecture would be welcome. Her chief purpose is to provide, for aficionados of Colette, an informed chronology, identifying the important events and forces in her evolution and the people who served as both models and friends. From the childhood in Saint-Sauveur, the paradise lost that was eventually regained through the art of the *Claudine* series, through the highly artificial turn-of-the-century Paris (which she is particularly good at evoking), to Colette's old age and death in 1954, Crosland has supplied a useful handbook to check against Colette's own fanciful, obscure, and gloriously distorted version of the same events. One can guess at Miss Crosland's enthusiasms in Colette's work, but she never forces them on the reader—an exercise of tact, perhaps, but also a pity.

The Thousand and One Mornings, translated by Crosland and David Le Vay, is also for Colette fans. Colette wrote about herself and what she knew, even when covering public events, but her autobiographical self-interest was, unlike most women's writing today, centrifugal rather than centripetal. Where we are locked in the chrysalis of our own consciousness, waiting to spread our literary wings, Colette flew.

In her first two articles, she recounts her airborne adventures aboard a balloon and on the airship Clement Bayard, trips that would have been daring for any journalist but particularly for a woman. Like the actress-pantheist she was, she entered into every living thing, feeling the pain of man's encroachment on nature, bringing to the landscape below the double vision of a god and a fieldmouse.

She has the new journalist's eye for the novelistic and the dramatic, an ability to gauge the precise mood of a crowd or the emotional temperature of a courtroom or to perceive a drama of passion being enacted in the tiniest of gestures. And there are studies of women's habits that convey, as vividly as any of Barthes' "Mythologies," the signs of French tribal bourgeois culture.

But in the last analysis, I remain less than ardent in my feelings about Colette, and I am not sure if the limitation is in me or in her. Perhaps if we were able to enter her world with less intellectual, and even masculine, prejudices, we would, after all, learn more about the nature of the female beast. For she is the female in her purest state. Yet no one is that purely female, certainly no one as professionally industrious, as dextrous at presenting herself on so many fronts, and as transparently driven as Colette. Isn't this what gives us pause, this sense of an elaborate creation, of undiluted femaleness as a canny projection concealing desires and ambitions even more forbidden than the ones she acknowledges!

A Woman for All Seasons

E M M A

To seize with romantic rapture upon a very ordinary young girl, a
plump blond beauty of malleable character and a humbler background
than oneself. To devote all one's attentions to winning her over and then to
educating and "improving" her according to current fashions in women. To
refuse to hear any criticism of her unworthiness and to ignore the young
woman's own murmured protestations. To suppose that this object of one's
idealization attracts the eye of every male beholder and to be blinded as to
the true feelings she excites.

What kind of sexist persecution is this? Pygmalion imposing his will on
womankind in the name of Galatea? Griffith and Gish? Sternberg and
Dietrich? No. Emma Woodhouse, the mistress of Hartfield and heroine of
Jane Austen's *Emma*, and her protégée, Harriet Smith.

Of course, intimacy between women, sometimes of the most passionate
kind, is a commonplace of nineteenth-century fiction, extending into the
novels of Henry James. It occurs not just in the intense sibling relationships
so characteristic of Austen (and of the Gish sisters in Griffith films, for that
matter), but in different kinds of "infatuation": the "older" (if only two
years) or plainer woman and the young beauty (Esther and Ada in *Bleak
House*, Olive and Verena in *The Bostonians*), the virtuous woman and the
sinner (Dinah and Hettie in *Adam Bede*), brains and beauty (Lucy Snowe and
the young French girl in *Villette*). In *Bleak House*, Esther's solicitude for and
references to her "beloved Ada" and her panegyrics to her beauty often
sound like the effusions of a suitor. On one level this is a convention,

*This review first appeared in *The Village Voice*, August 2, 1973. Copyright © 1973 by
Molly Haskell.

allowing women (much like the use of women in soft-core sexploitation films) to act out feelings with one another that were forbidden from heterosexual intercourse. But they were not just playing surrogate lovers. Women really entertained these feelings and relationships and seemed to take mutual pleasure in a range of sensations, from the sublimated erotic to the pure platonic, of a richness and variety that are beyond the imaginings of our supposedly liberated era, with its lepidopterist's need to pin down sexual typology with the bipolar terms of gay-and-straightjacket thinking.

But Emma is a little different. Her attraction to Harriet and her disastrous effort to match her up with the vicar of Highbury is not, like Esther's sponsoring of Ada, the impulsive surge of genuine affection coupled with that instinct for service that Dickens's "little woman" shares with other Victorian heroines, particularly orphaned or disadvantaged ones, even with the most independent-minded women of the Brontës and George Eliot or with Austen's own selfless Fanny in *Mansfield Park*. (Not that Emma is uncharitable: she performs "good works" with a lack of sanctimoniousness that is refreshing, but she often uses the ideal of service to mask ulterior motives.) Emma's attachment to Harriet—and how modern and understandable she seems—is willful, manipulative, neurotic, the folly of an overactive (but undisciplined) imagination, the game of a ferociously intelligent woman with no approved outlet for her drive to power . . . or at least none that she *cares* to cultivate. For if Emma is brilliant, she is also lazy, the spoiled and headstrong daughter of an overindulgent father. She is a happier and less malignant Hedda Gabler—if such a contradiction in terms is possible—whose restlessness arises not from disaffection with her society but from a too easy ascendancy over it. She is a mistress of mise-en-scene—how easily she mediates among the guests at her father's little parties, smooths rumpled feelings, orchestrates moods, and finally stages scenes and initiates symbolic maneuvers (the portrait painting of Harriet, her conversations with Frank Churchill about Jane Fairfax) whose ultimate meaning eludes her. These more elaborate projects come to mind when that faculty is so little taxed by her ordinary social obligations that she must cast about for a meatier challenge. She fastens, not uncharacteristically (for she has a good opinion of herself and doesn't want to "risk everything"), on a person—Harriet—who will only reinforce her sense of superiority.

She doesn't get along with her one female equal—the brilliant, accomplished Jane Fairfax, an orphan who regularly visits her aunts in Highbury (and who, more than Emma, illuminates the dreary plight of the impecunious single woman who is also an intellectual among philistines). There is, true, a touch of jealousy. Emma is sick to death of hearing Jane's praises and feels keenly the dilettantishness of her own attainments next to Jane's real achievements. But their incompatibility is one of temperament. Jane is cool, reserved, terse, an overachiever; Emma is outgoing, curious, responsive, and spoiled. Jane is like a New Yorker in the South, adrift in a cultural desert, ill at ease with small talk (determined to say nothing if she can't be "sincere"), unable to key herself to the languid rhythm or respond to the genuine personal warmth which she sees as excessive. But she has "made it"—her-piano playing is the talk of Highbury and points north—in a way that must be enviable to Emma. For the irony of Emma's "advantaged" position is that while it frees her from the oppressive alternatives of either marrying ("it is not my way, or my nature") or becoming a "poor old maid" ("it is poverty only which makes celibacy contemptible to a generous public"), it also removes the pressure, born of financial necessity, to develop her talents—to practice her playing, to read books from that impressive list she has drawn up for Mr. Knightley—so that she might be truly independent, i.e., intellectually self-sustaining.

By fortune and habit of mind, Emma is freed from the necessity of marrying and from the romantically indentured mentality of most of her sex. She doesn't give a hang about her beauty, laughs inwardly at the ludicrous posturings of courtliness, even lacks feminine intuition, failing to understand, in this most marriage-minded novel, that Knightley is her destiny. This true and gentle Englishman is a classic older man/mentor but also mother surrogate in that he supplies qualities like warmth and judgment and a moral compass that Emma has been deprived of since her mother's death.

As an independent woman she sees in her doting old father—an even greater misogamist than she is—the ideal mate: worshipful, undemanding, and conveniently dependent. More heretical for a woman, she harbors no discernible maternal feelings, admits that her sister's infants are not adorable and have muddled, indistinguishable features, and even betrays a slight aversion to the physical intimacy of family life.

By any traditional criteria, she is the least "feminine" of heroines, a rarity among her sex, someone who escapes the most severe inequities of a sexist society and who therefore cannot serve as a model of oppression or offer romantic wounds for our commiseration. She does not illustrate the anguish of the "homely" orphan like Lucy Snowe or of the disenfranchised woman like Jane Fairfax. Jane Austen herself thought she would find few friends among her readers. And yet why is it that we take her to our heart, identify with her more passionately than with any other heroine? How can we act in such defiance of our "female natures"? Can it be that women, no less than men, are capable of something called intellectual passion? (And, as corollary, that men resort to "sheer emotionalism" more often than they care to admit?)

The whole question of identification and the difference between male and female response was raised by Edmund Wilson and ultimately recoiled on the critic, in a fascinating essay on *Emma* written in 1944. He complained that women readers (represented by the two Englishwomen whose work had prompted his essay) failed to recognize the superiority of *Mansfield Park* over *Emma* because their inclination to identify with Austen's heroines blinded them to the formal virtues—or defects—of the novel. A woman, Wilson wrote, "rebels at the idea of being Fanny. The male reader neither puts himself in Fanny's place nor imagines himself marrying Fanny any more than he does the nice little girl in Henry James's 'What Maisie Knew' . . . " Wilson then proceeded to praise Austen for an objectivity and aestheticism that distinguish her novels from the "projection of feminine daydreams" that characterizes most women's writing. He declared that she is "almost unique" among novelists of her sex for being concerned "not with the vicarious satisfaction of emotion . . . but, as the great masculine novelists are, with the novel as a work of art."

Leave aside for the moment the problems that this division introduces (aren't all "great" novels by definition *formally* great, a fusion of emotion and intellect, of cool appraisal and hot intensity? Where do Lawrence, Dickens, George Eliot, George Sand, Gertrude Stein, the novel as prophecy or jeu d'esprit or self-expression fit in?). What is it that enables Austen to achieve this objectivity, and why is it that the character who most closely imitates her detachment (Emma being, as Wilson admits, her most autobiographical creation) is the one with whom we "emotionally" identify?

The fact that Emma is not interested in men (except as fathers) would seem to create an unbridgeable distance between her and her female readers, and yet it is women who "feel instinctively the psychological rightness of the behavior attributed to" her, and it is male readers who, according to Wilson, are bewildered. To satisfy them, he offers as explanation Emma's lack of interest in the opposite sex. Here of course, is the crowning irony: Wilson explaining his own dissatisfaction (for to my knowledge he is in the minority in preferring *Mansfield Park*) by judging Emma, the character, against those very romantic expectations that he has applauded Austen, the woman-writer for avoiding, and by elevating into an "aesthetic" those personal responses—here of a man (Wilson) to a woman (Emma)—that he has identified with "women readers" as a kind of corruption of the critical faculties.

His formal rationale for the failure of *Emma*, and the criticism most commonly leveled against it is the problematic nature of Emma's marriage to Knightley and his agreement to move in with her and her father. While I readily concede that living with the old geezer has its drawbacks, the notion that Knightley (never was there a man more secure in his sense of self) is capitulating or being emasculated by this arrangement is pure sexism. And Wilson's vision of Emma entertaining a whole string of sweet young ladies to Knightley's dismay doesn't convince me either. The young protégées were always intellectual rather than sexual playthings, and Emma has found in Knightley her spiritual stimulus, father-figure, partner, and even, covertly, her long-lost mother. Unlike her continental namesake, the romantically deluded Emma Bovary, Emma Woodhouse expects nothing from marriage—does not look to it for her fulfillment—and therefore stands to gain everything from it. She and Knightley may never execute the 103 approved Masters and Johnson positions, but I suspect their marriage may be more exciting for that. She is very much the type of independent woman who goes for the slightly older man, the Katharine Hepburn (or Audrey Hepburn, for that matter) of literary heroines. (Think of how often Katharine Hepburn was paired with older men, professorial types, fathers, and how right it seemed: in *Bill of Divorcement*, *The Little Minister*, *Little Women*, *Break of Hearts*, *Morning Glory*, *Stage Door*, *Sylvia Scarlett*, *Bringing Up Baby*, and, to a certain extent, *Christopher Strong* and all her movies with Tracy.)

But perhaps Emma's is the most romantic solution of all, the smart woman's ultimate fantasy: a man who sees her beauty but responds to her intellect. Feminists have taken to complaining that their relationship is not the perfect match that Austen seems to think it, that their marriage, far from being a delicious duet of mutual edification, is likely to be a grim series of home lessons, with the stuffy Knightley (he doesn't dance) scolding and molding a passive and pliant Emma. I don't think so. Knightley *can* dance (he has already taken his first step in that direction), he will unbend; while Emma will bend with more application to books and studies and discover in her mate a worthy adversary and conversationalist. They will draw each other out emotionally, expressing the warmth each had previously held in check. And perhaps what Emma found in Knightley is not too different from the emotional sustenance the celibate Austen found in her family, particularly in her sister Cassandra. To my way of thinking, these are no mere accommodations. They are as close to the sublime as two human beings ever get.

The art? That is the mystery. But there, too, we are enmeshed in paradox. Women are now finding in Austen an example of an authentic "female sensibility." In a recent article in *The Voice*, Vivian Gornick quoted Virginia Woolf to the effect that Austen, unlike Eliot and the Brontës, rejected the "male sentence" that was the common currency to fashion a "natural, shapely sentence proper." This is a lovely idea, if a little too all encompassing. Neither Woolf nor Gornick, perhaps, makes sufficient allowance for non-sexual (or rather, bi-sexual) differences—the spirit of an age, influences of class and ideology. But to the extent that Austen restricted herself to a world that was dominated by women and social events, captured in a style that paid tribute to all the finer points of dress and manners, social gatherings (no less did Balzac, or Tolstoy), it was, ironically, through a dissociation from the supposedly normal and natural concerns and events of a woman's life. Like Emma, she was free of the "instincts" and emotional dependencies that we think of as a crucial stage in the evolution of the female sensibility and the literature that grows out of it. And her life seemed devoid of those sexual tensions that are the matrix of so much contemporary women's writing.

Austen's "condition" was very different from ours; her balance, her irony, her serenity were as much an expression of a classical vision as of a female sensibility, and even her Emma, the most "neurotic" of her heroines, is hardly a figure on whom we can nourish our sense of injustice. She is a long way from the current pain and pressure and desperation of women, caught between the prison and promise of the independent self. More important, she can excite our intellectual passion and pride. As for all the modern heroines who express the numbness and confusion I feel, it's not that I love them less if I love Emma more.

The Nineties: Where Do We Go from Here?

. . . .

Lipstick Envy

F reud, as we all know, invented penis envy to account for women's supposed inferiority and their unconscious desire to be men. Melanie Klein came back with "womb envy," the idea that men harbor enormous fear and resentment of women's procreative powers. I herewith offer my own hypothesis as the *real* source of gender conflict: makeup envy. After all, the poor guys have to go out and greet the world day after day, year after year, with the same unadorned face, the only option being to shave or not to shave.

Not for them the delicious mutations of feature and coloring according to the dictates of fashion or one's own mood; not for their rugged plainfacedness the subtle shifts in self-disclosure brought on by concealers and revealers, or the endless mutually challenging duet between eye shadow and lipstick. Deprived of such joys, let it also be said they are spared the agonies of how much to wear and when and are immune—transvestites excepted—from the siren songs of the cosmetics manufacturer.

Makeup, like so many other things in our lives, has become fraught with meaning, a political act, a crucible of self-ness, a procedure whose implications we must agonize over and decode. We are caught in a blizzard of choices and interpretations, whereas our mothers—or so goes our alternately self-victimizing and glorifying myth—slapped on a little rouge and lipstick and swiped it off with Pond's cold cream at night. Each delicate blob of eye liner, each firm application of the lip pencil, each heretical foray into bright eye color is no longer an expression of sensual pleasure or a

*This article first appeared in *Self*, February 1995. Copyright © 1995 by Molly Haskell.

simple gesture toward looking good, but a statement of purpose, of *how much* one wants to look good and how much one is willing to be *seen* as trying to look good. Because of our radically changing roles, and a continuing conflict between inner and outer self, we find outselves caught up more than ever in the dilemma of what adorning ourselves *means*.

Part of this ambivalence comes from the association of makeup with frivolity, vanity, and general unseriousness—the domain of the "weaker" sex occupied by women—whereas men, in their unvarnished splendor, get to play the part of serious and essential beings. Color has itself been suspect in puritan cultures, and in different eras painting one's face has been enjoined as sinful or whorish by religious law. How different this is from the animal world where color-coding by gender is reversed: among the fish and fowl, who of course had no choice in the matter, dull gray and brown females lie lazily back while the males, desperate to attract their attention, flash iridescent sparks and exhibit lurid plumage, hoping to be chosen as sexual partner and sire for the next generation.

In other less democratic centuries, it was upperclassness rather than gender that was emphasized and celebrated. In eighteenth-century France and England aristocratic men powdered and perruqued, moled and dyed, but, with the rising middle class, masculinity came to define itself via a more sober and stripped-down bourgeois image. Could it be that male humans of the increasingly suffragist nineteenth and twentieth centuries have felt so keenly the erosion of their claim to power that they've devised an emotional blackmail to make women feel inessential and insecure? It was left to women to carry on with the plumage, and in the patriarchical terms of the ruthless get-ahead industrial world, the seriousness of men and the frivolity of women became mutually reinforcing opposites.

We have been molded by the idea that fashion and make-up are frivolous because appearances are part of what being a woman means—hence the decidedly mixed feelings with which feminists regard female impersonators. In emphasizing a retrograde and superficial femininity, in celebrating the socially constructed facade of our sex, the swoony and masochistic divas of Piedro Almodovar, the garish and corseted "queens" of drag shows haunt us with the grotesque side of female love scenarios. In fact, no less than Arnold Schwarzenegger carrying a fetus called (in the film of that name) "Junior," they represent a nostalgic fantasy of completeness, a yearning to be both male and female—a desire that seems to be ubiquitous in the spate of gender-bending and boundary-blurring images to which our century's end anxiety has given rise. Principal among them, of course, is the spectacle of women entering the police force and the army, women in positions of authority. But in giving up notions of women as the weaker sex, do we also give up the appurtenances by which that weakness has been defined, or can we gradually bring back pleasure in looks and beautification as a human glory rather than a womanly weakness? It may be that female impersonators, exulting in artifice, rendering questionable the whole notion of a pure biological determinism, have allowed us to see just how much gender is about playacting, and—once our sense of self and place in the world is more secure—how much fun we can have doing it.

Sometimes when I'm applying makeup in front of the mirror, I wonder, as I assume all women do, why I am doing this. Why am I buying all these products, taking all this time, wondering if I'm doing it right? Am I submitting to some ancient tribal practice or am I a slave to fashion and fantasy, wearing makeup because everyone else does it? Am I responding to the advertiser's message that there is some one product that is going to bring confidence and ensure, once and for all, my social success. With every touch of eyeliner or blush I'm giving myself away, saying to the world I want to be observed, I want to be thought pretty.

What would happen if I just stopped? Would dogs and humans run from me, clocks stop? Or would no one notice? More likely my friends would look at me more closely, wondering if anything was wrong. Thinking I looked tired, they'd recommend multivitamins.

On those days or nights that I'm not going out, why is it I greet with such inordinate relief the fact that I don't have to wear makeup? After all, the task isn't all that burdensome—for me, ten minutes at most. Is it because the act of making oneself up is itself so fraught with ambivalence: with pleasure at oneself and guilt over this pleasure; with the endless questions of *why* (is it a cover for flaws and insecurities or the proud assertion of a more colorful version of oneself?) and above all for *whom*! Is it for one's public, one's lover, one's friends, oneself, and—the implied subquestion—which of these is it better (morally superior; politically correct) to be for. The answer, of course, is all of the above, but their place on the hierarchy changes with fashion.

My mother, who belonged to the Protestant minimal makeup ethic, used three items—lipstick, powder, and rouge—and was thus a consumer society's nightmare. The lipstick was bright—a purply pink in winter, a salmony color in summer; the powder was Charles of the Ritz in a round box with a puff that was used until it was threadbare; and the rouge didn't pretend to be anything other than what it was. For her, it was "the face" she presented in public, and the main point was to show the flag, to know one's script, and to cooperate with the project at hand. It was a social contract: when you accepted an invitation to a party, it was your duty to your hostess to make it a success. That meant looking "your best," keeping up your end of the conversation, bringing out the shy people, and smoothing out any bumps that might arise. There was no sense here of the ignominy of self-sacrifice, of being phony or hypocritical: there was enough homogeneity in this world that appearance and reality were one. Doing things for other people was a reciprocal game: they would reflect her back to herself with *their* cosmetics, clothes, conversation, and make her party a success.

Now, however, we are suspicious of any notion of performing for others and seeking their approval—it smacks of narcissistic weakness, of needing validation from outside, of not having an inner self.

When my mother applied lipstick and powder, self and audience were one. She was part of an ongoing play whose moves were known in advance and whose lines were improvised according to a relatively narrow fund of topics and queries. With today's mixture of classes and sexes and a *seemingly* wide open field of talk and action, our every choice seems more weighted. Yet *seemingly* is the operative word here—we are not as free as we seem, our choices are more restricted and conventional than we like to think. So perhaps we should relax and enjoy our makeup ritual, see it as a tribal custom through which we connect with each other and with women throughout time.

One of Yeats's most beautiful and generous poems, "Before the World Was Made," describes a woman in front of her mirror:

> *If I make the lashes dark*
> *And the eyes more bright*
> *And the lips more scarlet,*
> *Or ask if all be right*
> *From mirror after mirror,*
> *No vanity's displayed:*
> *I'm looking for the face I had*
> *Before the world was made.*

What if I look upon a man
As though on my beloved,
And my blood be cold the while
And my heart unmoved?
Why should he think me cruel
Or that he is betrayed?
I'd have him love the thing that was
Before the world was made.

This is, among other things, a magnificent reproach to those who would judge women harshly and would dismiss the artifice involved in makeup as "mere" vanity. With sublime compassion for women, Yeats refocuses the question: women don't use makeup to deceive or disguise, but to create something magnificent, to add to the sum of beauty in the world. We are artists of ourselves, our faces a canvas onto which we dab and dash the lines and colors of a painter's palette, and in the sensuous act of making ourselves up we look for something beyond and before time, an ideal self. In looking into the mirror, we go back to before we were born and perhaps to being born, to the mother whose face was our first mirror—and from there to our first memory of *her* looking into the mirror. Each look in the glass invokes a chain of mirrors, of mothers and daughters, receding into infinity.

A poet friend told me that some ten years ago when bright lipstick had just come back in, she went to Cosmetics Plus and bought one. She applied it and when she looked at herself in the mirror, she almost shrieked. It was her mother's face. The bright color that her mother had worn in the fifties had disappeared, only to make a comeback. The return of the repressed! Could it be that the demiurge responsible for the material world has given it to the ebb and flow of lipstick styles to reflect the tidal moves of mother-daughter relationships? When we are in our teens and twenties our lipstick is either pale or dark, whatever the color of Mother's generation *wasn't*. Then, ten or fifteen years later, when we are beginning to make our peace with her, with the fact that we have in some very real sense *become* her, lipstick colors have cycled back again and there she is, staring at us in the mirror.

I know two women who wear no lipstick and very little makeup. One, a close friend, tells me she was repelled by the spectacle of her mother getting ready to go out, sitting at her vanity, applying endless coats of this and that, much *too* much as far as she was concerned. The other woman, a painter, had a complete and painful break with her mother. Her face, plain but lovely, its own stylish statement of antistyle, refuses all references to her mother.

Most of us, though, have some kind of charmed memory of watching Mother make herself up—it was part of what being a grown-up woman was, it smelled and tasted and looked different. Yet it also carried a warning or threat. I remember as a tomboy not liking that vanity with its silver comb and brush set (now in my possession), its lace runner (which I was forbidden to touch—it took hours to wash and iron), its exclusively female unguents and colors. It was all right for Mother, but I wanted a desk instead. At the time it didn't seem possible to have both.

We make up for others, ostensibly for men, but in fact it's one of the supreme bonds all women share—something we do *with* each other rather than *for* each other. More democratic and universal than fashion, makeup is a ritual that young girls submit to and take possession of. As adolescents, we bought our first lipsticks together, discussed them, and admired ourselves; and as we mature, the ritual threads through our days as we discuss the "latest" eyeshadows and lip colors. The *Iliad* spends pages describing the way the different warriors dress for battle, details upon details of colors and fabrics, the design and metal of armor and swords; just such an epic could be written about women painstakingly assembling their faces in the battle dress of lipstick and mascara.

My cousin Annie and her friend Catherine, extremely bright women both, could spend hours discussing the relative merits of Christian Dior foundation versus Lancôme, of Clinique's concealer versus some other label, the comparative merits of an eyeshadow brush or a sponge. They tried each other's lipsticks, took swabs of under-eye cream. Annie, with the tone of expert to novice, gave me makeup counsel, and I obeyed. Once she told me I would look infinitely better if I lined under my eyes, which was something I'd never thought of doing. I did, dutifully . . . until I read that eyeliner under the eye makes you look older, whereupon I stopped. Of course, that opinion will undoubtedly be reversed (was no doubt contradicted by other experts even then), which is what makes makeup so bewildering. It's not so much that the greedy cosmetics manufacturers are sitting up nights trying to hoodwink us into thinking our products are obsolete as that we ourselves start itching for a slightly different look. Like politicians, they want only to give us what we want.

I like makeup precisely because it's unnecessary. Clothes carry with them a functional justification—no matter how frivolous your attire, or how ridiculously expensive, you have to have clothes. But a nude face won't create a scandal or give you a cold. Making up is *always* gilding the lily; it isn't even as essential as icing on a cake. On the other hand, it's so much easier than choosing and assembling clothes. Take lipstick: I'm drawn irresistibly to those display cases with their little squares of color, each shading into the one next to it, each harboring a sample tube whose color you can try on your hand, even combine with another. Whatever tube I select is at that moment exciting, radical, like no other in my possession, a new lover: colors have changed since last year, my taste has changed, what looks good on me has changed. I imagine it on my lips and someone's eyes lighting up at this new but not entirely new me, I imagine the very act of talking (a stand-in for kissing, which is a stand-in for making love), now made more palpable by this new shade, this new song on my lips. Is my lipstick fetish actually a gratification of oral cravings? a displaced embodiment of phallic wishes? Or is a lipstick sometimes just a lipstick? I'm ready to entertain any kinky explanation, but I don't need to pay $175 an hour to find out: for ten dollars, I have a buzz.

One of the peculiar ironies of makeup is that as we get older and presumably need it more, we care less about how we look. Women in their late twenties and thirties, who have only to get out of bed to look gorgeous, will spend hours trying different products, getting it just so, whereas women edging into their fifties exhibit a kind of pleased carelessness. "I'm in a different play, now," they seem to be saying, "one that can be done on a bare stage." It's a play about peace, the merging of inner and outer, rather than about masks and special effects and self-display.

Until I embrace with mixed emotions this more austere role, I *enjoy* playing around with different combinations of emollients and colors. It's a frugal way of feeling reborn.

Working against the joy is the worry: will I look reborn or ridiculous? Will my obvious attempt to beautify myself make me vulnerable? Will I fail? A wonderful cartoon in a recent *New Yorker* showed a woman in front of her mirror, shoulders slumped with defeat, saying, "I looked better when I wasn't trying to look my best." In other words, it's preferable to look halfway good than to miss at looking good. This is another version of the taboo against Effort. Which is probably one reason we don't take lessons in makeup, or if we do, forget how to use them. We want to believe, in the words of another Yeats poem, that they love us for ourselves alone and not our yellow hair. Or rosy lips. The effortless look has always taken more effort than anything, in makeup no less than in clothes. I have never achieved it. On me, lipstick quickly evaporates, and then I fade into sickly beige, so I quickly apply some more. Probably too much, setting myself up for the trying-too-hard that leads to rejection.

I remember once being out sailing with a man I was interested in and another couple. We were all in shorts, shirt, beach attire, I with no makeup except lipstick. Peter, the man I was interested in and our captain, passed around a beer and, noticing traces I'd left on the can, asked me why I was wearing it. "Because I get chapped lips," I said. I couldn't say "because you're attractive and I want to look good for you," but I might as well have. He knew. Insecure himself, no doubt, and wanting me to make the first move (and prepared to run if I did), he would take any obvious effort I made to look good as a sign of interest, an overture.

This is a sobering thought. On the other hand, there's something liberating in admitting we want approbation, admiration, etc. If Peter was afraid of my lipstick, he was the wrong man for me anyway (and he was, by the way!). Fashion *is* self-display, clothes and makeup are part of the game, so why pretend otherwise. If we want to be be loved for who we are rather than for our yellow hair, why is everyone blond? Certainly we don't want people to take us for "just another pretty face" (one of the most puritanical and hypocritical phrases in our culture), but if a face made more arresting by a bold shade of lipstick or a tantalizing eyeshadow can bring them a little closer, whet the interest, impose awe, or up the ante in the game of seduction, then wouldn't we be fools not to take the opportunity—and the makeup case—and run with it?

Nude with Attitude

T ime was when you could pretty much get through an entertainment
season without having to confront the human body in its unadorned
state. Now you'd need Bible-belt blinders to escape the omnipresent spectacle of flesh. Male and female nudes, separately and together (and sometimes artfully made to look either or both), confront you in Cinemascope
dimensions on buses and bus shelter ads, posters over Times Square, movies
and ads for movies. On the small screen, grappling bodies appear as often
on network shows as on porn channels. Print advertising offers its own
slightly more decorous eyeful in ads for brassieres, suntan lotion, perfume,
and jockey shorts. Even the runway models last spring in Paris looked less
like a display of haute couture than a trade show for foundation garments
or a sci-fi film promotional *(Star Trek: The Fashion Show?)*. They slithered
down the runway in satiny bras and shorts, transparent dresses, see-
through tops with pasties on the nipples, flesh-colored garments, slits up to
the crotch—all of it either suggesting nudity or downright brandishing it.

And then there are the arts: nude paintings, nude sculptures, and nude
photographs, and the occasional nude performer and nude self portraitist
—all seen fit to print in family newspapers. Display and self-display run
riot among us, but for how long, and how much nudity can we take?

As the ocean is governed by incoming and outgoing tides, so society is
prey to the push and pull of conflicting currents regarding violence and
nudity; we are constantly testing the waters, plunging in, stretching the
boundaries of the culturally acceptable and then retreating before the
winds of counterreaction. (Will the ascendancy of Newt Gingrich and a

*This article first appeared in *Self*, May 1995. Copyright © 1995 by Molly Haskell.

newly conservative congress cause fig leaves and other skin protection factors to come out of the closet?)

The forbidden, in becoming acceptable, becomes boring. Already there seems to be a turning away from the female body and from such overexposed exhibitionists as the oxymoronic Madonna. "In: male nudity; out: female nudity" pronounced a columnist in a year-end report, and an eye cast over the recent scene would seem to confirm this. Male genitals, once protected by a sacred mystique regarding the phallus (and the potency of the invisible), are the latest part of the anatomy to emerge from taboo. The most dramatic unveiling occurred in last year's *The Crying Game*, when the "heroine" played by Jaye Davidson flashed an erection in the face of a surprised lover played by Stephen Rea.

In public discourse, the dismembering of Mr. Bobbitt brought the penis out of the closet and onto the six o'clock news, and since then it's been a gleeful addition to the media vernacular. In a recent episode of *Cybill*, the star, consoling Ira, her ex-husband, about the theft of his new Porsche, says "It's only a car, Ira," to which he replies,

"Only a car, Cybill! Where have you been? It's a 70,000 dollar penis!"

From off-Broadway to Broadway the male strip tease continues. There are seven actors and almost as many penises on display in Terrence McNally's *Love, Valour, Compassion* (seven brides for seven brothers), not to mention more groping and caressing than has been seen outside a homosexual porn film. The *New York Times Magazine*, once dubbed "the Girdle Gazette" for its prurient lingerie ads, could be renamed the Deltoids Daily for its images of men in various states of undress. One ad that leaps off the page features a man with bench-press-perfect proportions lying on a Caribbean beach, his buffed and moisturized torso gleaming under pearls of sweat. Too rich for me, at least over breakfast coffee.

Ostensibly these are addressed not just to a gay readership but to the newly liberated and licentious female. However, as far as I know, most women are still more turned on by a man's personality than by his pectorals. The display of perfectly rounded muscles signals narcissism and self-involvement, whereas shared tastes, a sense of humor, and a liking for women are the aphrodesia of romance. When Clark Gable took off his shirt in *It Happened One Night*, it was sexy as hell, but only because it was Clark Gable, and only because he didn't go all the way.

Still, what's the harm in seeing what we can get away with, if we can strike a blow against the double standard and small-town puritanism. That would be fine, but this flaunting of flesh has little to do with a celebration of sensuality and everything to do with shock value, i.e., puritanism by another name. In a vicious circle, nudity wouldn't be shocking if we weren't deeply uncomfortable with our bodies, saddled as they are with all the guilt-ridden taboos of Judeo-Christian morality.

There's a punitive element that is also part and parcel of our inherited puritanism: in the case of the male ogling the female, which is the way it has usually been, what is revealed is never as wonderful as expected, and when that happens, when nudity turns out to be anticlimactic, the voyeur feels a little dashed and ashamed.

At a dinner party, some of us were talking about *Nell*, the movie in which Jodie Foster plays a wood nymph raised in the mountains of North Carolina without benefit of language or clothes. "It wasn't prurient enough," one man sheepishly joked. "Why would Jodie Foster do it?" wondered his wife. "Box office calculation," said a third member of our group. This man, a professional voyeur and student of Eros, offered the explanation that "the promise of nudity gets us into the theater while the reality invariably disappoints." How puny the body is compared to the swirling and complicated fantasies that surround it.

Because our first desires form around parental figures, eroticism is always tinged with shame and taboo, and the wish to evade and suppress the erotic is almost as strong as the need to express it. Women, as the central figures in the drama of desire, have also borne responsibility— established forever in the transgression of Eve—for the attendant shame and guilt.

Thus the dichotomy between nudity as a pure and prelapsarian state of innocence (econudity, as in *Nell*) and nudity as wickedness incarnate (nudity lib) is perhaps even more profound in our culture than the classic distinction identified by the British historian Kenneth Clark between *nakedness*—simply a state of being unclothed—and *nudity*, which is an art form. From Renaissance painting onward, the nude as a staple of figure painting has developed certain conventions and meanings—what the contemporary British essayist John Berger has called, in the title of his now-classic pictorial essay, *Ways of Seeing*. In looking at the treatment of the nude in Western art he shows a woman depicted as supine and pandering to the voyeuristic tastes of the emerging bourgeois male consumer. Her status as someone who sees herself being seen encapsulates the way woman, conditioned from birth to appeal to the male eye and to see herself in the mirror of male desire, has split herself into the surveyor and the surveyed, in the process denying her own appetites and desires. Berger contrasts conventional male-flattering nudes with the more idiosyncratic shapes and poses of certain models of Titian and Rubens, suggesting that the former are nudes while the latter, radiating a kind of authority and insolence we might now dub as "attitude," are "naked," i.e., they commune with themselves in ways the other models do not.

While granting the differences between these two types of nudes, I would suggest that none of them are really "naked." The moment nakedness goes public it is no longer nakedness, and even when we look in the mirror we carry a public image of ourselves within us. Thus, in our mirror images, we are not quite "naked," so busy are we screening out flaws (or overemphasizing them, if that's your game). The ideal of portraying nakedness as something whole, intact, and innocent of the desire to please is itself an impossibility, because nakedness *becomes* nudity as soon as it goes public. Once the image is given over to another—even a public of one— that person's fantasies and criticisms inevitably go to meet and reshape it.

An example of the difficulty of the problem emerges in the anticlimactic ending of Robert Altman's *Ready to Wear*. The director wishes to pay homage to "real women" (as opposed to all those phony fashion clotheshorses) by having the models walk down the runway nude—or "naked," because shorn of the finery in which they have previously catered to our senses and consumer appetites.

The result is an embarrassment, a spectacle from which you want to avert your eyes. In fact, the women who awed us with their style and authority now look like birds plucked of their feathers. Wanting to celebrate Womanhood, Altman does individual women a disservice by depriving them of what they do best. Taking from runway models the clothes, the stride, and the haughty aloofness that go with the turf is like asking a Shakespearean actor—say John Gielgud—to do pantomime.

Clothes are complex and seductive; one of the great things they do is suggest the nude female underneath. Conversely, nudity, as Anne Hollander points out in her fine book *Seeing Through Clothes*, is always referring to clothes. We look at nudes of the past, and in their awkwardly posed legs we see long concealing dresses, in their voluptuous folds we see the folds of material, in their era-specific anatomy we see long waists or high breasts.

All nudes, she says, are "wearing the ghosts of absent clothes, sometimes highly visible ghosts." Their ghosts are friendly, however, while the "naked" women of Altman seem to have been abandoned by their clothes ghosts.

The best moment in *Ready to Wear* combines fashion and sexiness, nudity and dress. It's when Julia Roberts, who has been lumbering around in a terry cloth robe for the whole movie, finally puts on street clothes. The camera, starting at ground level, focuses on her shoes and works its way up her endless, stocking-clad legs until it reaches her skirt—short but not micro—and then takes her all in, including her radiantly smiling face. She's a knockout, of course, but she's not just a passive receptacle for male fantasies. She has gumption, personality, and an inalienable sense of equal rights (to the room she refuses to surrender to Tim Robbins, the phone, room service, the bath); a working woman with a husband back home, who's had a hell of a nice interlude and is ready to get on with her life. In her final dazzling chic, she's also a cunning, if inadvertent, testimonial to the world of fashion to which she is supposed to be an outsider (she has spent the whole week in her hotel room; she's not the fashion editor of her paper) but to which every inch of her perfectly and stylishly decked out body renders tribute.

For women, the new emphasis on nudity is less likely to signify the freedom to be oneself than competition on yet another terrain. Will this star do nude scenes, will that one have to have breast implants, will yet another have liposuction? Women, as Berger pointed out, end up turning *themselves* into objects in order to exercise some control, but this process is much more difficult if one has no props to work with. In a world in which body shape matters, clothes offer protection, make us less vulnerable. Marlene Dietrich, epitome of glamor and perfection, had special undergarments made to correct her flaws, and, as daughter Maria Riva tells it in her biography of the star, when Marlene took one of her lovers to bed, she *always* made sure the lights were off.

As the frankly and gloriously middle-aged actress-star of her show, Cybill agrees to do a nude shower scene in a made-for-TV prison movie. We watch the woman lathering her gorgeously curved waist and flat tummy as Cybill, with glasses and ponytail, looks on and then confides to assorted exes and friends that it was a body double. Perhaps *this* is the sort of exposure we need, a huge laugh at the expense of titillation; and maybe the new male nudity, the strutting and competing for the body perfect, will make all those imperfect men in the audience appreciate the rack on which women have long been strung.

One stratagem currently in fashion is to preempt the voyeur's perspective: expose a body part here and there in a blunt, provocative way, half joke, half statement of ownership. Acting out the dual roles of surveyor and surveyed, the woman is taking an I'll-make-myself-into-a-fetish-before-you-do approach. If the results are bizarre or unpleasing, that may be the point: a square of bare thigh between the over-the-knee sock and micro-skirt, a shaved head. These are like images of rape or humiliation turned on their head: the white upper leg sandwiched between swatches of black carries a whiff of s & m, but the woman is somehow playing both parts. It's a "buzz off" rather than a "come-hither" look. Similarly the nude head: it evokes the ultimate wartime mortification whereby women accused of collaborating with the enemy had their heads shaved; only now, it's the woman doing the shaving. I can brutally subtract what would seem to be the most essential trapping of femininity, hair, the skinhead seems to be saying, and still be me. I dare you to find me repugnant. Even women who've undergone chemotherapy sometimes choose not to wear the covering of hat or wig, in a powerful, take-me-as-I-am gesture of self-exposure.

A similar message turns up in a Hanes hosiery ad in which a woman's legs take up half the photograph, and her body, in tiny black sheath, takes up the other half. The woman is young and black, her arms are insolently folded and you can practically smell the don't-mess-with-me pheromones. A gigantic caption reads "nude with attitude." She's still selling a product, of course, only the product (aside from the stockings) is Woman with Her Own Agenda (and purse strings) rather than woman waiting for man to give her an agenda (and the wherewithal to go with it).

But she's not really nude, though, and that's the point. If she were, all sorts of confusing feelings would come into play. Is she being exploited; is she a force of self-assertion? To what degree does this image belong to: the photographer, the advertiser, the viewer/consumer?

How do you feel about Julianne Moore in Altman's *Short Cuts* flashing a furry red pubis; a pregnant and nude Demi Moore on the cover of *Vanity Fair*; Sharon Stone, ditto, covering her breasts with her hands; the woman with a mastectomy on the cover of the *New York Times Magazine* bringing breast cancer and nudity into the home with one shot. They're "controversial"—which itself plays into the hands of merchandisers and publishers.

Some women cry Brava! (a taboo coming out of the closet); others cry Horrors! (offensive and demeaning). The best that can be said is that the subjects have negotiated a contract whereby they gratify their *own* needs while colluding with the director or editors to sell a product. A stand-off.

Generally, the partially or fully clothed body will always be more tantalizing than the nude, which simply provokes nervousness or self-congratualatory tolerance, but rarely erotic pleasure. In the plastic arts, nude images, being two-dimensional and aesthetic, can be examined with a certain one-on-one dispassion. The fierce nudes of modern artists—Picasso and Giacometti, Dubuffet and de Kooning—are women who represent a whole palette of emotions, thrust before us with the intensity of their creators' ambivalence. They don't represent womankind, and, for all the unease some of these images evoke, they speak more for female power than powerlessness. They are also set at one remove from "real" women by form and material: the stylizing cubism of Picasso, the pinched bronze and elongated figures of Giacometti, and so on.

When a woman goes nude on the screen, however, her self, her character, fly out the window. We can analyze performances, but how can we evaluate nudity? Even the French, habitually more adept in the languages of love and passion, lose all their sureness of touch when they dwell on the beauties of the unclad body. The more skilled the movie (or novel) at drawing character and involving us in event, the more let down we feel when characters take off their clothes and become "mere" bodies. Narrative could be considered the living room of story-telling, where certain decorum and rules prevail, while pornography is the bedroom, the place where we feel comfortable with scenes that are meant to turn us on.

The one glory of nudity in real life is that it brings lovers together in a sharing of self and a sense that one female body is not all that unlike another, even what Berger calls its reassuring "banality"—a loss of mystery which at that awesome moment is precisely what we seek. This sharing, this "forgiving," is what we don't get in spectacle, where the person seems isolated, no longer partnered by someone on the screen but appealing directly to the spectator. Even when the nude is loved and adored and "forgiven" by her lover/director—Marianne Sagebrucht, the enormous yet somehow attractive star of Percy Adalon films for example—the director can't control how she will be received according to the fantasies of the viewer. The artist or director or photographer starts out with talent and a view of women shaped by primal experiences with mothers or mother figures, all of which emerge in the definition and emotional coloring of his females.

It's safe to say that women, who also have good and bad mother memories, don't see themselves with any less ambivalence, and certainly our nudes will be as controversial as those of men, and as subject to fashion. Who controls the image? No one person, so beware of those who promise to show you, or show you as, the essential woman. Nakedness, in the public eye, is just a less protected form of nudity—Madonna, Christy Turlington, or Kate Moss to the contrary, notwithstanding. I'm thinking of the ad in which Ms. Turlington, helping out the Animal Rights campaign, is lying lengthwise in the nude, her gorgeous body stretching for miles. The caption reads: "I'd rather go naked than wear fur." Some choice!

Bearded Ladies

WOMEN IN COMEDY

Because they live in a world in which serious-minded folks can still get points for claiming never to watch television, Respected Culture Arbiters, when they come out of the closet with their secret addictions, do so with a certain elegantly tortured defensiveness to placate the highbrows. Just so, television's superior serial dramas—crime shows *(N.Y.P.D.* and *Homicide)* and the hospital shows *(E.R.* and *Chicago Hope)*—have recently been getting some well-placed attention from the literati. These long-running series, with their ethnically varied casts, superior women's role, and feeling for complex characters evolving over time, deserve all the accolades they get. But these shows aren't the only ones that are beating Hollywood at its own narrative game. I'd suggest that it's in the field of comedy, including that much despised genre the sit-com, that television is exploding all over the place. Both within the precincts of network television and in the outer reaches of cable, there are uncommonly raunchy, innovative, sophisticated shows, many of them women-driven, that are tackling male-female conflict and sexual taboo and the undercurrent of women's rage, subjects that mainstream movies won't touch with a ten-foot pole. Hollywood's only concession to the "transgressive" is that reassuring staple, a big male star in fright-wig drag.

What movies rarely give us is the other side of the coin, the funny and terrifying spectacle of a woman taking on the coloring and aggression of the male. The tacit assumption was that, unlike the female impersonator, the male impersonator, the strident female comic, just wasn't funny. A little tough-guy bravado, a little blatant penis envy here and there was okay, even flattering, as long as the bounds of femininity remained in place. Well, I'm here to tell you that there's a new breed of women comics who are crossing the lines and testing boundaries, not just of what's taboo and what isn't, but—more dangerously—what's funny and what isn't.

IN A RECENT PROFILE on the television star Roseanne, a fellow comedian recalled a riotous bit she'd performed at a Denver club where the two were both doing stand-up and waiting tables. According to the admirer, now a writer on her show, she had gone onstage to do a routine about bikers when she looked and saw the place filled with them—fifty black-clad bruisers and their girlfriends. Hesitating a minute, but urged on by her backstage buddies, she went through with it. "I really hate bikers," she said. "You know, they all got tobacco juice in their beards. They piss on the side of the road. And the men are even worse!"

The audience fell out of their chairs. This little outrage from the early Roseanne (she was making a dollar and a half an hour, plus tips) was a foretaste of the uproariously rude down-and-dirty comedian to come: the special twist on sexual machismo, the need to blow things up from the inside and substitute "uterus power" for "penis power."

Just as I was pondering the humor of ladies with facial hair, Brett Butler came along with a similar routine. She's talking, in her southern drawl, about New York being a Bigots' Buffet. Rednecks from her native Dixie have come to visit, and they're in the Bronx when they are startled to behold "mustachioed Sicilians . . . and their boyfriends."

What was going on with hirsute women? Even Woody Allen had a hairy unisex gag: "I [was] hitchhiking west and being picked up by two native Californians," he recalls in a monologue in his collection, *Side Effects*, "a charismatic young man with a beard like Rasputin's and a charismatic young woman with a beard like Svengali's."

These jokes obviously tap into our confusion about sex roles in the age of androgyny: that moment when, walking along a sidewalk, we see two people ahead of us, arm in arm, both with pony tails, and we wonder which, if either, is the woman. Remember the Bearded Lady at the circus? She was a freak of nature, supposedly, but also a cautionary figure. As we stood there, transfixed and giggling with adolescent anxiety, she seemed to be saying: This is what could happen to you if you don't give up your tomboyish ways and become All Female.

Women with male hormones, women with male secondary sex charac-teristics, might be a metaphor for these new women comics, the bearded ladies who are crossing gender boundaries and breaking the rules of humor. They are an aggressive bunch and they would have to be: comedy, particularly the stand-up variety, is an act of aggression, a violent ripping apart of the conventions and clichés by which we live. We watch with equal parts discomfort and glee as someone else's beliefs, color, eccentricities are ridiculed, and our fears—mostly of embarrassment, of exposure—are vicariously exorcised. Without overindulging in the romantic fantasy of the wounded artist, it seems logical to assume that this kind of savagery comes out of pain cauterized, or transmuted, into comic revenge. There have been far fewer women comics over the years for obvious reasons: Women are on earth to mend, not rend, the social fabric. We are the healers, the civilizers; we nurture, mediate, sympathize, tame, and domesticate.

Or so goes the myth, now being given a run for its money by one woman comic after another. Why indeed should men have all the fun and the fury? Giving vent to the rage and disillusionment that was previously papered over by the will to please or channeled into political activism, women comics and women in comedy series are letting it all hang out in ways that once might have provoked retaliation by censors. Roseanne mocks and ridicules the sacred cows of mainstream America, those very institutions whose products her show is pushing. Murphy Brown's pregnancy without benefit of husband caused a high-level snit and still pinches nerves in the body politic.

In the past, women comedians might exaggerate, even tumble, but there was a clear division between the clowns (Bea Lillie, Martha Raye) and the ladies. Well, Mae West was no lady and would be insulted to be so labeled, but her act was more femme than butch, even if it bordered on female impersonation. There was a kind of either/or governing comedy and women: comedy was the last resort of the homely woman. You were either favored by fortune: pretty therefore popular, therefore normal, Daddy's little darling; or you were a plain Jane, therefore a misfit who needed to develop wit and personality to claim the attention and love denied you.

There were a few anomalies: Carole Lombard, being both gorgeous and goofy, was an exception that proved the rule.

The screwball tradition, in which women like Lombard, Katharine Hepburn, Claudette Colbert, Rosalind Russell could be brainy, nutty, *and* beautiful, was unique. For the most part, movies didn't know what to do with women who combined such powerhouse qualities. The most successful gambit for a smart funny "looker" was to play dumb: Judy Holliday was an adorably shrewd fluff, while Lucille Ball, of gorgeous gams and model good looks, turned into the screwball Lucy, blithe savager of Ricky's best-laid plans. They slyly put the torch to all sorts of conventional expectations but had to do it by pretending to be dopier than they were. Like Carol Burnett, they put on their comic personae like clown suits: Burnett could never have gotten away with some of her more acid numbers—the corrosive Mama-and-Eunice feature, for example—if she hadn't been so high-spirited and congenial as partygiver-hostess for the Carol Burnett show.

The seventies were self-consciously serious, an era of political activism: we marched, signed petitions, stormed the barricades to win reproductive rights and equal pay. We were too focused on the business at hand to laugh at ourselves. Even that decade's queen of comedy, Mary Tyler Moore, was notable more for the emotional intensity and guiding conscience she brought to the workplace than for her own intrinsic funniness. Her seriousness was a foil, her anxiety that of the single woman not yet comfortable in her singleness, still waiting for Mr. Right to make his entrance. Now two decades later, we've come far enough to be able to jeer at our own romantic illusions, to take a rueful view of the idea of "having it all," and to acknowledge that the results of the so-called sexual revolution have been ambiguous at best.

Okay, so we've emerged from the repressions of Victorianism wherein sex was unmentionable, contraception barely existed, pregnancy out of wedlock was a social tragedy, and women weren't thought to have libidos at all. But how free are we? That is, are women who like sex or have multiple lovers really exempt from the taint of being thought "loose," promiscuous, even tarts? And are women who *don't* want to have sex really free to say No? From the evidence of series like Grace Under Fire and Cybill, surely men had even more to be grateful for: there being (theoretically) no onus attached to the pursuit of sexual pleasure, they could now get all they wanted without having to get married or even say I love you. They could play the field forever and if suddenly seized by an urge to settle down, they could lie down till it went away; or they could marry and then, when the urge wore off, get a quicky no-fault divorce. And women might find themselves "free" once again, but this time with a couple of kids and a drop in income, scratching out a survival existence and harassing her ex for child support.

Is *this* what equality means? asks one harried woman after another. To be saddled like Grace with three children, a factory job, and little faith in marriage or men? Or like Cybill, with two children, one grandchild, and two ex-husbands in one's twilight years! And still feeling sexy. To be friend, employer, den-mother, and unpaid shrink to a group of egomaniacal me-decade drop-ins running a barely profitable bookstore-coffee bar *(Ellen)*. To be raising a child or children alone *(Murphy Brown, Absolutely Fabulous)*. To be trying to have a child without sacrificing a high-powered career *(Mad About You)*.

Classic comedy came from the head-on collision of men refusing to grow up and women insisting that they do. The gags of Chaplin and Keaton, or W. C. Fields or the Marx Brothers, radiated from the basic premise of turning order into chaos, busting up the living room furniture, and fleeing the terrifying stultifying rule of The Wife. Even *The Simpsons*, that durably funny cartoon series by MTM and *Rhoda* guru James Brooks, is a kind of smirky triumph of dumb-male entropy over what, in the gender dynamics of the show, is seen as the earnestly civilizing influence of wom-en. Such sacred cows as upward mobility, self-improvement, and the im-portance of education, along with the smarts of Lisa and the sweetness of Marge, hold little weight against the boorish cunning of the male side of the family, as Bart follows Homer's slackerish footsteps into a downscale spiral of screw-up, goof-off, loserdom.

If women are fighting back, it's partly against having been cast in the role of nag and relationship-bore. As women in power roles become more common, and men as helpmeets and supporters become less taboo, we can exorcise our nervousness through gags and storylines that play on these very reversals and fears.

Women's comedy is the continuation of consciousness-raising by other means, with all the issues that once formed the agenda of group therapy and editorials now incorporated into the ongoing drama of frustration and comic release. The continuing imbalance of power, the refusal of men to commit, form an ongoing leitmotif: "A friend of mine asked me how I get rid of a guy I don't want," said Rita Rudner. "I just tell him I love you, I want you to be the father of my children. He leaves skid marks."

Or Brett Butler's rueful line: "You know Bill Clinton, you've met guys like him at a bar. You know that every word out of his mouth is a lie, but you just don't want to go home alone."

The humor is directed at men, but it is also directed at ourselves, at "smart women who make foolish choices," at the conflicts that just won't go away. A "Guerrilla Girls" cartoon says: "Don't agonize over whether to work or stay home with your kids—you'll feel guilty either way." And suddenly, hearing that truth, realizing the absurdity and *universality* of our predicament, we feel better. With humor, we share emotional burdens together.

In one show, Roseanne, wanting space to "create," isolates herself in a basement office in an attempt to write. By emphasizing the truly limited condition of the working class woman, she shows in extremis the harrowing truth of most women's existence: the desire to express oneself, to be independent, is one that can be fulfilled only intermittently or in rare circumstances. We are bound, if not by biology, then by those very forces of *wanting* to care for the young, for others, that fuel the ire, or comic inspiration, of male comedians. What the retrogressive, still-yearning princess in us would deny, comedy forces us to look at, over and over again. We can no longer depend on the kindness and staying power of husbands; besides, in a society that values remunerated work, it feels good to bring home a paycheck. The paradoxes of women's position, the contradictions within ourselves, are brought into the open, and in the catharsis of laughter we feel a momentary release from pressure and relief at the realization that others are in the same boat.

Old myths and expectations die hard, and ancient impulses lie in wait to ambush us like phantom limbs. On one episode of *Ellen*, she decides to entertain in grand style—a Martha Stewart fall dinner, complete with an autumn foliage centerpiece and Martha Stewart herself as honored guest. Only it's California, so they have to use palm fronds instead of autumn foliage, and her oven has a breakdown, so instead of Cornish hens, they send out for pizza. Martha, sharing the joke of which she is also the butt, smiles benignly and unflappably as Ellen chokes and sputters, unable to execute this newest version of society's ideal woman. Setting a gorgeous table with crystal and iron-only linen—just like the one Mom did or didn't—is a fantasy we all entertain from time to time, but let's admit it's beyond the grasp of most of us, so why not leave it in the realm of fantasy.

Comedy writing, most people in the business will say, comes out of anguish, of being dissed or dysfunctional, a misfit in school or abused at home. Even such apparently nice girl–nice guy types as Mary Tyler Moore and Kelsey Grammer have written autobiographies of childhood torment, substance abuse, loneliness.

At a panel on comedy at Columbia University's School of the Arts, Fred

Wolf of *Saturday Night Live* claimed, "They're all dysfunctional. I've known a lot of them, and every comedy writer I've ever known is seriously dysfunctional."

Roseanne maintained that if she hadn't become a comedian, she would have become a serial killer—perhaps not realizing that a serial killer, in a different form, is just what she *has* become. This is a woman who revels in firing employees of her show, who rakes her abusive family over the coals at every opportunity, who beheads and castrates like a mythic monster . . . or a ruthless CEO or a bloodthirsty tyrant! Revenge in the form of a scorched earth policy, taking no prisoners—isn't this a form of homicide? The tip-off is the language comedy uses to describe itself. "We murdered them," "They died laughing," "We almost croaked," that joke "killed" them.

There's a spectrum of women comedians, ranging from the Nice Girls (Ellen De Generes, Helen Hunt, Cybill Shepherd) to the Furies, with various forms of survivors in between. When they lapse, when they find themselves waiting by the phone or tippling over into masochism, they're the first ones to realize it and make a joke about it. In fact, you might say that each character is really two characters: yesterday's woman who self-destructs, sabotages herself, and clings, and her emerging self—probably wrung through the wheel of psychotherapy—who sees and jeers and resolves to do better next week.

Even the women who play second bananas—Roz on *Frazier*, Elaine in *Seinfeld*—refuse to get stuck in some subordinate, spear-carrying role. Roz is not a lead, but she has her scars and her smarts. She's like the Eve Arden sardonic-foil, but less sexually marginal than those comic women of the forties who played the heroine's best friend. Even the English cutie who is dad John Mahoney's aide is a peppery antidote to the father-son and brother-brother hugfest. Elaine on *Seinfeld* is both pal to the guys and balloon-puncturer of some of their more fatuous flights of self-congratulatory fancy. It's true that their wise-ass mystique usually triumphs over alternate versions of reality—what's one dame to a bunch of perpetually adolescent guys?—but she strikes a blow for common sense. Murphy Brown with her slow burns and delicious sarcasm, her shameless egocentricity, dominates her show, but Corky has evolved from cupcake to serious reporter.

At the other end of the spectrum are the Furies, women like Roseanne, Brett Butler, and Jenifer Saunders's Edina on the British series *Absolutely Fabulous*. They give vent to a kind of free-floating rage at everything:

husbands, ex-husbands, lovers, children, neighbors, parents, the System, the politically correct.

For these women anger is mother's milk; their style represents a major defection from the femininity program. Once it was the better part of valor, where "ladies" were concerned, to control your temper. It would have been no more seemly to display your anger in public than to go to a party with a bra strap showing. Now women ("ladies" no longer) are expected to sound off regularly, whack an offending male, and keep a good pot of bile on the perpetual boil. "Rage," as Brett Butler says, "is not born overnight. You have to coax it with rusty forceps from a womb of malcontent." We go into therapy to cultivate our anger, as if it were a rare plant in need of careful nurturing.

On one show, Roseanne and family are visiting Disneyland, when a brief altercation with an unctuously smiling official occurs. Roseanne, imitating the professional grin and niceness of the guard, the behavioral equivalent of the squeaky-clean, ultra-sanitary theme park atmosphere, resolves the problem. "This polite stuff really works," she says. Pause. "But I feel so dirty."

The "womb of malcontent" proves endlessly fecund on that wildest and funniest of comedy series, *Absolutely Fabulous*. Edina, the fortyish mom played by writer-star Jennifer Saunders, ignores her ultra-straight teenage daughter (Julia Sawalha as the marvelous Saffron) when she is not actively ridiculing her.

Eddy is flamboyantly and relentlessly narcissistic. Boundless is her appetite for shopping, eating, drinking, drug-taking, traveling, abusing all and sundry—indeed almost any activity in preference to the glum prospect of spending a caring moment with her daughter, or one of fleeting filial devotion with her tiresomely sweet mother.

On the night of the Super Bowl, Comedy Central offered re-runs of *Ab Fab* billed as "Not the Super Bowl." Refugees from the Pittsburgh-Dallas grunt-off and its attendant hype found relief in beserk matriarchal mayhem as Eddy and longtime pal Pat (Joanna Lumley) wreaked havoc on Eddy's mother and the vengefully sane and unflappable Saffron. This was presumably as far from the Super Bowl as you could get. But was it? As Eddy pushes Pat away from the breakfast table and throws her things on the floor; as Pat, with Eddy and Saffron in Morocco, prances around with an old British dipsomaniac who has just jumped Saffron; as Eddy, on her fortieth birthday, takes an aerosol can to her candle-bedecked cake and blow-sprays the candles *and* the cake to kingdom come; as one of her ex-husbands, in a rage, fills her bed with cigarette ashes; I thought: and they call *football* violent!

Ab Fab, like *The Simpsons*, sometimes makes me uncomfortable, since it quite deliberately and audaciously throws out the baby of responsibility with the bathwater of social pieties. Eddy and her buddy Pat send up women's obsession with weight, with style, with hunky younger men, with the miracles of cosmetic surgery, even as they celebrate flagrant derelictions of duty in the form of falling-down-drunkenness, slovenliness, smoking, and not using recycled paper—all on more or less the same level. But that's what makes it so exhilaratingly cutting-edge. For one thing, no matter how remiss we feel in our own lives, we *have* to be doing a better job of it than Eddy! That, and the enormously vital bond the two women share, a kind of updated post-sixties flipped-out version of Lucy and Ethel.

This glorious sisterhood, as well as the specter of fortyish women, ripely sexual but anxious about aging, marks its American counterpart, the softer but often enchanting *Cybill*. Christine Baranski's Maryann, like Lumley's Pat, is tall, stylish, sardonic, her slender body made to hold a champagne glass in one hand, a cigarette in the other, political correctness be damned. Maryann plays the embittered divorcee and mischief-maker to Cybill's no-nonsense very contemporary Earth Mother, an out-of-work actress who is trying to hold the split ends of her life together. The show closely parallels the real Cybill's own life, and its trump card is Cybill's refreshingly un-*angst*-ridden reaction to aging. However ambivalent we may be about blond beauty queens, the spectacle of an aging "looker" touches female nerves and brings discomfort. Not relying on the gallows humor of many age-obsessed comediennes, Cybill seems glad to be where she is. Her thigh-slapping sense of fun, and our feeling that she is having a grand time and has really come into her own as a *performer*, invigoratingly redeems the hollow old cliché about aging with grace!

The subject and tone of comedy differs significantly according to the age group (and gender): the twenty-somethings are still dreaming about romance and having it all (see *Friends*); the over-thirties are wrestling with lost illusions; and the over-forties, with lost illusions *and* lost youth. These, as you might expect, are the angriest and the funniest. On one *Ab Fab* show, Eddy and Pat imagine themselves twenty-five years down the road: hunched over, shrewish, thrashing the air with their canes, cackling like witches. Together, they have turned the holy terrors of aging outward, unleashed their combined womanpower upon the world.

If stand-up, at its most ferocious, is still more men's terrain than women's, it may be that something in its agressiveness is still anathema to women. I know that at one time, a man of my acquaintance would watch Comedy Central for hours on end, whereas after the first two or three solos, I would feel pinned to the sofa, gasping for air. It brought back that terrifying childhood feeling of being tickled against your will. It was as if the comedian hadn't succeeded unless he had his hand around your throat, while you begged for mercy. The determination to "slay" you, to pile on one gag after another until you scream "Stop! Stop!," becomes a kind of assault: war by other means. And that kind of all-out aggression seems to have been testosterone-driven . . . and best appreciated by that half of the human species who are hormonally attuned to cutthroat combat.

There's a connection here, whether you want to call it women's innate need to hold things together, their Darwinian strategy for passing their genes along, or simply a habit that dies hard. When a woman comic loses her empathy through an obsession with her own hurts—as in the case of Roseanne—then the womb of malcontent turns sour, uterus power becomes an excuse for megalomania, and there's a danger of failing to connect with the vulnerabilities of the audience. Roseanne's extremism becomes a form of blackmail: "If you're not as angry as I am," she seems to be saying, "then you're a sellout." Taking herself too seriously as a one-woman revolution, she's in danger of losing that sense of humor about herself which is the essence of comedy—and is the all-important ingredient in the surge of women into the field. Where once melodrama (the "weeper") was the form best adapted to the emotional needs of women and their restricted status in the world, now the resources of comedy and its cerebral approach to opportunity and failure signal a transcendence over experience, a triumph over victimhood. Holding a stage alone, making jokes, carving out a persona that says "take me as I am"—women are throwing down the gauntlet not just to men but to the little girl inside, raised on the age-old command, best said by the French: "Sois belle et tais-toi" (Be beautiful and be quiet).

You might say women for the first time have the luxury of contemplating themselves as human beings as well as women: instead of just reacting to men's initiatives, or sharing in men's reflected glory, they are acting on their own. Constance Rourke, in her wonderful 1931 book *American Humor*, quotes Henri Bergson to show how the Yankee as a comic figure entered the national stage. " 'The comic comes into being just when society and the individual, freed from the worry of self-preservation, begin to regard themselves as works of art.'" Rourke dates the emergence of "embellished self-portraiture which nations as well as individuals may undertake" at 1815: America was coming into its own as a country, and with sufficient detachment to examine just what it was. The comics were, of course, male. It is only now that the American female is sufficiently disengaged from her biological destiny and domestic vocation—her mandate to live through and for others—that she can stand back and wonder who she is and where she is going.

The "deconstruction" of traditional roles that academics engage in—the perception that women are not born but made (Simone de Beauvoir) or, in the current parlance, "constructed"—is merely a fancy-talk way of describing the taking-apart that women comics do every night. Ellen both displays and mocks women's excess of empathy when, after watching and commenting on the monotonous to-and-fro of her pet goldfish, she suddenly leaps (figuratively) into the bowl and *becomes* that pet goldfish, now watching Ellen's lumbering maneuvers with goggle-eyed tolerance. Cybill is so attuned to daughter Zoe's rage that when the fiery adolescent treats her mother too sweetly, Cybill becomes suspicious and sends her off to school with the words: "You better come home with some abuse for your mother!" Eddy makes fun of collagen lips and liposuction by having a fantasy in which she grotesquely sucks and morphs into a woman who is all lips and microscopic body.

Through our comic surrogates, women can now see themselves as works of art in a funhouse mirror, beauties and beasts along a spectrum of roles that defy political correctness *with a vengeance*.